TEACHERS IN ACTION

The K–5 Chapters from *Reading and Writing in Elementary Classrooms*

PATRICIA M. CUNNINGHAM
Wake Forest University

SHARON ARTHUR MOORE
Peoria Unified School District, Arizona

JAMES W. CUNNINGHAM
University of North Carolina, Chapel Hill

DAVID W. MOORE
Arizona State University West

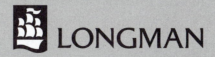 LONGMAN

An imprint of Addison Wesley Longman, Inc.

New York • Reading, Massachusetts • Menlo Park, California • Harlow, England
Don Mills, Ontario • Sydney • Mexico City • Madrid • Amsterdam

Editor-in-Chief: Priscilla McGeehon
Senior Acquisitions Editor: Virginia L. Blanford
Supplements Editor: Joy Hilgendorf
Full Service Production Manager: Eric Jorgensen
Project Coordination, Text Design, and Electronic Page Makeup: Electronic Publishing
Services Inc., NYC
Cover Design Manager: Nancy Danahy
Cover Designer: Joseph DePinho
Senior Print Buyer: Hugh Crawford
Printer and Binder: The Maple-Vail Book Manufacturing Group
Cover Printer: Coral Graphic Services

For permission to use copyrighted material, grateful acknowledgment is made to the copyright holders listed throughout this book, which are hereby made part of this copyright page.

Library of Congress Cataloging-in-Publication Data

Teachers in action: the k–5 chapters from reading and writing in elementary
    classrooms/Patricia M. Cunningham…[et al.]. p. cm.
  Includes bibliographical references and index.
  ISBN 0-8013-3424-1
    1. Language arts (Elementary)—United States Case studies. 2. Elementary school
teachers—United States Case studies. I. Cunningham, Patricia Marr.
  LB1576.T3753 2000
  372.6′044—dc21   99-22406
                                                                   CIP

Please visit our website at http://www.awlonline.com

ISBN 0-8013-3424-1

12345678910—MA—02010099

For all the determined, hard-working, caring, smart, real
teachers after whom we fashioned the fictional
Helen Launch, Rita Wright, Norma Nouveau, Vera Wise,
Yetta Maverick, and Ed Dunn

And for supportive, engaged, underappreciated, real
administrators and supervisors after whom we fashioned
the fictional Tip Topps and Sue Port

CONTENTS

Preface   *vii*

The Retreat   II-1

Miss Launch: Kindergarten   II-10

Mrs. Wright: First Grade   II-54

Miss Nouveau: Second Grade   II-106

Mrs. Wise: Third Grade   II-135

Ms. Maverick: Fourth Grade   II-167

Mr. Dunn: Fifth Grade   II-213

Index   *I-1*

PREFACE

Teaching children to read and write at high levels of literacy is a complex, long-term commitment that our society and our schools must make if we are going to remain competitive in the twenty-first century. The field of reading appears to be continually under siege by various factions arguing for one approach over another. That children learn in different ways and that acquiring high levels of literacy is a complex long-term process mitigate against any single, narrow approach. Research, experience, and common sense indicate that a balanced diet of authentic reading and writing activities along with instruction in appropriate strategies is the most effective framework for literacy. The best literacy instruction blends features from a variety of approaches to reading and writing. Most teachers know this, but knowing it is easier that doing it.

Teachers often bemoan the fact that children have many more skills and strategies than they actually use. The same can be said of teachers. To use knowledge, one must know not only what to do but when and why, for how long, with which children, and in connection to what! These story chapters were created to give teachers concrete examples of how a variety of ideas and activities might be implemented in different classrooms at different grade levels with a variety of different children by teachers with a range of different teaching styles.

To accomplish this, we have created an imaginary school, Merritt Elementary School, where an imaginary class of children progresses from kindergarten to fifth grade. With help and support from the principal, Mr. Topps, and the central office facilitator, Sue Port, the various teachers use a variety of approaches to make literacy a reality for all their children. The children emerge into literacy under the enthusiastic tutelage of their kindergarten teacher, Helen Launch. Rita Wright provides a balanced approach in her first-grade classroom. She emphasizes shared and guided reading, words, writing, and self-selected reading, and demonstrates how the instruction changes as the children's literacy develops. Norma Nouveau, a first-year teacher, takes the class through second grade. She gets off to a somewhat rocky start, but with help from Mr. Topps, Sue Port, and other teachers, she makes great strides by the end of the year. Vera Wise, the third-grade teacher, has through all her years of teaching acquired huge stores of knowledge and books, and she carries out an integrated language arts program with literature as the centerpiece. The fourth-grade teacher, Yetta Maverick, also integrates, but her focus is on integrating across the curriculum. Ed Dunn, the fifth-grade teacher, carries out a balanced program that emphasizes studying, independence, and technology.

Our imaginary teachers keep a monthly journal, which allows us to see what they do and why they do it. Just as in real classrooms, not everything works out perfectly—or even at all—the first time. So the teachers problem solve, ask advice from colleagues, and try again. We join our teachers now as they are beginning an end-of-the year retreat to try to clarify, solidify, and articulate guiding principles with which they can all agree and which will help shape their daily instruction.

ACKNOWLEDGMENTS

We would like to thank the students and colleagues who have read and commented on earlier editions of this book. They have helped us improve it. We would also like to thank the following reviewers for their helpful suggestions: Val Christensen, Valley City State University; Particia H. D'Agostino, Seely Place Elementary School, Edgemont School District, Scarsdale, New York; Jarene Fluckiger, University of Nebraska at Omaha; Karen Huff, Shenandoah University; Linda E. Martin-Squier, Ball State University; Joan Simmons, University of Wisconsin–Green Bay; John A Smith, Utah State University; Lynn C. Smith, Southern Illinois University at Carbondale.

The Retreat

Mr. Topps looked over the agenda for the faculty retreat on teaching reading and writing. Getting the money for stipends for the whole faculty had taken some finagling, but he was a problem-solving principal! A district-level grant and some money his site council had raised provided the funding he needed to add two workdays to the school year just ended. He believed a retreat was needed because he and his faculty had never really taken the time to work on instructional principles for literacy. Though the teachers were ready for their summer break, everyone had agreed it was better to do major work like this now so they had the summer to plan the coming year.

In preparation for the retreat, Tip had papered the room with posters he called his "brainwashings." These were the things he believed in and that helped guide his daily practice as an instructional leader in the school. He knew the teachers were somewhat familiar with them because he regularly brought them up during his conferences with them after observing their teaching.

> They can ALL learn to read and write.
> More children are "instructionally disabled" than "learning disabled."
> You are a gifted teacher of gifted children.
> Teach children not the curriculum.
> Think outside the box!

As the first group of teachers began to arrive, Mr. Topps put them to work distributing markers, paper, note cards, and other supplies they were going to need for their work together. Some teachers had also gathered around the brainwashings, and as he walked around, distributing copies of the agenda, he heard them wondering whether they were all supposed to subscribe to these ideas. He also overheard conversational bits as teachers arrived and glanced over the agenda. Someone at Helen Launch's table of kindergarten teachers remarked that there was no way this agenda was going to take all the time scheduled for the retreat; but when he passed by the third-grade teachers' table, he heard Vera Wise say that there was no way they could finish all the agenda in the time scheduled for the retreat. He hoped the truth was somewhere in between.

Mr. Topps welcomed the group of teachers before him and told them he had always wondered about the word "retreat" because his intent for these few days is to make progress, but when he asked for funding for a "progress" nobody bit. After the light laughter died down, he placed an overhead transparency on the projector and read it aloud.

> *I am only one.*
> *Still I am one.*
> *I cannot do everything.*
> *Still I can do something.*
> *Because I cannot do everything,*
> *I will not refuse to do the something I can do.*
> *Edward Everett Hale*

After a pause, he continued, "These are some of the words I try to live both my professional and personal life by. Imperfectly, at times, I admit. Hale's poem causes me to accept responsibility and to not give up in the face of overwhelming circumstances. Take a bit of the problem and deal with that. At least try, he says to me. I'd like each of you to take a file card and write down some words you use to help guide your life. We will be sharing these in a few minutes." Mr. Topps leaned against the table and watched the group. At the end of three minutes he told them to share their guiding words with their grade-level group. Then he called on some of the teachers who volunteered to share with the whole group.

"Well," began Helen Launch, "I had never really thought about it like this before, but when I was in college I read some of Haim Ginott's work, and one thing really stuck with me. He said, 'Treat every child as if he already is the person he is capable of becoming.' I know I try to live those words as I teach children. I really do believe they can all learn to read and write, and I know if I act that way, in my behaviors, the language I use with each child, and in the instructional choices I make, then they all will learn." The murmurs around the room showed how impressed her colleagues were with Helen's explanation.

Yetta Maverick chimed in from the fourth-grade teachers' table. "Helen, I didn't know that quote before, but I copied it down on my card right next to Hale's poem. It just feels right to me! Oh, Tip? How many cards are we each allocated? Anyway, what I wrote was a quote attributed to Martin Luther. He purportedly said, "Even if I knew certainly the world would end tomorrow, I would plant an apple tree today." What Luther says, to me anyway, is similar to Hale's poem—do something, don't just sit there, but it goes further than Hale. Be hopeful; there's always a chance; don't give up; make the world different because you were here."

Frank Lee piped up from the table of fifth-grade teachers to say, "You know, the words that have meant the most to me are, 'Every child has a right to a safe and orderly environment in which to grow into a physically and mentally healthy adult who is an eager lifelong learner.' These are the words that have meant the most to me as I teach," Frank finished as the room erupted in laughter to hear their school's mission statement used in this context.

The sharing of guiding words continued for several more minutes before Mr. Topps cut into the lively discussions and told them they had to get on to other agenda items. Anyone who wanted to share their guiding words with the whole group could put them in the center of the table, and he would have Ms. Mainstay, the school secretary, type them up for everyone. He suggested that teachers take their own guiding words (and any that were appropriate from others) and put them on posters in their classroom next year. "Start the year by sharing the words with the students and telling them how you live out the words in your daily life," Tip suggested.

Next, Tip directed them to his posters. "Some of you recognize these things from conversations we have had. I call these my brainwashings because I really like them. Talk with your grade level about any relationships you see between the guiding words everyone shared and the brainwashings. Also decide if any of the brainwashings make sense for your grade level. If not, why not? If so, how?"

After this activity, Mr. Topps helped the teachers think about what makes avid readers and writers. "You all know avid readers; you may even be one. Take an index card and write the names of five avid readers—yourself, children you have taught, anyone."

"Only five, Tip?" queried Will Minter, a second-grade teacher, with a grin.

"Only five," he responded.

Mr. Topps paused for them to jot down names. "Now, circle one name. On the back of the card, write down how you know that person is an avid reader." He again paused to allow them to respond. "Now, talk with the others at your table about the person you selected and the evidence of avid reading you have observed."

Tip listened in on the discussions at various tables. When he heard them winding down, he switched on the overhead again. "Tell me what you notice about avid readers," he asked. Tip began to record their comments on the overhead transparency.

stacks of books around	always has a book
talks about books	has a good vocabulary
knows lots of stuff	owns lots of books
gives books as presents	wants books as presents

"Now write the names of five avid writers you know, and we'll go through the whole process again."

"Do we have to have five names, Tip?" asked Will.

"Try," Mr. Topps responded.

The teachers settled back down to brainstorming names, selecting one name, and then finding evidence of avid writing. Sadly, many teachers could not think of five avid writers they knew. As the process continued, they also discovered that the evidences of avid writing were not as clear to them either. They did finally produce a short list which Tip compiled on a transparency, too. They discussed why it was harder to know who writes a lot and enjoys it. They decided that readers are more likely to talk about what they are reading than writers are to talk about their own writings. While both reading and writing may be solitary endeavors, writing is even more so, and the joy of writing less obvious to the observer.

Mr. Topps continued, "If this is what avid readers and writers are like, let's keep this in mind as we do our curriculum planning. Everything we do ought to be with the goal in mind of creating avid readers and writers. Use these behaviors to gauge your students against. Are you helping to shape avid readers and writers with each instructional decision you make?"

A quick glance at the clock showed him that the morning was already over. The salad-and-sub-bar lunch was quickly set out, including some cheesecake that Frank Lee's sister Sara had sent, and the group settled into talking about the morning's activities and their upcoming summer plans.

When the teachers returned after lunch, they found that name tags had been placed on all the tables. "Ah ah ah!" Tip waggled his finger as Linc Toomey and Ed Dunn tried to get their name tags together at a table by trying to trade places with Vera Wise. "No trading! You think I went to all this trouble so you could mix them up any way you want?" He grinned to take the sting out of his comment.

"Gee, Tip. Ed and I need to be together. We're working on that big tech project in his room, y'know," Linc implored. No soap! Ed and Linc gave in to the inevitability of the grouping and went around warning others of the dire consequences that would befall switchers.

"What do you notice about the people sitting with you at your table this afternoon? Isn't that a good multilevel question, Helen?" Tip asked a kindergarten teacher as they were starting the session.

"It is a good multilevel question, Tip! I noticed we are from different grade levels," said Rita Wright, her first-grade self squeezed into a space between a fourth-grade and a kindergarten teacher.

"Exactly so," he responded. "For this afternoon's work, we need thinkers representing different experiences and understandings about a range of student abilities, ages, and curricula. The instructional principles we formulate must reflect our whole school, and if you only worked with your grade level, you would be less likely to consider the full range of students we deal with. Our students come to us with a range of individual, cultural, and language differences. We must teach all of them. Among us we ought to have a pretty good idea of what that will take.

"That is not to say we must all teach reading and writing alike. Shared instructional principles simply means we have agreed to some overall guidelines that give our program continuity and integrity. You all know how much I believe that teachers are professionals, and as such, you should have freedom to select instructional materials, methodologies, and practices that fit your unique perspectives, abilities, and philosophies. However . . ." Tip paused for effect, then continued, "However, we must agree to some instructional principles because we have a responsibility to do our best to ensure that all students learn to read and write as well and as much as they can.

"Each table has a sheet of chart paper. Designate a scribe for your group. The writer will put 'Children learn literacy best . . .' at the top. Also designate a speaker who will explain your list to the whole group. Your group, including the writer and speaker, is to generate as many things as you can think of that finish that sentence stem. Use the brainwashings around the room, any other products we created this morning, and your own understandings and experiences. For example, were I in your group, I would suggest that we write, 'Children learn literacy best when actively engaged.' I would also suggest that we include 'Children learn literacy best through repetition with variety.'

Teachers talked together, generated lists, posted their lists on the wall, and then shared information about their lists. The activity took them up to their break time. When they returned from break, they found another blank sheet of chart paper on their tables.

"This time I want you to think about the instructional implications of all these wonderful things you believe about how children learn literacy best. If you believe that children learn literacy best when actively engaged, which, by the way, I see made it onto every group's list, if you believe that, then what must teachers do to ensure that this occurs? Writers, label this sheet 'Teachers should . . .' Now, spend 25 minutes again creating your chart. First 15 minutes on talking, last 10 finalizing language and writing it out."

"That's harder!" protested one table.

The sharing by groups of the ideas on the second chart took them up to the end of the day. Mr. Topps introduced Sue Port, the district curriculum supervisor, in case any teachers had not met her. She was going to join them for tomorrow's sessions. The teachers hung their "Teachers should . . ." charts on the wall and headed home.

The next day, Tip kicked off the session. "Okay. Ready for the next step. We are going to work on this all morning. Your group needs to schedule your own 15-minute break. Agree first when that will be. Second, start generating a list of the literacy instructional principles every classroom teacher in this school ought to be guided by. For example, in the past we have agreed as a school that we would all have self-selected reading daily. Maybe you think we should keep that or maybe you think it should be history. We have always said that we believe in having high expectations and that all children can learn to read and write. Do we still believe that? Do you get the level of specificity and language I am asking for here?

"Again, designate a scribe—get someone else this time—and begin talking through what we are going to all agree to. Spend at least a half hour trying to integrate the various posters and charts with your own experiences and expectations. What does our community expect? Come up with no more than 20 to 25 instructional principles max. Put these on file cards, one principle per card. Once you have identified your set of instructional principles, start sorting them into categories and paring them down to the most essential ones. By lunch time, you must have a list of about 10 items that you all understand and any one of you could explain to the whole group this afternoon. Sue and I will be sitting in with different groups so we can hear what the issues are and what you are thinking about them."

Each group settled in to work. To give them time to get started, and to orient Sue to what had gone on the previous day, Tip showed her the agenda and explained the wall hangings, handouts, and some of their discussions. Then they split up and began to sit in with groups of teachers, asking clarifying questions and encouraging them to consider additional issues before moving onto another group. When they had all left for lunch, Tip began to clean up the area, set up the room, and put out materials for the afternoon. He couldn't help but read the lists that had been left on the tables. He was pleased to see the instructional principles they were formulating and how much similarity there was across tables. This afternoon would be much easier than it could have been!

After lunch, Tip gave directions for their work up to break time. Tables of teachers had been paired to form half the number of this morning's tables. Their task was to resolve their two lists to devise one list of instructional principles between them. Same rules, no more than 10 instructional principles, which the groups would post on chart paper. After break, the groups would resolve the list into one final set of instructional principles and give three examples of instruction that reflected each principle. They got to work. Tip and Sue circulated again, listening in on the discussions.

Comment: "Okay, so we agree. All of us think it is a no-brainer that we need daily writing and that we need time every day for us to read to kids and for them to read to themselves."

Another comment: "How can we *not* put on there that we will have a safe school environment? If it isn't safe to be at school, nothing else can happen."

"Do you mean safe emotionally or physically?"

Another group: "Reading and writing *are* thinking, feeling, and language. I mean, what else could you put there?"

"I'm not disagreeing, but why? What does it mean? What does it mean for our teaching? How do we teach so that reading and writing are thinking, feeling, and language?"

Another group: "But reading and writing are learned in a variety of ways. If there were only one way, we would have found it a long time ago. Because kids come to us different in individual, cultural, and language ways, we have to have a range of approaches."

Another comment: "I cannot imagine how we would set schoolwide literacy instructional principles and not address decoding and spelling. Those two are crucial for kids to become independent with literacy tasks."

"I didn't say they were not important. You know how much time I spend on both in my room! However, the issue is should they be separate instructional principles or are they included within other areas?"

Another comment: "We have to say something about grading or report cards or something. Parents want to know how their children are doing. They want grades."

"Yeah, they want grades because they think they know what an A means."

"But don't you think what they really want is to know 'Is my kid doing okay or should I be worried here?'"

Overheard elsewhere: "I don't see the need for a goal on having groups. I lived through the bluebirds, redbirds, and buzzards era. I don't want to go back to that."

"I'm not talking about ability groups. There is something other than ability grouping and whole-group teaching. Doesn't it frustrate you that some kids already know what you're teaching and others are left in the dust? Whole group usually just teaches to the middle."

Throughout these discussions, Sue and Tip made notes on the issues that were coming up at the various tables. At their meeting during the break, they would take the literacy instructional principles identified by the teachers and the issues they were struggling with today and create some inservice topics to offer during the year. Both were very impressed with the quality of the discussions and the professionalism with which the teachers handled the areas of disagreement or misunderstanding.

Following the break, groups began to reconcile the instructional principles from their various charts. Tip told them, "The final list can be no longer than 12 items—it must fit on a single sheet of paper. The final list must be in plain and clear language we can share with parents and school board members who don't know educationese. Let me first, though, go across the charts and find those things which are on all the charts." He began circling items that were similar and then rewriting those onto a clean piece of chart paper.

The groups worked hard for the rest of the afternoon. While the teachers worked, Tip removed all the posters, except the final list, from the walls, leaving plenty of room for their products. When Sue and Tip perched at different tables, they heard teachers saying over and over, "Yes, but when you . . . , you have to . . . ," and "But what I thought that meant was . . ." Even though these very smart and dedicated teachers all agreed to the same instructional principles, their personal interpretations of what that meant or how it looked in the classroom varied a lot. The three examples of instruction that reflected each principle were really a selection from the ones each group had written during their various deliberations.

At the end of the session, the teachers gathered up their personal items and said their good-byes, making arrangements to meet for additional planning or for social events. Tip took down the 12 charts the teachers had created. He loved the tone of his school. There was a positive atmosphere that reflected the learning attitude of the teachers. But to help all of this happen, he, Sue, and the teachers had a lot of work ahead of them.

1. Provide a balanced Literacy program.

Use a variety of methods to meet one goal.

Balance teacher led and student centered activities.

Build on children's multiple intelligences.

2. Make instruction multilevel.

Let students make choices whenever possible.

Use a variety of whole class, small group and partner arrangements.

Use a variety of materials on different levels.

3. Use language as the foundation for reading and writing.

Speaking and listening should often precede reading and writing.

Use a variety of oral language strategies like discussion, sharing, and dramatization.

Help children know that reading, writing, listening, and speaking are social and cultural.

4. Teach reading and writing as thinking.

Teach students that the essence of reading and writing is thinking.

Model essential thinking processes of connect, self-monitor, predict, organize, generalize, image, evaluate, and apply.

Use these thinking processes all day, every day.

5. Use feelings to create avid readers and writers.

Use student interest to engage them with reading and writing.

Help students realize their success comes from their effort and procedures, rather than their ability or luck.

Ensure success with appropriate reading and writing materials and tasks.

6. Connect reading and writing to all subject areas.

Provide real rather than artificial purposes for reading and writing.

Help students to develop their own purposes for reading and writing.

Have them read and write a variety of different kinds of text.

7.
- Read aloud to students daily.
- Select high interest books and articles.
- Select a variety of authors, genres, and topics.
- Read expressively.

8.
- Schedule daily self-selected reading.
- Set aside time just for self-selected reading.
- Teachers must help students get better at choosing books they will like.
- Teacher conferences with individuals or groups during self-selected reading.

9.
- Have students write everyday.
- Teach and use self-selected writing.
- Teach and use focused writing.
- Provide opportunities for students to respond to one another's writing.

10.
- Teach the decoding and spelling strategies reading and writing require.
- Stress transfer in all activities.
- Assess by what they actually use in reading and writing.
- Help students develop "word wonder".

11.
- Use observation to assess learning and plan instruction.
- Assess, evaluate, plan, then teach.
- Adjust instruction based on student strengths, limitations, and needs.
- Track student progress by observing their task performance and evaluating their work samples.

12.
- Inform parents of expectations and progress.
- Meet with parents in conferences.
- Hold a parent curriculum night at beginning of year.
- Make positive phone calls and send notes home once a month per student.

Miss Launch:
Kindergarten

THE PARENT MEETING

Over at last! Helen Launch glanced at her watch and noted with surprise that it was only 9:00 P.M. As she moved about the room, collecting materials and getting out other supplies for the next day, she thought over what had taken place. She had talked to the parents about her program for approximately half an hour, and then some of them had asked questions. To her amazement, many parents had stayed longer for a private chat. But now, even they had gone, leaving her to her reflections. She decided she would also need to contact the absent parents at a later time to discuss her kindergarten program with them.

She had known that this should be one of the most important encounters she would have with parents this year, and that this meeting would set the tone for all future parental cooperation. Mr. Topps had told them all to relax—these meetings went much more smoothly if they were informal and casual. To Miss Launch, with her penchant for food, that meant cookies and coffee! While the parents were assembling in the classroom, she had announced that refreshments were in the rear of the room, as was a sign-in sheet for their names.

Miss Launch firmly believed kindergarten to be an essential and integral part of the total school program. She had told the parents that kindergarten was *not* play time for which she was the baby-sitter. Further, she had emphasized that the foundation for all future school success was laid in kindergarten.

She had outlined some of the experiences that the children would have in her room and the reasons for them. This had been an important part of her presentation, for she wanted and needed parental support and cooperation. She had pointed out to the parents the various centers for learning. In addition to providing the traditional block, art, and house corners she had included other areas that she felt would enhance the educational program for the children. There was an animals area, an area for puppets and plays, one for reading, and a things-to-do corner that would include activities ranging from math, to science, to cooking and other topics. Much of the learning would take place in these centers.

Learning would also occur outside of the classroom. Miss Launch had told the parents that she had planned two field trips a month to various places in the school and community. Follow-up activities for these field trips would include making thank-you cards, drawing pictures, and having shared writing/language experience lessons about what they learned. These field trips would comprise most of the social studies curriculum of her kindergarten program as well as some science and much reading, writing, and math.

Miss Launch also had informed the parents of her concern with oral language development. She said that there would be many and varied opportunities for the children to talk and listen to each other. One of the mothers questioned why talking was important.

"Miss Launch, I don't know much about how they do school now, but when I was in school they didn't take learnin' time for talkin'. I don't see how that can help Chip learn to read! Readin' and talkin' are two different things as I see it!"

Miss Launch had replied calmly to Mrs. Moppet. "Not so different as you might think. The language children can speak and listen to is the foundation we build on to teach them to read and write. Children are already speaking many thousands of words when they enter kindergarten. They will be able to read all of those words within the next few years and spell most of them. In addition, they will be reading and writing other words that they do *not* yet know. But almost without exception, those new words they will learn to read and spell will also be words that they have used in speech. If they do not learn to *say* new words, or if they do not learn to use old words in new ways, then they will read and spell only at the level at which they now speak. That is why I do so much with oral language development. In reading and writing, I want to build from what the children know to what they need to know. That is another reason, by the way, for the two monthly field trips. Not only will the children become more familiar with their community, but these trips will also expose them to new words and new ideas that they will need later for reading, writing, and other subjects."

She had gone on to say that there would be much dramatization and storytelling. Some of the children's stories would be written on chart paper, some might appear in individual storybooks, and still others might become part of one of the class books of original stories. Each day, before the children left, she would sit with them and discuss all the activities engaged in that day. She felt this discussion would help them develop a sense of sequence, the recognition of main ideas, and a memory for things they had accomplished, all important requisites for reading and writing. Besides, she had said, when parents ask children what they had done in school all day, she wanted to prevent the old "Oh, nothing!" response that children often give.

Miss Launch explained to parents that she wanted to give the children many experiences in identifying, sorting, and classifying. These activities help children develop vocabulary and see conceptual relationships. They would work with letters, colors, numbers, their own names, and many other concepts that would help them learn to do the thinking crucial for success in reading and writing.

Miss Launch indicated that she would use a variety of techniques to prepare children for the very important idea that one reads with the expectation of understanding what is read. They would construct charts of their animals' activities, of the weather, and of other things they knew about or could observe. They would be dictating stories and "reading" them to one another and to her. They would cook in the classroom and follow simple recipes. While she did not believe that kindergarten is the place to establish reading groups and use commercial reading programs, she did believe that each child should have constant exposure to things that can be read.

Miss Launch told them that she would read to the children to develop their listening skills. ("Good luck," she heard Butch's mother mutter.) During these listening lessons, she would model for the children her thinking processes as a reader. While reading good children's books, she would model how to connect, organize, self-monitor, predict, image, generalize, apply, and evaluate. She showed them a copy of a Big Book of a nursery rhyme she would be reading to the children the first week of school. Parents exclaimed over the size and joined in as she modeled how she would do these shared book readings with the children. Even parents in the back row could see the words as she pointed to them.

She planned to read to the children a great deal, and she expected them to "read" to her. For some children, this reading would consist of picture interpretation; for others, actual words would be read. Everyone would be reading when they were in the reading center and, later in the year, during their self-selected reading time. By the end of the school year, they would be able to read to themselves for several minutes each day. She had also planned many literature response activities for the children. These activities would be extensions of stories read to them, and they would be tied into other classroom activities such as music, art, and cooking.

MISS LAUNCH: Children first of all need to develop a desire and purpose for reading. Reading is a difficult task at best, but without proper motivation, it is even more so. We're all going to read, read, read in this class and not just during reading center time or self-selected reading. I will read to the children and they will "read" to me and to one another. Even if they're only reading pictures, they are still acquiring abilities they will need to be good readers. They can determine the sequence of story events, what the important ideas in the story are, and what might happen next in the story. We will write and, I hope, receive letters. We will label things around the classroom and set up a post office for messages. We'll make books of all kinds. Some will have only pictures, like Mercer Mayer's "Frog" books, and others will have words. We'll follow recipes for purposeful reading. In addition, we'll be working with rhyming patterns and letter names and sounds. As I said earlier, I believe that a firm background of oral language is the most important contribution I can make to your child's future success in reading, so I will do much with that. I have lots more planned, but I hope that you have the general idea.

Horace's mother held up her hand. "Could you explain that in a little more detail, Miss Launch? I'm not quite sure that I understand what our children will be doing."

MISS LAUNCH: Children who are ready to begin reading and writing have certain characteristics. They know why people read and write, they have a broad background of knowledge and concepts, they know that words are made up of sounds, and they know many letter names and sounds. They know how print works and how we describe print, they know 20 to 30 sight words, and they want to learn how to read and write. Children are at all different places with these critical knowings; I'll be working to make sure I develop them during the school year. The main activities I use are reading to the children shared book experiences such as I modeled earlier, language experience and shared writing, and having the children write. Through these activities and many others, I will be helping your children to better understand how words, letters, and sounds work.

MR. MARTIN: You've mentioned cooking in kindergarten a couple of times now, and I can't for the life of me figure out what cooking has to do with reading and writing. Can you explain it to me?

MISS LAUNCH: Would you believe that it's really because I like to eat? [Chuckles around the room] Actually, I do justify it educationally, though I must admit that I enjoy the food too! Cooking in this room will be done for several reasons. First, since children eat what they prepare, they learn that it is important to follow directions carefully; second, the food produced is the incentive to do the work well, so there is meaning to doing it; third, there is always more language produced as we discuss why a particular sequence is necessary and why certain ingredients are added, what they do together; and fourth, new science concepts are observed and dealt with, such as the evaporation of liquid, or the nature of change as we observe it with popcorn. Maybe I should add a fifth one—because it's fun, and if language, literacy, and science learning can all result from an enjoyable activity as well as it can from a pencil and paper task, well, I'm all for it!

MRS. PENN: I recently read an article about . . . , is it phonemic awareness? What is that anyway? The article made it look like that was just about all that mattered in kindergarten.

MISS LAUNCH: Yes, it is important, though not more important than other critical knowings. *Phonological awareness* is the term that phonics researchers have used to refer to whether children are conscious of the elements in the language they speak and hear. So, *word awareness* concerns whether children are conscious of the individual words in the oral language around them. All children who can talk can speak and understand separate words—the question is, are they aware of those separate words? The reason word awareness is important is simple. How could a child learn to read and spell a word unless you could link them up to the separate pronunciation that word has in oral language? *Syllable awareness* concerns whether children are conscious of the separate syllables in spoken language. *Rhyme awareness* concerns whether children can tell whether two spoken words rhyme, as opposed to when they don't sound alike or when they sound alike at the beginning rather than the end. Finally, the *phonemic awareness* you asked about, Mrs. Penn, concerns whether children are conscious of the smallest individual sounds in the words they speak and hear. Phonemic awareness seems very important as children are learning phonics. Obviously, they cannot learn to associate sounds with letters unless they are conscious of the sounds in spoken language. This year, we will do a number of activities to help your children develop these different kinds of *phonological awareness.* It is one of the critical knowings I talked about a few minutes ago.

MR. MARTIN: Will the children be studying a letter each week, the way my older children did when they were in kindergarten?

MISS LAUNCH: No, because I have not found that to be a particularly effective approach. By the end of kindergarten, children should know almost all of their capital and small-case letter names, they should know the sounds of almost all the consonant letters, and they should be able to form almost all of their capital and small-case letters on unlined paper. If we try to teach everything about a letter during a single week, we miss the wonderful opportunity of revisiting the same letter over and over again throughout the year, which all the children will benefit from. Programs that teach a letter a week often have children who really don't remember much about the letters they studied earlier in the year. Also, when we teach letter-names and letter-sounds together, children are more likely to confuse them. Letter formation is harder than letter recognition, so it is better taught several months later. Now, we will do some letter-a-week instruction starting in January, but only for the consonant letter sounds. Then we will review, review, review!

Miss Launch then explained that there would be at least two parent conferences this year, and that at the end of the year, parents would receive a written appraisal of their child's performance in various areas.

MR. GRAHAM: I have no questions as such, but I just want you to know that I am amazed that so much can be done with kindergartners! You have a very ambitious year mapped out. Is there anything we can do to help you?

MISS LAUNCH: Is there ever! Thanks so much for asking, because I was just about to ask for your help. I can use parents and other relatives to help with taping stories, typing books, helping children write, field trips, cooking, and all sorts of things. I'll be sending a request-for-help letter home soon, giving you the opportunity to volunteer. Some of the jobs can be done at home, so that even if you don't have a lot of time, you can still help me out. As to all that the children can do, I have found that many adults tend to underestimate the capabilities of young children, and for that reason we do not help them to attain their full potential. I hope to help them do so without the attendant pressure that we sometimes place on children.

As Miss Launch evaluated the evening, she found that the meeting had gone rather well. Many of the parents had remarked to her that they were pleased that the emphasis would be on learning through creative means. She was certain that she would have a great deal of support from the parents whenever she might need it. She hoped she had convinced them that kindergarten was "real school," but not like first grade. Oh, well, if not now, then by the end of the year they would be aware of it! She glanced around the room. Yes, all was ready for tomorrow morning. She allowed herself the luxury of a stretch and a yawn; then, she turned off the lights and left for home.

MONTHLY LOGS

September

September is always a bit of a shock to my system. Each year I am taken aback at how small and shy the entering kindergartners are. I quickly realize that I am using the children of the previous spring as my criteria. How much they do grow and change in one year's time! It always takes so long to deal with some of the school socialization processes, such as how to use the water fountain and what "line up" means. Those can be difficult areas for children to deal with for the first time. Fortunately, most of them are already "housebroken"!

Starting the year is the difficult task, and as I look over the list of all I have set out to accomplish, I wonder somewhat at my audacity. The 12 instructional principles we formulated at our retreat in June have been in my mind ever since. I know that a certain road is paved with good intentions and that if I don't structure myself, I will probably not do all that I now plan to. Therefore, I have taped a list of factors inside my plan book so that I will be reminded to include specific activities for each in my planning. These factors are my way of turning the 12 instructional principles into a form that will guide my kindergarten program throughout the year.

THE SEVEN CRITICAL KNOWINGS

1. Children need to know why people read and write.
2. Children need to have a broad background of knowledge and concepts.
3. Children need to know that words are made up of sounds.
4. Children need to know many letter names and sounds.
5. Children need to know print conventions and jargon.
6. Children need to know 20 to 30 concrete words.
7. Children must want to learn how to read and write.

DAILY INSTRUCTION TO ACCOMPLISH THE KNOWINGS

Read to and talk with children.
Use shared book experiences.
Use shared writing and language experience.
Have children write regularly.
Help children understand how letters and sounds work.

My class of 25 includes some very interesting young people; I can tell already! The list of children follows:

Alex	Daphne	Mike
Alexander	Hilda	Mitch
Anthony	Horace	Mort
Betty	Jeff	Pat
Butch	Joyce	Paul
Carl	Larry	Rita
Chip	Mandy	Roberta
Daisy	Manuel	Steve
Danielle		

One child was so withdrawn that I was immediately aware that his problem was more than fear of coming to school for the first time. Paul wouldn't speak to me or any of the others for three class sessions, and then he merely uttered his name in a group game. When this happened, we were so excited that we gave him a "silent cheer" (that is, we raised our hands into the air, shook them up and down, and formed our mouths as though we were cheering). Paul cried often during those first two weeks, but they were strange, silent tears that rolled down his cheeks. There was no sobbing or screaming—just a sad, sad look and those tears running down his cheeks. (I have asked the school social worker to investigate the home situation. Something is drastically wrong; perhaps we can discover what it is and then remedy the situation.) Alex and Daphne began to sniffle when they saw this (tears are among the most contagious of childhood afflictions), but Hilda simply told them to be quiet, that she had looked around and it was obvious that there was nothing to be afraid of! The sniffling subsided, but Paul continued his silent crying despite all my efforts to comfort or distract him.

Although he is quite friendly and willing to play with the other children, Manuel apparently does not speak one word of English. He may understand a few words from watching television, but even there I am not sure. So far, he gets along with the others because he relates well non-verbally, but I feel the challenge of teaching him what kindergarten exists to impart.

I read to the children every day, usually more than once a day, and sometimes the whole morning is built around one book. First the book is read to them, and then we do other activities to tie the book into the other curricular areas. As an example, one of the first books I read to them was Mirra Ginsburg's *Mushroom in the Rain*. After reading it, we talked about their favorite parts of the story, and they drew with crayons or painted at the easel the one thing they had enjoyed the most. We hung these up and let children tell what the part was and why they had chosen it. The fox section was the most popular of all, for children like to be scared just a little. Then we dramatized the story by playing the parts of the various animals. When I asked the children what we could use for a mushroom, they cleverly decided to use an umbrella that they would open out more and more as the various animals came under. In addition, we counted the number of animals in the book. We looked for certain colors ("Find all the red things on this page"). We made up a song that we could sing to the tune of "Are You Sleeping?":

Is it raining,
Is it raining,
Little Ant?
Little Ant?
Hurry to the mushroom!
Hurry to the mushroom!
Drip, drop, drip.
Drip, drop, drip.
Is it raining,
Is it raining,
Butterfly?
Butterfly? (etc., for all the animals up through the rabbit. Then:)
Here comes Foxy!
Here comes Foxy!
Poor Rabbit! (two times)
"No, he is not here, Sir." (two times)
"Go away." (two times)
See the rainbow. (two times)
In the sky. (two times)
Now the sun is shining. (two times)
Warm and bright. (two times)

We tested the hypothesis that mushrooms grow in the rain, and we planned additional adventures for the characters in the book. We talked about who else might have come to the mushroom, what might happen next, where Ant would go when the rain finally stopped, and what other scary things might happen to the other animals. After we did a lap story with *Mushroom in the Rain*, I placed the characters, props, and the book in the puppets and plays center so they can retell the story individually or in small groups over and over.

At their seats, they drew a picture about another animal that might try to get under the mushroom. I encouraged them to write a word or more on their paper that would tell others about their idea. Then I had them think of a statement to dictate about their picture, and I circulated among their work tables, writing statements for them on the page. I can really see how it might help to have a parent volunteer help me with this part! Chip seemed not ever to have seen a crayon, and so Danielle helped him learn how to hold it and mark with it. Paul could not come up with an animal to draw or a word to say. Most children drew but did not try to write any words. Larry wrote his own sentence!

(An elephant tried to get under the mushroom.)

We have established a daily pattern or schedule. Establishing a routine that children can depend upon is a critical aspect of school. The morning is mainly spent on math and language arts, so I have only three hours in which to do a lot of things. The morning schedule is:

8:30   Attendance, sharing, read a story or poem
9:00   Work time—centers, oral language lessons, etc.
10:00   Physical education—outside if possible
10:15   Snack and story
10:30   Work time
11:15   Group together for review of work sessions

Most mornings at 9:00, we begin by singing "The Alphabet Song." In addition to having a book- and print-rich classroom, I have had the capital letters displayed large over the marker board and at eye level two or three places around the room since they entered my classroom on the first day. For a few minutes each morning, I use an empty can, carton, or wrapping of a product I think they may be familiar with. I ask if anyone knows what it is—someone usually does. One of the first packages I hold up is an empty *Cheerios* box. After we share briefly about whether we have had them, like them, or prefer another kind, I ask them to volunteer to come up one at a time and point to something on the box they notice that no one else has noticed yet today. Some children point out a color, some a picture, and some a letter. Rather than asking who can point to the letter C or who can point to the color yellow, I use this multilevel task because it helps every child be successful. After the children are finished, I "notice" anything else on the box that I want to draw their attention to but which no child pointed out. I emphasize letters during this activity, making sure that every child is paying attention when a letter is noticed and noticing any myself that the children did not.

During the third week, at work time the children were to find pictures of red things in magazines and catalogs. Larry, who is already reading, I've discovered, found the word *red* also. We pasted the things they found on a chart labeled "Red Things." Most of the children could already identify the colors without help, but some could not. I paired Joyce (who could) and Chip (who couldn't), so she could help him find red things. Daisy, Jeff, Paul, and Butch also worked with other children to find red objects. Once Manuel understood what we were looking for, he was able to find pictures of red things independently.

We took the first field trips of the year right in our own school area. It is important for children to become oriented to the building, the grounds, and the personnel as soon as possible. The first day the children came to school, we spent part of the morning walking through those parts of the building we *had* to know—the restrooms, the office, and the janitor's room—so that when (not *if*, but *when*) a child throws up I can stay with the child while someone else asks the janitor to bring a mop. We have our own kindergarten-sized playground equipment, and that also had to be shown. We went to the office on subsequent days and met the secretary, Mrs. Mainstay, and the principal, Mr. Topps. I prepared for these trips by first going there myself and making sure that someone who knew precisely what it was I wanted children to learn about that particular place would be on hand. I prepared the children by telling them the highlights of each place, alerting them to what to look and listen for, and urging them to try to remember everything, so that we could talk and write about it when we got back to the room. Upon our return, I asked them to tell what we had seen and done. As each child made a contribution, I wrote it down on chart paper with the child's name after it, so that he or she could see the very words contributed. I repeatedly drew their attention to the chart by reading aloud what I wrote while I wrote it. Afterward, I wrote the sentences on sentence strips, cut these into words and let children glue them back on another piece of paper in the proper order. Finally I read it all back to them and they agreed that they had done a fine job!

It has also been a busy month with some of the activities that I have been doing with the children to help develop visual discrimination of letters. We have learned to play some new games. I wrote out six copies each of the capital forms *P*, *H*, *A*, and *R*. I made each one about six inches high so that the children could readily see them from across the room. They are on sheets of oak-tag and covered with clear plastic adhesive paper so that they are durable. The first game was one that the whole class played together. I shuffled the cards and gave out one to each of the children. I told them to find the other children who had the same letter. When two children got together, they had to stay together while searching for other children who matched them. If they thought that they had found one that was a match, they carefully looked at the parts to see if they were correct. After all groups had been formed, I checked them: Perfect the first time, just as I had known it would be, for the abler ones helped those who could not yet match. (I had set the timer for three minutes. They enjoy the timing—it gives activities a little added excitement.)

It was interesting to observe the differences among the children as they formed their groups. Paul stayed put and was found by Mandy and Horace, who also had *P*s. They dragged him along with them until they found or were found by the other *P*s. Daisy dashed wildly around the room, ostensibly looking for the other *A*s, but in fact making it only more difficult for them to track her down. Mort sat in a chair, apparently not wanting to exhaust himself, being fully confident that the *H*s would get to him in time. Chip and Manuel held hands and went from group to group checking the letters, even though Chip was an *A* and Manuel an *R*. I suppose they just needed the extra confidence that they gave one another. The children begged to do it again, so we shuffled the cards and went through the same process. This time, Hilda tried to organize the thing a little more by shouting out, "A! A! A!" apparently as a clue to those who might know the name of the letter. Larry formed his hand into the letter *P* and said, "Do you look like this?" Ingenious children I have!

For another game I used the same cards and placed three cards of the same letter on the chalkboard tray with one that was different. I arranged the cards like this for ease the first time: *A A A P.* I then asked Rita to come find the ones that were the same. She chose the first three. "Terrific! Let's all give Rita a silent cheer!" (The silent cheer is a good reward for children, and it's also easy on the teacher's eardrums.) I continued the game with other children, making the letter combinations harder or easier depending on a child's capabilities. I then put the cards into the things-to-do center and suggested that they were available to play with.

October

October is over—I didn't think Halloween would *ever* arrive, and neither did the children! Every day it seemed they asked if it were here yet. Well, at least I was able to channel some of that interest toward school activities. Many of the books I selected to read to them and ones they chose themselves were about Halloween or monsters. One of my favorites, *Where the Wild Things Are*, was one of those with which we did literature response activities. The children made monster masks, and we had a "wild things" parade. We also had a word gathering for scary words—I asked them to tell me all of the scary things they could think of. Since this was our first word gathering, the children had trouble getting started. After only a few suggestions by other children, everyone joined in. Even Paul gave me one—*night*. When they started to bog down, having given me several words and phrases, I asked them for scary colors, then for scary smells, sounds, and looks. This is their completed list. Leo Lionni's Frederick the mouse, the original word gatherer, would be very pleased with this compilation.

SCARY THINGS

blood	monster	bad dream	nightmare
howl	bloody	black cat	Boo!
ghost	scream	witch	mummy
giant	storm	red	fire
dogs	growl	night	orange
purple	blue	scared	afraid

something touching me in the dark
when my night light burns out
footsteps in the dark
my mom's closet without the light on
my window with the curtains open
noises outside in the dark

After we had completed the list, I read the words back to the children, running my hand under each word or phrase as I said it so that they would have more opportunity to observe left-to-right progression with the return sweep to the next line. "Now," I told them, "we are going to write a poem!" I had read many poems to them and they did enjoy poetry. Now it was our turn to produce. I used a concrete format since it is the simplest one I know. I drew a random number and arrangement of lines on the chalkboard, and the children helped me to fill them in with words and phrases. To show them what I wanted us to do, I had them count the number of lines I had drawn, and I told them that I was going to use some of the words from our scary things chart to help me make up the poem. There would be only one word written on each line, so since we had counted 21 lines, I needed to write 21 words. This is what they saw:

‾‾‾   ‾‾‾

‾‾‾   ‾‾‾   ‾‾‾   ‾‾‾   ‾‾‾   ‾‾‾

‾‾‾   ‾‾‾

‾‾‾   ‾‾‾   ‾‾‾   ‾‾‾   ‾‾‾

‾‾‾   ‾‾‾

‾‾‾   ‾‾‾   ‾‾‾   ‾‾‾

The children were intrigued, particularly when they saw me begin to write words on each of the lines. This is my finished poem:

> *I felt*
> *something touching me in the dark.*
> *I knew*
> *my window curtains were open.*
> *I screamed.*
> *Bad dream go away.*

We counted the number of words that were on each of the rows of lines. Mort pointed out that the first line in the second row had nine words on it! At that point, to help them distinguish between words and letters, we talked about how some words have one letter (pointing out "I" in the poem) and that some words have more than one letter. The word *something* has nine letters. I wrote *Mort* on the board. "What is that word?" I asked. He did know his name and told me that it said *Mort*. "This is one word and that word is your name. But your name has four letters in it." Of course, it was necessary to do the same with the names of several other children, since all of them wanted their names written. But it was also important to count the letters in the names of several children in order to show children the concept of *letter* versus *word* in lots of examples. Obviously they didn't all get it this time around, but with lots of examples throughout the year they should all have the idea by the time they hit first grade (I hope!). With a little help, this is what the class was able to come up with:

One Night

> *Black cat scream, black cat howl!*
> *Why do you make that noise?*
> *Growl, purr, growl, purr*
> *Dog and cat*
> *fight.*

I copied both my poem and their poem onto sheets of chart paper and hung them near the scary things chart. I find it fascinating that Danielle will steer her wheelchair over and pore over the poems with Roberta and Alex. They seem fascinated with the idea that there is one word on each of the lines, and they try to count how many letters are in each of the words. Occasionally Mort will wander over and watch them for a while. I heard him say, "But how do you *know* which ones are words and which ones are letters? I don't get it. I think you're making it all up." Clearly, there is a range of abilities within this classroom.

We also did a concrete poem on the color black. First we had a word gathering of black words, sounds, and smells to get them prepared.

Black

> *Black, black is the night,*
>   *blacker than black*
>   *is*
>   *my window.*

While we were gathering black words (which was, of course, the color chart they were working on that week), a discussion took place. The children were coming up with all kinds of black things when Butch contributed three words: *Joyce, Danielle*, and *Jeff*. Some of the children turned around and looked at those children as if they had never seen them before. Others started murmuring—this *was* a revelation!

Larry said, "No, I don't agree. Some people call them black, but I think they are actually more brown."

The three were asked by another child what color *they* thought they were. Joyce responded, "Well, what color do you think *you* are?" There was a general comparing of arms, but little agreement. Finally Jeff said proudly, "Well, I don't care what color I look like; I'm black." So his name went up on the chart, and though he tried to hide it from them, he smiled! Later I saw him tracing the letters of his name on the chart. He was the only child to get listed on the chart.

I sent a letter to all my parents at the beginning of October to solicit help. Parental response to the letter was overwhelming. For the most part, parents want to be involved in their children's education and will volunteer if there is something specific that they feel confident in doing. In some cases, parents prefer to or *must* do things at home. For example, Chip's mother must stay home to take care of an elderly aunt and uncle who live with them. She thus offered to cut out things for me if I would send the materials to her. *Where* it's done matters not to me! I'm just delighted that parents are willing to do it at all!

I have labeled many things around the room: window, door, mirror, desk, table, chair. Children seem to enjoy finding labeled objects that have letters like those in their names. I was working with each of the children so that they would recognize their own names. I wrote each name about three inches high on unlined paper. I then took each child's hand and traced over the name with two fingers. All the time we did that, I said the name over and over with the child. Then, after we had done that a few times, I let them go to the chalkboard where they could write it, using the paper as a model. I stayed with each child until the name was mastered and then went to work with the next one. With that technique, almost all of the children can recognize their names when they see them, and several can write their own names without looking at a model. As a further incentive, I labeled the bulletin board with their names and then asked them to draw a picture

Dear Parents,

As I told you at our September parent meeting, I am most eager to provide your children with a year full of good learning experiences. In order to give them the kind of program I have envisioned, I am asking for your help in many ways. Would you please put a check mark beside those things which you would be willing to do for us this year. The space for "other" is one in which you might suggest to me any possible aid or special talent you would like to contribute.

Thank you so much for your prompt attention to this matter. Your children and I will gain much from your participation in their education.

Sincerely,
Helen Launch

....

Please detach here and return.

I would be willing to help in the following ways:
____ helping in class one hour a week
____ typing at home (or school)
____ cutting out paper at home (or school)
____ transporting children for field trips
____ helping with the cooking projects at school
____ donating scrap materials (cloth, pretty paper, etc.)
____ tape-recording stories, music, etc.
____ making puppets
____ contributing art materials
____ contributing materials for house corner
____ contributing books, records, pictures, etc.
____ contributing scatter rugs, pillows for floor, etc.
____ other:

Name: _____
Telephone: _____

of themselves and tell me where to hang it. Mort, Paul, and Daisy were the only three who needed extra help. Mort got confused because of all the names that began with *M*, as did Daisy with three *D* names. Paul just didn't have a clue! Another activity they like is to dip one-inch paint brushes into clear water and write on the board with those. They have fun, they learn, there is no erasing to do, and at the end, the chalkboard is clean.

A device I started this month to also help the children identify their own and each others' names, as well as to help them develop responsibility, is a *job chart*. There are always many tasks to be done in a classroom, and by this time of the year I try to involve the children even more than previously. There are enough jobs for everyone, even though several children have the same job simultaneously, as the cleaners do. So that children have a variety of jobs during the year, the job assignments rotate weekly. Some jobs can be done by the children only if their teacher instructs them. For instance, they must be told how much water to give the plants that are so important for the science we teach in kindergarten. One tip that I found helpful was to color-code plants to soup cans used for watering. I draw a line inside the soup can with permanent marker to indicate how much water is needed for a plant. A small square of color on the plant container that matches the line drawn in the can will clue children so that they will have a hard time going wrong. I learned, however, that with a color-blind child like Butch, you may have a drowned cactus and a droopy ivy! Using this kind of a coding system is the beginning of learning to follow "written" instructions. Though no words are used, children learn to decode the meaning of the symbol being used (in this case, color) in order to follow some specific instructions.

Here is the job chart for one week. Every week new assignments are made:

Water plants	Chip	Paul	Anthony		
Room cleaners	Betty	Butch	Daisy	Rita	Hilda
Messengers	Manuel	Daphne	Alexander		
Mail	Larry and Danielle (they knew all of the names)				
Line leader	Mort				
Group work leaders	Roberta	Horace	Carl	Alex	
Feed animals	Pat	Mike	Steve		
Special helpers	Mitch	Joyce	Mandy	Jeff	

I now have the capital letters of the alphabet also spread out on a wall of the room, and I have placed the first names of all of the children by the letter that begins their name. I wrote each name on a sentence strip made of colored tagboard. They are large enough to read from anywhere in the room. All the activities I do with children's names help them become aware of letters and words. These activities are highly motivating because children are always interested in their own and other children's names. I often see them standing alone or in pairs or triples near the job chart or name wall, looking at or talking about one or more of the names.

Another popular hangout is the "Words We Can Read" bulletin board. Children have been bringing in words from advertisements that they can read. Of course, if "the golden arches" are missing, Betty can't really say "McDonald's." Nevertheless, being able to read the word with the logo is a beginning step for successful later reading. They love bringing in words, which they share with the class during our morning opening time, pinning them to the bulletin board. I've had to place some restrictions on them, however, ever since Butch brought in the condom ad. They must show the word to me first; I decide if they can share it with others. Along with this, the children are making their own *Words I Can Read* books by pasting logos and words to pages. I often see them reading their books to other children.

During work time, I frequently ask the class to go one at a time to the "Words We Can Read" bulletin board and point to one word we know and say it. I ask them to point to one no one else has pointed to today, which helps them try to pay attention to what others are doing. We have done several other activities during work time this month.

We have used Cheerios to "count" the words in oral statements. I give each child six Cheerios. After modeling for them several times, I make a statement to them and ask them to push out a Cheerio for each word they hear. In the statement "I love you," they should push out three Cheerios. At this point, I don't use any words with more than one-syllable, and I don't use any statements with more than five words. I help the ones who are having trouble by "stretching" my statement, "I-love-you." This activity helps children acquire word awareness.

Instead of singing "The Alphabet Song," as we did regularly last month, this month I often have the class say the capital letters while I point to them in order with my yardstick. I pace it so they have to look at the letter to know when to say it, rather than just saying the alphabet without looking at the letters.

During teacher read-aloud time this month, I read lots of alphabet book to them. I made sure it was a very simple one like *The Timbertoes ABC Alphabet* or *Alphabetics*. After I had read one of these a couple of times, I encouraged the children to consider where they had seen a particular letter or whether they had that letter in their name. Such discussions, though brief, help children become more aware of particular letters in their environment outside of school.

Our two field trips this month were to places that supply us with food—the grocery store and the farm. I had taken my class to these same two places last year, and I made extensive notes to myself about the kinds of things I wanted them to notice and learn about. I spend a lot of time listing for myself what concepts and vocabulary I anticipate will be developed. After each visit, then, we make language-experience charts of things seen and learned.

I made arrangements for the manager of the grocery store to show us around at 8:45. I planned to spend half an hour there, so the children would be able to observe some shoppers, but the store wouldn't be too crowded. I prepared the children for this trip by discussing with them the various services and goods the store has to offer. Daisy was the greatest contributor, for she had spent a good bit of time in stores with her mother. I put down things the children said, so after the trip they could look at their list and add to it. Upon our return, we wrote this summary that hangs on the bulletin board surrounded by all of the children's pictures.

We went to the store. (Daphne)
We saw lots and lots of food. (Daisy)
The fruits and vegetables are called *produce*. (Larry)
We saw lots of meat. (Chip)
There were sweet things to eat. (Carl)
The store man showed us many things. (Pat)
We had fun and learned a lot. (Rita)
My mother and Larry's mother drove. (Roberta)

In addition, the children drew pictures and wrote thank-you letters that I mailed along with a copy of their summary and a personal note of thanks from me. Some of the children were even able to write a few real words.

We did the same kinds of activities for our visit to the farm. So many children do not associate the farm with the grocery store that I made a special effort to talk about where butter, milk, meat, and vegetables come from. When I first asked them where milk comes from, Butch replied, "From the carton." But where did the milk for the carton come from, I persisted. Jeff told me that it came from the store! In the whole group, only four—Larry (no surprise!), Steve and Anthony (the science buffs), and Daphne (who lives on a farm)—knew that cows are milked and that is the source of milk.

We received several pumpkins from both the farm and the grocery store, so it seemed only reasonable to try out some of the recipe and craft ideas in *The All-Around Pumpkin Book*. Two of their favorite recipes were roasted pumpkin seeds and pumpkin milk (believe it or not!). Here's the adapted recipe for pumpkin milk, which they did in groups of six:

Pumpkin Milk

We Need:
2 cups of plain yogurt
3/4 cup pumpkin sauce
4 tablespoons honey
1 1/2 teaspoons nutmeg
1 1/2 cups milk
2 tablespoons wheat germ
We Do:
Put everything in the blender and turn it on.
Turn the blender on whip.
When it is all mixed up it will be all orange.
Turn off the blender and pour the pumpkin milk into 6 glasses.

I thought it turned out remarkably well. All the children except Anthony tried it. However, I was a bit chagrined to overhear Butch muttering, "I'd rather have some coffee."

We ended the month by starting to do "The Five Steps," my version of Bobbi Fisher's "Four Steps" (in her book *Getting Started with Writing*, 1991). The Five Steps are: think; draw a picture; write something; write your name; copy (or stamp or get an adult to write) the date. At first, I do a minilesson to teach The Five Steps. Using an overhead projector placed on the floor so as not to obstruct any child's view of the screen, I do The Five Steps while the children sit together on a large rug and watch me.

I begin the minilesson by turning on the light to reveal a blank transparency with no lines on it. I say something like this:

"Boys and girls, in a few minutes I want you to do The Five Steps. So you will know what I want you to do, I am going to do The Five Steps and let you watch me. Before I do that, repeat after me what The Five Steps are: think [they repeat as I raise a finger]; draw a picture [they repeat as I raise another finger]; write something [they repeat as I raise another finger]; write your name [they repeat as I raise another finger]; stamp the date [they repeat as I raise a fifth finger]. So, what's the first step? ['think.'] All right, the first thing I have to do is think about what I will draw today. Have I seen anything interesting in the past few days? Have I done something interesting that I would like to draw? Let me think."

At this point, I pause and then mention one or two things that I have done or seen lately that I might draw. I make sure they are things that the children can relate to. An example might be for me to say something like:

"I know. We have a new baby in our neighborhood. I went over to see her when they brought her home from the hospital. Maybe I'll try to draw her asleep in her bassinet."

After mentioning a couple of examples like this one, I decide out loud to the class which one I will draw. Then, I say something like,

"I've thought about what I'm going to draw. Now it is time for me to do the second step. What is the second step? ['draw a picture.'] Right! Now I have to draw my picture."

I pick up a colored marker appropriate for use on acetate—any bright color but black—and begin drawing. I am careful to draw a very simple and primitive picture that will not intimidate the children into thinking they must be artistic to do this step. While drawing, I tell them what I'm trying to draw. I might also say something like,

"I won't draw my picture too big, because I need to leave room to write something later."

It is important for me not to take too long drawing my picture. When I have finished drawing, I put down my colored marker. Then, I say something like,

"I've thought about what I wanted to draw, and I've drawn a picture. Now it is time for me to do the next step. Does anyone remember what the third step is? ["write something"] Now it is time for me to write something about my picture."

Using a black marker, in my best handwriting, with correct spelling, capitalization, and punctuation, I write something about the picture I have drawn ("*I went to see the new baby.*") while saying out loud what I am writing.

At this point, I explain to the students that, if they aren't sure what letters to use to spell the words, they should write some letters they know how to write. The children are told that whatever they try to write will be okay. I model for the children what their writing might look like by writing a few letters or squiggles near what I have printed.

I say something like,

> "It is time for me to do the next step. Does anyone remember the next step after we write something? Yes, now it is time for me to write my name."

I write "Miss Launch." I tell the children that it is okay if they are not sure how to write their whole names. They should just put any letters they know are in their first names. I model what theirs might look like by putting one or two letters from my name near where I have printed my name.

For the fifth step, I model for the children how I want them to get their paper dated after they have finished the first four steps. I use a date stamp to stamp the date on my writing.

Immediately after this minilesson, I give the children unlined paper and drawing implements and tell them to begin doing The Five Steps at their seats. Again, I have them repeat The Five Steps aloud chorally after me. For a couple of minutes at the beginning, I tell them they are to think about what they will draw today. During this time, I do not let anyone start drawing. After the couple of minutes have elapsed, I tell everyone to begin drawing their pictures. I walk around the room, encouraging individual children as they move through the steps.

If they ask me to spell a word for them, I encourage the children just to write letters on their paper. It does not matter to me at first whether those letters bear any relationship to the sounds the children may want to represent in writing or even that they are real letters. Several children may look around the classroom in order to copy letters or words they find displayed there. At this point in the year, I am happy for them to do that, even though what they copy has no relationship to what they want to write or think they are writing.

From the time the children begin the thinking step until I end the activity is about 15 minutes. At the end of each Five Steps lesson, I make sure that I can read the name on each child's paper. If not, I turn the child's paper over on the back and write the name there. I do not have the children tell me what they were trying to write so I can write it down correctly, because I don't want them to compare what they did with what an adult can do. At this point, that would teach them nothing but frustration. I write down what they dictate to me during language-experience lessons, not during writing.

After The Five Steps is over, the children often want to show me and any other adults in the room what they drew and wrote. I take a few minutes and look at what they produced. I encourage everyone, but am sure to single out the children for praise who completed all five steps. I take up all the children's papers for filing in their individual writing portfolios.

I have the class do The Five Steps at least two days a week at the beginning. I always start with a minilesson that has a teaching point. My teaching point for the first several minilessons is "what The Five Steps are" until I am sure that every child knows and understands the steps in order. After that, my minilessons have other teaching points such as "ear spelling" (phonic spelling) or "look around the room to find letters or words to put on your paper."

All of these activities seem to be helping Manuel learn English. It is amazing that he has already learned to say and read most of the other children's names and the names of certain objects around the room.

November

I have been having so much fun with Big Books! The other kindergarten teachers and I have a number of highly predictable big books to use during the first half of the year. Every week since the middle of September, I have been doing shared reading with the children, using one of these enlarged-print books. Because a Big Book makes it possible for all the children to see the print and not just the pictures of the same book, it is invaluable in helping children learn concepts about print. Left-to-right directionality is the first concept about print I emphasize during shared reading, and the concept of word is second. Of course, I sometimes have them do "One Thing I Notice" after shared reading, because that is a multilevel task that enables everyone to be successful, regardless of how much or how little they know about print. For example, one day Paul noticed a *P*, while Roberta noticed a question mark.

One week this month, I *made* a Big Book of Little Miss Muffet by using shapes to represent the characters and props: Miss Muffet was a red circle, the tuffet was a green square, the curds and whey were a yellow triangle, and the spider was a black rectangle. The book had five pages, with the appropriate shapes on each page. Here's what page 3 looked like:

I wrote the lines of the rhyme in very large print, so that children could read the book from about 12 feet away. I used white tagboard that was 18 by 24 inches. After gluing on the shapes, I laminated the book for durability.

I had also cut out pieces of felt, using the same shapes so that I could retell the story on the flannel board and show children how the spider moved beside her and how Miss Muffet ran away. In addition, I had duplicated the pages so that the children could create their own small book by pasting on the appropriate shapes as we went through the story page by page. Children helped one another at each table, and I had a parent-helper in that day too. In about 45 minutes, I had gone over the story with the Big Book several times, as children joined in, and with the flannel board once, and all of the children had completed their own books. They then went to Mrs. Wright's room to read to the children there.

Other creations like that took much less time. Now they know the process, and it really goes much faster to make the small books. I guess we must have made a half dozen or so by now. The parents really love them!

Finally! Colors are finished! Our room looks like a rainbow gone crazy. Because Joyce and Danielle had finally declared themselves brown, I changed the order to the colors we were working on. We did brown the first week of November, and their names were the first words put on the chart. They helped me spell them, too, which made it even more important to them. We did purple and white things during the second and third weeks, which led to further discussion among the children of which ones were white. Some decided they were pink, some orange, and some light brown. Mike (of course!) declared himself purple and used some of the finger paints to prove his point. What an unexpected way to have gotten into such a serious issue—I think the children have a better idea now of how complicated the notion of skin color is.

Larry is able to read a great many of the things we have listed on our charts. I'm amazed that he can read so well. He often chooses the reading corner in which to spend his free time.

The reading corner is furnished with an old bucket seat from the car of a friend of mine. (My friends are well trained—they never throw any unusual items away without checking with me first. Over the years I have asked them for odd items, from popsicle sticks to eggshells.) The children love the car seat—two can sit together cozily, reading or looking at books. There also are a small rug, some pillows donated by parents, and a small table with three chairs. A shelf contains a variety of books, ranging from those with pictures only to those with quite a long story line. The children can sometimes choose books they want me to read to them, and often we do literature response activities with these books.

The blocks area is another one that the children enjoy and use frequently. It lends itself to all sorts of language experiences as the children build and discuss what they have done and why. Sometimes they ask me to write signs for them or write down stories that the constructions trigger. By the end of November we had enough of those stories to make a book, which we placed in the reading corner. The children were really pleased that I valued their work enough to put a cover around it and give it a title. Nearly everyone in the class had contributed something to the book, and even those who hadn't had worked in the block corner and could enjoy the stories and illustrations.

The art area has paint, easels, clay, crayons, colored chalk, *lots* of paper, odds and ends for constructions, and various other materials for artwork. I have a section of the bulletin board reserved for paintings and a small table nearby for displaying constructions. Very often, artwork acts as a stimulus for story writing. One of the children might ask me to write down his story about the horse he or a classmate had made of clay. I am often asked to label their work; not only is there further language concept development, but this labeling also seems to add value to the work.

I have never called the house corner the doll corner or dollhouse, as some of my kindergarten colleagues do, for lots of boys don't want to play there if it has that name. They learn too soon to shun the so-called feminine playthings. By calling it the house corner, there is a greater opportunity to draw boys in. They experiment with all sorts of housekeeping experiences, even arguing over whose turn it is to vacuum the floor. Of course, they get real cooking and dishwashing experiences from the cooking sessions we have.

For the time being, every time we do a language experience chart, I underline and then point to each individual word with my finger as I read back the completed story to the children to emphasize the concept of a word. Our latest one dealt with one of our more disastrous cooking experiences.

> We had a messy time cooking today. (Anthony)
> We made cranberry-orange relish to take to our Thanksgiving dinner
>   with the first graders. (Danielle)
> We got juice and seeds all over the floor. (Alex)
> It tasted yucky. (Butch)
> Nobody wanted to eat any but Miss Launch. (Carl)

After each language experience chart, I usually have them do "One Thing I Notice." I am amazed at how well this activity reviews different concepts about print and letter names that we have covered, yet my students who know so much feel so successful in being able to notice things they really couldn't be expected to know for a few years yet.

We continue the quest to distinguish between letters and words, as well as trying to emphasize the return sweep to the next line of print. Paul, Mort, Daisy, and Chip are still unable to figure out how children like Roberta, Danielle, and Larry can always tell which marks mean words and which ones mean letters. Most of the group are able to figure out questions such as "How many words are in the first sentence?" if they can come up to the chart and put a finger on each word in the sentence as they count. The chart here allowed me to get into another concept with them. Danielle's sentence continued onto another line. When I asked, "How many words are in Danielle's sentence?" most of the children said 12. A few, Betty and Larry and some others, disagreed. There were 15 words, they contended. Alexander, who thought he had finally caught Larry in an error, volunteered to come to the chart and check it out. It took a lot of convincing, with

Danielle chiming in for support, to try to convince some of them that Danielle's sentence was indeed 15 words long. Eventually, I know, all of them will understand the difference between words and letters, but for now . . .

Daphne's grandparents, with whom she lives, are farmers. In fact, it was their farm I have taken my class to visit each of the past two Octobers. They told me that they very much enjoyed having the children come to the farm and that they felt somewhat guilty they did not have enough time to come to the school and volunteer some of their time. Despite my protest that it was fine, they insisted that they wanted to help out in some way. Could I use two bushels of apples from their orchard? I love questions like that!

Need I tell you that every one of our cooking activities for the month of November involved apples? I did have to alter the cooking plan that I had made for the year, but it was worth it. One of their very favorite recipes came from *The Taming of the C.A.N.D.Y. Monster.*

Candy Apples

We Need:
  1 apple for each person
  1 popsicle stick for each person
  A bowl of honey
  Toasted wheat germ on waxed paper
We Do:
  Pull the stem off your apple.
  Push the stick in where you took out the stem.
  Dip the apple in the bowl of honey and turn it 2 times.
  Hold the apple over the bowl of honey until it stops dripping.
  Roll the apple in the wheat germ and eat it up!

All the children seem to know what "The Five Steps" are, in order, so now the teaching point of my minilessons before they write is no longer just what those steps are. I am now teaching them how to "stretch" words they want to write and listen for the sounds, so they can use one or more letters to spell out those sounds. This "invented spelling" or "phonic spelling"—what I teach the children to call "ear" spelling—is somewhat controversial, but an essential instructional activity in kindergarten and first grade.

First of all, I find it to be the best activity to help children develop phonemic awareness. By stretching words and listening for sounds, they increase their awareness of those sounds. Once they get in the habit of doing it regularly when they write, nothing can provide them more or better practice with phonemic awareness. Second, by stretching words and listening for sounds, they also increase their phonemic sequencing ability—the ability to hear the sounds in order from beginning to end. Third, ear spelling makes it possible for them to write more, to remember better what they wrote, and after they get pretty good at it, to write something I can actually read. Nothing is better at encouraging children's self-confidence and desire to learn to write than being able to write something someone else can read! Fourth, their ear spellings, and the writings those spellings make possible, provide me with an invaluable diagnostic and assessment tool. If, for example, a child writes:

Midg nm Sm

the child and I can each usually read it to say, "My dog is named Sam" or "My dog's name is Sam." From this writing, I can tell that child knows, among other things, that letters go from left to right when words are made, that many sounds have been matched with their letter forms, that letters are grouped to make words, and that there is an understanding that words are written so that others can read them. Clearly there are many things for the child still to learn; however, it is easier to teach from a base of what is known and gradually introduce new information than to try to teach everything at once or separated from real applications.

This month we continued to "count" words in oral statements by pushing out Cheerios or sunflower seeds. We began clapping or ruler-taping the number of "beats" (syllables) in their names to help them develop syllable awareness. Each child loves it when we do his or her first or last name. Again, I praised the children who were getting it right and helped the others by stretching the words to make it easier to hear the separate syllables. I just started using the name wall with syllable-awareness activities—I ask the children to guess which child I mean when I make statements like, "The name is on the wall, begins with an R, and has three beats in it." They love these activities and are getting very good at using the number of syllables in a child's name as a clue.

The children continue to read the alphabet chorally as I point to each letter. Now, however, I have placed the small-case letter beside each capital, both above the marker board and at eye level around the room. I point to the small-case letter with the yardstick, even though both letters are there together. In addition, I put five letters in order on the marker board each day and had several children come one at a time and track (point to) each letter while saying its name. I carefully observed whether the children were pointing to the correct letter as they were saying it, or just saying the same five letters as the previous child.

The children have been working since the beginning of the year on matching uppercase letters to uppercase letters, and recently they have been matching lowercase letters to lowercase letters. I waited to have them do this until I felt I had taught the capital and small-case letter names well using alphabet books, choral reading of the alphabet while I pointed to each capital or small-case letter, use of the name wall, and letter-name tracking.

One of my tricks is to tell them that while they were outside, an elf came in and mixed up all those nice letters we had been playing with—could anyone help us to get them straightened out again? Of course, there are always several volunteers! We concentrate on three pairs at a time, which is a workable number for them. Also, I always begin with those upper- and lowercase letters that tend to resemble one another except for size (such as *Ss*) to further ensure success.

I also play a game of "Memory" with the one capital and one small-case letter card for each of the three letters we are currently working on. I shuffle the six letter cards and place them face down in a two-by-three array. The children take turns selecting two of the letter cards to be revealed. They are then turned over. If they match, they keep the cards. If they do not match, the cards are turned back over to be chosen at a later time by someone who can remember the position of the letters.

December

Despite the holiday rush and clamor, we did manage to accomplish some things this month. It does seem to me, though, that the break can't come a minute too soon, for we have been in a holiday whirl since before Halloween!

We did another very easy poetry format this month. First, I asked the children it they knew what opposites were. Horace volunteered. "That's when my mom puts money into the bank."

"Pretty good guess," I replied. "That is called a *de*posit."

Larry said, "You know, they're words that mean just the different thing, just the, well, *opposite*, like hot and cold, wet and dry, up and down."

"Very good, Larry. Can you think of any other opposites, children?" They came up with several pairs: warm and cool, summer and winter, big and little. I asked them to choose a pair so that we could make up a poem. They chose up and down. I told them that this time we would start and end the poem with those words and fill in with others. We would put the words in one long column, one word per line. There was an uneven number of words, for the middle word, the transition word, had to have something to do with both of the opposites. Together we talked for a short time about some possible words for the slots in the poem. I chose from among their ideas to complete the poem that follows:

Up (Larry)
Sky, (Joyce)
Clouds, (Pat)
Flying, (Mike)
Swing, (Hilda)
Falling, (Butch)
Dirt, (Mitch)
Rocks, (Steve)
Down. (Larry)

I read their poem to them, phrasing it to make the most of the poetic elements. Notice that the middle word is the one where the transition is made between the opposites. The words from the top to the middle build images for the top word; the words from the middle down build images for the bottom word.

Rhyme awareness is considerably more difficult for children to acquire than word or syllable awareness. We began working on that this month. We did an occasional game with rhymes or riddles. Several times, we did the "Head or Knee" rhyming game. I had all the children stand, and then I would say a sentence containing a word that rhymes with either head or knee and then repeat just that word ("I fed the gerbil. Fed. Now, point . . .). They respond by pointing to their head or their knee after I repeat the word. It is fun and helps them get the wiggles out. Variations on this game include "Arm or Toe" and "Hand or Leg."

Their favorite Big Book this month was *Brown Bear, Brown Bear*. I introduced it in the usual way, by showing the cover and having them predict what the story might be about. I asked them to image with me as I conjured up the bear lumbering through the forest, lifting his nose to sniff for honey. Then I began to read the story in a fluent and expressive way. I told children that this was my turn to read, and they should not try to join in with the reading yet. They were to listen to the story first. I read each page of the book, pausing to allow them to comment on the pictures and the story line. I used a pointer to touch each word as I said it. The second time I read it, I invited children to join in when they could. By the third reading, nearly everyone was chiming in. The fourth time I asked them to try to read it without my help, and I had to step in only a few times to help them.

After we read the book together for three days (the other two days took much less time), I gave the children small copies that they read together in pairs. They love this part the most! They really feel like readers as they go off together to a special corner and read with a friend. I have put capable and struggling children together so that the modeling continues for those who need it. They continue to read the book with their partner until they feel very comfortable with it. At that point they read it to me, and if they do well (which means they sound fluent, not that each word is necessarily perfect), they may check the book out to take home to read to their parents and others.

Predictable big books like *Brown Bear, Brown Bear* seem to be helping Manuel learn English. I believe that the repetitive sentence pattern with different words being substituted that are shown in the pictures are helping him learn English syntax. Certainly, he can help "read" these kinds of Big Books during shared reading time. I am just so pleased at how his self-confidence and interest in reading are growing along with his ability to speak and understand spoken English.

Since we began "The Five Steps" in late October, I have been loudly praising everyone who attempted to complete all five steps in the time allotted for writing. In minilessons, I have modeled looking around the room and copying letters and words off the wall, as well as modeling ear spelling—stretching a word you want to write, listen for letters, and write down the letters you hear. By now, almost all of the children are doing all five steps most days.

I have been working on small-case letter names with the children even more this month. I have read to them several times a couple of alphabet books in which the small-case letter is prominently displayed on each page. I have had them take turns each day tracking five small-case letters in order on the marker board, the way we did it last month with capital letters. We finished the classroom alphabet book we began the middle of last month. I put a photo of every child on the page his or her first name begins with, and then we put a photo of an object from our classroom on the pages for the other letters. That only left us the hardest three letters to have to get "creative" about.

This month we did one of our recipes as a chart very much like the ones that are in some of the children's cookbooks that I showed to the class. They had almost all seen cookbooks at home, but they had not really noticed how the recipes were written. The form we now use includes the headings *Ingredients*, *Utensils*, and *Preparation* (written with numbered steps). The recipe was for "Happy Holidays Egg Cones," a kind of egg salad that we scooped into ice cream cones. Recipes certainly help work on the essential thinking processes as we *connect* new and old cooking experiences; *generalize* about what we have learned about how to cook so far; *apply* reading as we cook different recipes; *image* how this might look, taste, feel, or smell; *organize* the directions in a logical sequence; *predict* what might be added next or what step to do next; *self-monitor* if the directions or proportions make sense, and *evaluate* the product.

This was one of our better experiences this year. The children learned so many things while putting together this recipe. For example, we looked at raw eggs and hard-cooked eggs and talked about how the cooking changed them from a liquid to a solid. We measured the water after the first batch of eggs had finished cooking. Evaporation was discussed when they noticed much of the water gone. This recipe format allowed the introduction of quite a few new words, such as *ingredients*. There was much more measuring than in other recipes we had tried. All in all, it did go well. It amazes me to realize the number of concepts being developed.

I feel better about my assessment this year than I ever have before. No longer am I concerned about what to report to parents during our conferences or on my written summary of progress sent home to them at report card times. I use my observations and samples of their work, particularly their writing portfolios, to characterize each child's current status on each of my seven critical knowings. I make sure to point out each child's main strengths and weaknesses and then to summarize how well I think the child is moving toward ultimate success in first grade and beyond.

January

The children seemed really glad to be back at school—two weeks is a long time to be away. I find, too, that they usually have become bored at home and come to miss the routine we have so carefully established. Furthermore, most of them are anxious to share their holiday "goodies" with the other children. Pat got her wish and received some new books, which she assured me she could read. I asked her to bring them in and show them to us and perhaps read them to the class. Pat brought in a predictable-language book, *The Napping House*, that she had received for Christmas. First she read it to me, and then I let her read it to the class.

This month I began self-selected reading. Most of the teachers in this school set aside a time period during which the children silently read in materials of their own choice at their own pace. I explained to the class that I was going to set our timer for three minutes, and during that three minutes everyone was to be looking at a book. We went to the school library to select books just for self-selected reading. I aided some in their selections so that Larry, Roberta, and Danielle had books they could read, and Paul and Daisy had some bright picture books on topics they found interesting (a children's cookbook for Daisy!). At self-selected reading time, it all went rather well, considering that this was a first for them. After it was over, I pulled aside the children who had had an especially difficult time sitting with a book for three whole minutes. We discussed again how they could look at the pictures to try to figure out what the story was about or to name the colors they saw on the pages, or how they could go through and think of the names of as many things as possible pictured on each page. I encouraged these children to try to decide if they liked the book enough to want me to read it to the whole class. I had to do this several times with various children in the room (not always the same ones), but by the end of the month the children really could sit still with a book for three minutes.

Children are getting the idea that what is in books should make sense to them and to others. By "pretend reading" the books over and over, many of them are even able to identify some of the words that occur repeatedly in each book. Certainly the motivation of reading to their peers has helped some of the children to become more interested in reading and in words. They also are becoming exposed to a variety of book types.

There was a flood of stories from the children after our field trip to the fire station this month. *Now* everyone wants to be a firefighter! They tell gory stories about how brave firefighters save helpless people and little babies—the influence of television, I think, for the fire chief certainly did nothing that would have aroused such stories.

Our second trip, a visit to a restaurant, couldn't compare with the excitement of the trip to the fire station. The children were fascinated with the huge appliances in the kitchen, and informed the chef that they too were cooks. He asked them what they could cook, and they proceeded to catalogue our entire year of cooking for him, complete with the description of the mess we had with the cranberry-orange relish!

I am still having problems with Alexander. He often removes his hearing aid so that he can get out of work by claiming he doesn't know what to do. He is one of the children most in need of the language activities we do. He still doesn't talk in sentences; mostly he grunts and points. I suspect he can understand more than he appears to, because his mother told me that they communicate this way at home often. He points and she fetches! He is really getting to be a pill! His hearing loss wasn't discovered until two years ago. He is so delayed in language because he missed so many important concepts. He really has the language development of a three-year-old child. Even Paul may be ahead in this area.

I've been continuing to work hard on visual discrimination and visual memory. They really have become quite good at matching letters to one another and at being able to tell which letters are different in a row of letters. I put up four words on the chalktray, and they have to locate the different one and group the three that are alike to one side. I also write selected words from our language-experience charts on cards and put these cards in the chalktray. Putting my hand underneath the word *snail* on the chart, I say, "Carl, this word is *snail*. Can you find another word that says *snail* in the chalktray? If you can, bring it here and we'll check it letter for letter." Carl, finding the word, brings it to the chart and we check first by counting how many letters are in the card he has brought and comparing that to the number of letters in the word on the chart. Next I have him check to see if the first letter looks like the first letter of the chart word; then we check the second letter, and so on. If each letter matches the letters on the chart word and all are in the same order, ta da, a match! Hooray for Carl!

Another game for group work is "Go Fish." We have two different groups of cards, one each for upper- and lowercase. The cards are shuffled together, and three cards are dealt to each player. If the player has a match of letter forms, the cards are put on the table. After everyone is given a chance to do this, the player to the left of the dealer asks another player if he or she has a particular letter. If the answer is yes, the card must be relinquished. The player continues to ask for cards until he is told to "Go Fish" by a player who doesn't have the card asked for. The first player then picks a card from the remainder of the deck, which has been placed in the center of the playing area. The first player to have all his or her cards matched and on the table is the winner.

I have begun to check letter name knowledge with the children, too. I have been calling them to me one at a time and showing letter cards with both the upper- and lowercase on the same card and asking the children to name the letter. I use a system of putting the known and the unknown in separate piles. Then I write down on that child's card which letters he or she still doesn't know so that I can begin direct instruction. Up to this point, the letter names that the children have learned have been through exposure to lists of their classmates' names, letters and words they have matched on the chart stories, and their writing. Eleven of the alphabet letters were easily learned by most of the children just because those letters begin the names of the 25 children. Paul is the only child who knows only two letters: *P* and *C* (for Paul and Carl). Larry, Danielle, Pat, Roberta, Hilda, Joyce, and Mandy can name all the letters, capital and small-case, very quickly. Rita, Betty, Horace, Alex, Steve, and Anthony know most of the 52 letter names with the exception of the least frequent ones. The other children are at varying points in the number of letters they can name and how quickly they can name them.

Sometimes, after I write a language-experience chart, I tell the children that I am going to cover up the chart with another sheet of paper and we're going to play the "How Many Words?" game. I peek at the first sentence so that I can say it aloud to the children. As I read it to them, they are to raise a finger for each word I say, so that they can tell me how many words are in a sentence. They tell me the number (or numbers!) and I remove the paper covering so that we can count the number of words. Then I count on my fingers with them so that they have a model for what we are doing, and we do another sentence on the chart the same way.

Distinguishing words that rhyme and coming up with rhymes is one of the major phonemic awareness abilities we work on. I find that children can begin to make sense of the concept of rhyme when I use one of my favorite books, *The Hungry Thing*. In this book, we meet the Hungry Thing and find that he will eat only silly rhymes for real words, so that if they want to feed him "noodles," they tell him he is eating "foodles"; "soup with a cracker" is "boop with a smacker," and so on. As we read the story, the children try to guess what the Hungry Thing is eating throughout the book. When we finish the book, I tell them it is our turn to feed the Hungry Thing. I tell them to think of their favorite food and then to try to find a silly rhyme for it, so that the Hungry Thing will eat it. They enjoy playing

"Feed the Hungry Thing," and it is increasing their awareness of rhyme and ability to come up with rhymes.

I think that Big Books and The Five Steps have totally changed the way I view beginning reading and writing instruction. Everyone can have success, and I can tell so much more easily who is acquiring which of the critical knowings. In writing, we have begun a formal sharing time after The Five Steps. Before, I had been going around as they finished and let them share with me what they had done. This month, however, I started allowing four or five children to share each day. I have found in the past that nothing motivates kindergarten children to write like having an opportunity to share with the whole class what they have written. To ensure the motivational value of sharing, I carefully observe to make sure that sharing time is very positive for every child. If it is not, I take immediate steps to make sure it becomes positive for that child.

Jeff burned himself slightly during a cooking adventure the other day, so I took him over to the plant shelf, broke off a piece of a leaf, and rubbed the cut end of the leaf over the burned area. Immediately a crowd grew around the scene, fascinated children observing that the juice of the plant had made the burn feel better. "What is that?" "How did you know to do that, Miss Launch?" "Wow! Magic!"

Ah ha! The teachable moment my college professors were always talking about! "Let's sit down and do a chart about this plant," I suggested. "Plants are really wonderful things. Not only do they look nice in our room, but some of them can be used for food, some for medicine, and some to make clothes and houses. What are some questions you have about this plant?" For the next five minutes, they asked questions and I wrote those questions on the chart.

Some of their questions were related to the name and characteristics of the plant (color, size, etc.), some dealt with the care of the plant, and some concerned how new plants were grown. After all their questions were on the chart, I cut them apart and we grouped them according to the type of question they had. Based on this grouping, I sent Danielle, Paul, and Horace to the library to bring back books on plants. I sent a note with them to Miss Page, the librarian, telling her we were trying to get information about the aloe plant. With books before us, we came up with the following chart about aloe plants.

The Aloe Plant
Our plant's name is "aloe vera." (Anthony)
Aloe vera means "true aloe" because there are more than one kind of
    aloe. (Larry)
Aloe vera is a succulent because it has fat leaves and likes water. (Danielle)
It can grow one or two feet. (Paul)
It is all green. (Chip)
It likes lots of light. (Carl)
You can make new plants by planting the baby shoots called suckers. (Steve)
Aloe is special because it can help the burn places on you. (Jeff)

I was impressed with how much they really got into the aloe plant. Now they keep asking me if the other plants we have are special in any way. We may be making our own book about our classroom plants. This was a highly successful science lesson, and I told the students so. I want them to see science as interesting and valuable knowledge.

Another really successful cooking experience was tied to one of the many books I read to the children each week. I had brought in several versions of the old story "Stone Soup," and we compared how the stories were alike and how they were different. After those discussions, I told them that we were going to make some stone soup in the slow cooker. Their reactions ranged from Butch's "Yuk!" to Hilda's "How fascinating!" Everyone was told to bring in a vegetable, any vegetable, the next day.

"But what do we need, Miss Launch? How can we cook if we don't know what we need?" asked a worried Betty.

"Well, in the book they didn't have a recipe. They just put in whatever was brought to them." That, clearly, was not very satisfying to Betty.

The next day most of the children had remembered to bring in a vegetable, and Daisy brought a loaf of Italian bread. Oh, well, it should go well with the soup. Next we went out to the playground, and each person was to find one small stone to put in the soup. Alex was appalled! "But they're dirty. People have been walking on them, and I even saw Mort and Butch spitting on the rocks!" "Yuk too," I thought, though I dared not show it! "We will carefully wash each rock in hot, soapy water so that they are nice and clean for the soup," I told him. And wash we did. The rocks were then placed in the bottom of the slow cooker, and I added 12 cups of water and 12 beef bouillon cubes. Joyce's job was to turn the cooker to high heat.

We began acting out the story with three children pretending to wonder what else they could put in the soup and how good it would be if only there were a carrot or two. In this way, we went through each of the vegetables the class had brought. Whoever had brought the vegetable had to wash it and cut it into pieces to put into the soup. I helped cut off the tops and bad places, but the children did most of the work. When all the veggies had been added, we put on the lid of the slow cooker and left it until nearly time to go home. Daphne gave it a stir with a big wooden spoon and put the lid on one more time. I took it home with me to continue cooking and then to refrigerate. The next day, we heated it up in the slow cooker by snack time. Needless to say, the soup was pretty good, much to Alex's amazement. Daisy's bread was just the right touch, and all of the children plan to make stone soup at home with their mother's help.

This month, I began to systematically teach the consonant letter sounds. We have been noticing sounds letters make in all our activities and particularly when I model for them how to "ear spell" words as they stretch them out to write them. I am now going systematically through the consonant letters. For each one, we identify all the children who have that letter in their name and stretch out the names to see if we can hear that letter's "usual sound." We are putting up key words for each letter—a favorite food and an action—a great teaching device I learned from Mrs. Wright. We have also read some tongue-twister books and are writing a class book of tongue twisters. The first ones we wrote use the names of the children, and later we will add some for those letters we don't have names for. In teaching the letter sounds , I don't go alphabetically, because *b* and *d* are so confusable, as are *m* and *n*. Rather, I pick ones that have very different sounds and for which I have name examples. This year, the first four I taught were *m, p, l,* and *j.* Here are the tongue twisters for them:

> Mandy, Mike, Mitch, Mort, and Manuel make meatballs.
> Pat and Paul pick peaches.
> Larry loves lemonade.
> Jeff and Joyce jump and juggle.

The children are learning these sounds quite easily. I attribute their success to all the work we did from September through December. Had I begun teaching these sounds in September, some of the children would simply have been unable to learn them, and almost all of the children would have had more difficulty.

February

Our poetry writing is coming along so well! I read Mary O'Neill's *Hailstones and Halibut Bones* to the children and discussed with them that O'Neill thought colors could represent things and feelings as well as thoughts. Then we did a poetry format (again as a group) that has this configuration:

> I feel _____
>
> I see _____
>
> I hear _____
>
> I smell _____
>
> I taste _____
>
> I feel _____

The unifying factor here is the repetition of the phrase "I feel." To help the children recognize the five senses the poem deals with, I told them that I would give them several days to work on a collage of pictures from magazines, newspapers, and other sources that portray the five senses. They were to find as many pictures as they could that would finish the phrases I listed. It was a messy assignment, but the children helped to create several poems and collages. In addition, the children were proud because the collages described *them* as individuals. I had the children work individually on this project, so I did have to help out some of the more unsure children such as Paul and Chip. Paul struggled—with my help—to find one example for each phrase; Chip kept asking the others to save any pictures of peanuts that they found for him—he wanted to finish each phrase the same way! When some of the children wondered if they could finish the phrase with just one word or a picture, I told them that they could. Others complained that they couldn't do that—they needed to say more! I told them that the only rule was that they finished the phrases, no matter how many words they used.

Last month's interest in the plants did indeed result in a science book we made for the classroom and the school library about the plants we have. Steve, who has a remarkable eye for drawing nature objects, did the illustrations. Actually, he did the outlines in pencil and then asked certain students to do the coloring in. We made one book for our room and another for the library, since Miss Page had been so helpful all year.

I have been doing some "think link" listening comprehension lessons with the children recently. Sue Port, the curriculum supervisor, was in last month and complimented me on the way I asked children to use the essential thinking processes as I read through a story. She really liked relating the listening to those processes. But, she said, what about Paul and Chip and some of the others who never contributed to the discussion? It was clear that children like Larry and Danielle were dominating the discussions. I told her that this had concerned me too. "Give me a week," she said. "I've got an idea for another way to use those thinking processes that I'd like you to try out."

Well! Sue Port's idea has revolutionized my classroom listening lessons. She told me that she wanted to try out a "Think Link." In Think Links, the teacher models what she is thinking about by talking through the story, stopping at appropriate places to tell children which of the essential thinking processes were triggered by the text. In this way, children like Paul and Chip can get an insight into *how* people think, not just *what* they think. She asked if she could model a story with my class.

Sue Port began her lesson by telling the children that when they went on to first grade, people were going to be asking them to tell about things they were reading. She wanted to show them how she understood things she was reading by reading a story and telling them what her mind was thinking about throughout. She showed them the cover of *Swimmy* and said:

> This book is called Swimmy, and it is by Leo Lionni. I know that I am probably going to like this book because I have liked other books by him. If I went into the library and found this book, I might pick it up and look at the cover and think, "Hmmm. Swimmy. I see a fish on the cover and since fish swim, I'll bet that's the name of the fish in this story. I wonder where the fish lives. Maybe a river. Maybe a lake. Maybe this fish lives in the ocean. Maybe Swimmy is a pet. I don't know yet if the fish is a girl or boy. I'd guess, though, that it's a make-believe story because Lionni writes a lot of make-believe stories."

She continued to go through each page of the book with the children, talking about "what is going on in my mind" as she read the text and looked at the pictures. I was particularly intrigued by her imaging with the children, because I had found that to be the hardest of the essential thinking processes for me to use with children. After reading about Swimmy's family being eaten and Swimmy going off on his own, she said:

> I can just see Swimmy gliding through the water, slowly, sadly. His little tail is hardly swishing at all. Close your eyes. Can you see him swimming? Ooooh! The water is getting colder as he goes deeper. I'm shivering as I feel that cold water all around his body. Can you feel it? Close your eyes. Feel that cold water. Are you shivering?

The children responded so well to what she was doing. Mike even said, "So that's how Larry knows so much! His brain is thinking of stuff!" As we talked later, Sue told me that she did not cover all of the thinking processes because not all of them were appropriate for that story. In fact, she really spent most of her Think Link on imaging and predicting, because the story fit those two quite well.

After she left, I dug out some books I had planned to use with the children and developed a skeleton of a Think Link for several of them. I plan to do Think Links once a week.

Self-selected reading continues to roll along smoothly. We are up to five minutes of reading time, now. We will hold at that level for a while, since Butch and Mort are at the upper limit of their ability to sit still. Larry and Danielle, however, continue to read after the class time is up. They both are reading almost a book a day. Danielle's father told me that he thinks Danielle is such a good reader because she was in the hospital for so long after the car accident in which she was hurt and her mother was killed. Her father, the nurses, and all her visitors read constantly to her and had her try to guess about story events, and they sat beside her so that she would always see the words as they were reading.

Again this year, I find it wonderful to see the consonant letter-sound relationships I am teaching show up in so many of the children's writing. Because I now require ear spelling of every child, when they stretch words to listen for letters to write down, they are naturally more likely to hear the sounds they have been learning to associate with particular beginning consonant letters. Often they hear them elsewhere in the word besides the beginning! Children's ear spellings during writing are the best means I can think of to assess children's developing phonemic awareness and phonics knowledge.

I praise the children who stretch words and listen for letters to write down during their writing. Moreover, I often point out to the other children when I can read a word or even a statement that a children has written using ear spelling. This not only encourages them to apply their developing phonics knowledge during writing, but it is part of my overall strategy to build their self-confidence to learn.

The first several months of the year, I wouldn't allow anyone to denigrate children's pretend reading or initial efforts at writing, even though they weren't really reading or writing. I wanted all the children to feel that they were doing exactly what I wanted them to without thinking they were inadequate, and I also wanted them to use these pretend experiences to begin to enjoy reading and writing as activities.

Beginning last month, however, and continuing on for the rest of the year, I am helping the children come to understand that how well they do is a result of their effort and how they go about it. So, when children use the pictures to figure out a word or part of story, I not only praise them, but I point out what they did and how it helped them. Likewise, when children use the beginning letters of a word along with its context to figure out what the word is, or when they ear spell a word so that I or another child can read it, I not only praise them, but I explain that their success on that word resulted from a good strategy that they made the effort to apply.

The favorite cooking experience this month was making whole-wheat pretzels. Children shaped the dough into letter names they knew and baked them. What fun and what motivation! Even Mort seemed to want to learn some more letters so he could make more pretzels.

March

I noticed this month that I don't even look at the seven critical knowings in the front of my plan book anymore. It has become so automatic to think of everything we do in terms of my knowings that I was well into the preparation of the cards for a game when it suddenly occurred to me that this simple game was facilitating some of my seven ingredients. In fact, all around me are opportunities to exploit learning!

I started this month with a game that the children really enjoyed. I told the children that we would be playing a game that might take all morning to finish, but that it didn't matter because they could play the game while they worked.

Surprise, surprise! Each child was going to have the picture of an animal pinned on his or her back, and they were to guess the animal. They could ask only two questions of each classmate, and the questions could only be answered yes or no. The purpose of this restriction was to encourage a maximum use of language on the part of the one guessing and to discourage unnecessary hints and clues. The children seemed very excited by the idea and were ready to begin immediately. I reminded them that they were to continue their work while trying to guess, and that it would be a good idea to think carefully before asking questions so that the questions wouldn't be wasted. I gave the following demonstration: "Mandy, will you please pin the picture of an animal to my back?" She did so, and I turned so that my back—and the picture—were toward the children. There was much giggling from some of the children.

"Okay. Steve, do I have hair? No? Hmmmm. Steve, do I have six legs? No? Thank you. Let's see now—Rita, do I have wings? No. All right, do I have scales? Ah ha! Now we're getting someplace. Mandy, do people catch me to eat? No, that means that I'm not a fish. Do I crawl? I thought I might. Horace, am I a snake?"

The children were amazed that I guessed the animal so quickly. I explained that animals are in groups and that I was trying to find which group my animal was in. One large group that includes bears, cats, dogs, beavers, and people was the one I was asking about first—they all have fur or hair. When I knew that the animal didn't have fur or hair, I knew that it had to be an insect or an amphibian (living both on land and in water) or a bird or a reptile (an animal with scales). "Listen carefully" was my last injunction before pinning on the animals. And the game was on! Larry, Hilda, Roberta, and Steve guessed theirs rather quickly, for they had paid attention to what was told to them and tried logically to figure out what to ask next. Daisy used up all her questions by running from person to person, asking questions like "Am I a deer? Am I a goat?" rather than trying to find the category and proceed logically. It took most of the children the entire morning to determine what they were. Paul managed to find out that he was a dog, though his guess was based on luck rather than system. Mitch never figured his out because he kept trying to start arguments with those who answered his questions.

He wanted so much to own a horse that he was convinced that a horse must be the animal pictured on his back. Whenever the children gave him an answer that didn't fit his mind-set, he argued with them, insisting that they must be wrong. Carl guessed "deer" fairly early, partially, I think, because he likes deer so much. And so it went—an interesting exercise for the children. They've already asked to play it again soon.

So many things are going on with this particular activity. Children are engaging in an identifying-sorting-classifying game that helps to develop further their understanding of animals and animal characteristics. They are developing the essential thinking processes of generalize, predict, and apply as they work on this background information. I think I'll do this again next week with forms of transportation or foods.

Anthony's mother has been riding me all year about making sure that I am teaching the children all they need to know to go into first grade. She and I have had a few points of departure this year in our assessments of his abilities. He is her brilliant, only child and she wants to make certain that he will be ready to attend MIT when the time comes! She has been taking books home from the school she teaches in for him to read with her. No wonder he is so intractable some mornings. She had told me that they have one hour of reading every night, and that she has been having him copy the words he doesn't know over and over. I told her that he had many opportunities and materials to explore and read at school. However, because he is so focused on science, she believes that we are not providing enough science stuff here. I haven't been able to budge her or she me. Oh, well!

All the things we do every day are moving along just as they should be for March. Self-selected reading is up to seven minutes, and all the children are writing stories about events or objects in their lives that they choose. Steve and Anthony have been trying some science experiments and writing down what they do and how it turns out (I am unable to read most of it, but they generously share what their markings mean).

The Big Books continue to be popular reading material with the children, and their favorite Big Books are the ones we made that were parallel to stories read in class. We wrote a version of *The Three Little Kittens* called *The Three Little Goats* who had lost their boats. They came up with some very nice ideas. I put it on the large tagboard and let the children illustrate the book. They worked in small groups so that every child got to add something to the book. We went through the same process with their book that we had done with the others, practicing it together before they read it to a partner. Although we had no small versions, the children seemed to love lying on the floor, turning the Big Book pages.

Manuel has come such a long way! He is now able to converse with the other children fairly well, unless he is trying to explain something that happened at home. Even then, he often succeeds. A literacy- and language-rich classroom seems to be one thing a child learning English needs!

The third-graders from Mrs. Wise's class have been writing books for the children, as well as coming down to take dictation so that the kindergartners can get *their* stories into print. The third-graders have been studying bookbinding and have made some very handsome books for the children to take home or to put in our classroom library. To thank them for all their help, we invited them to come help us eat the peanut-butter cookies we made.

April

Spring, spring, spring!!! I love it. We've been outside a lot lately, which has been good for the children as well as for me. We do some of our work out there when we can, such as our lesson on poetry. The poetry we composed this month used an "I wish" format. I told the children that they were to think of four different things they wished for. The poem was to have lines beginning with the words *I wish*, but the first and the last lines were to be identical. Here is the large-group poem that we did before breaking up into small groups for more poetry writing using this format.

> I wish spring was here. (Steve)
> I wish that the sun was warm. (Manuel)
> I wish that the frogs would make noises. (Butch)
> I wish I could go out without my coat. (Alex)
> I wish spring was here. (Steve)

The children have been creating greeting cards all year long, but some of the birthday cards for Jeff were just too much! Someone got the notion that even if he couldn't give Jeff a present, he could *wish* to give him a present. I don't know who began it, but children began to write things such as "I wish you could have this" with their ear spellings. Some children became the "experts" at the table, offering their help to those who wanted to write messages. In walking around later, I noticed that they were cutting pictures out of our catalogues and magazines. The picture of a bike, swimming pool, motorcycle, or some other luxury would appear at the bottom of the written message, which was then passed over to Jeff for his birthday. Jeff was grinning from ear to ear all day long!

I am still trying to help the children develop their reasoning and questioning abilities by such things as the "feely" box. I have constructed the feely box by cutting a hole in one end of a shoebox and attaching to the hole a sock with the toe end cut off. I placed a comb in the box and permitted the children to reach in through the sock and into the box where they could feel the object but not see it. Each child was permitted a few seconds to feel the object and then report what the object might be. I changed the objects frequently, so that the children would have many opportunities to use the sense of touch. The next project was somewhat harder for the children, for I had arranged the experiences in order of difficulty. This time a single child would feel the object, describe it in three different ways, and then guess what it was. The third kind of experience was to let a child see an object, describe it to the other children, and let *them* guess what was being described. The fourth task was even more complicated, for this time the child felt an object, described it to the other children, and they had to guess what it was that he or she had felt. Occasionally, as a variation, I would let several children feel the same object so that they could help one another with the description. The rest of the group had to try to guess what it was that was being felt. This worked out very well, particularly when Paul, Chip, or Joyce, who have a great deal of difficulty verbalizing, described the object. However, it is obviously easier for the group if the clues are clearly stated, a skill these three were unable to demonstrate yet.

The three gained from listening to the descriptions given by the more verbal children, however, for they experienced the same object and could compare their own perceptions with what was being said. The fifth task with the feely box was to have a child feel an object and then give a one-word clue, and so on. A particularly interesting game was one that took place this week. Steve reached into the box and felt the object. He said, "Prickly." There were guesses of *porcupine, cactus,* and *pins.* The next clue was "Woody." The children were stumped for a moment, until Larry guessed that it might be a plank from the workshop. The next clue: "Tree." Something from a tree that is wooden and prickly?

"Oh, I know, I know!" exclaimed Hilda, who had been putting all the clues together. "It's bark from the tree!" She sat back smug and confident.

"No, that's not it. 'Seeds.'"

The crestfallen Hilda began muttering, "Seeds? Seeds. Seeds! It's a pinecone! Am I right this time, Steve?" Steve's nod reassured her that her deduction skills had been well utilized.

The most difficult of all was the last project—identifying the object within a wrapped box by asking questions of me. They found this to be a very challenging task. They knew that it could not be a chair, for instance, for the package would not accommodate that large an object. The questioning techniques of the children had increased with the readiness activities that they had been doing for the few weeks prior to this exercise, and they did guess that the object was a shoe. I got the idea for this project from one of the other kindergarten teachers at a recent meeting. The teacher said she had presented a wrapped package to the children for them to determine the contents. The task was too difficult for them because they had not had exercises leading up to this game. As a result, the children were unable to figure out what was in the box, the teacher was frustrated and embarrassed, and she had tried to figure out what had gone wrong. She concluded that the activity was incomplete and useless until she set up the other activities.

Our consonant letter-sound instruction is going quite well. I am seeing all the consonants occur in the ear spellings that almost all of the children are now including in their writing. Of course, I review, review, review these letter-sound relationships. When I first taught each consonant, I taught them a key action that begins with that letter and sound. "Leap" was our *l* action. Each day for a while, we would all stand by our seats and leap to help us remember the sound *l* makes. Likewise, I taught them key actions for each of the other consonants, along with the other means I used to help them remember the sound of the letter. Before long, one of the ways we reviewed each of the single onsets we had learned so far was for me to write either the capital or the small-case letter on the board and have them (on the count of three) perform the key action for that letter. I will continue this type of "action" review of the consonants until the year ends.

This month we began to study capital letter formation. Of course, all the children have been writing the capital letters all year, but with no standards to meet. Now, I am systematically teaching them how best to form each capital letter on unlined paper and having them practice them. Their previous writing makes it easy for them to learn to improve their letter formation, yet they haven't been writing long enough without formal handwriting instruction that their habits are too ingrained to gradually change.

This month, we made "Ants on a Log" by cutting celery using a premeasured length and then filling the hole with peanut butter and putting on the ants (raisins). A great snack and E-A-S-Y, even for Paul at this point.

May

It is just amazing to me how much my children know about every aspect of reading and writing! That retreat last summer, and my translating what we agreed on into the seven critical knowings for kindergarten, has really paid off. I have never had a class end the year knowing so many letter names so fluently. I have never had a class with such a grasp of consonant letter-sound relationships. Yet I also have never had a class so turned on to reading and writing and with such developed language and thinking abilities. And yet, Mr. Topps said this was an unusually difficult group!

This month we studied small-case letter formation. I didn't go straight through the alphabet, but rather taught the easiest ones first and separated the reversible ones—*b, d, p,* and *q*. This year, I have fewer students making letter, numeral, and word reversals, though you always have some with kindergarten children. I attribute this improvement to all the shared reading with Big Books, language-experience lessons and charts, and writing that the students have done. Directionality has to be learned, and contextualized reading and writing are the main tools for teaching it.

We had two really nice field trips this month. The trips were preceded, as usual, with a listing of words they could think of that were associated with the location. We also generated questions for the inevitable question period that guides always have. Afterward, we did a whole-group language-experience lesson, and some children dictated or wrote individual remembrances. Same old stuff we always do prior to and following these trips, but such activities are crucial to concept development. As usual, several of the children choose to write about the most recent field trip, and since children's writings are shared with the rest of the class, there has been a steady increase in the number of children who do that.

The first was a day trip to the zoo with the children as well as many parents. They took sack lunches. Everyone returned exhausted but exhilarated (and only two of the children got sick on the bus).

For the last field trip, I asked the two first-grade teachers if they would permit our children to visit their rooms to acquaint them with the teachers and also to give them some idea of what they could expect to see in first grade. Both teachers agreed and gave the children a fine overview of the first-grade program. Mrs. Wright had one of her students act as guide around the room, and she had others who explained the various things that they were working on. The kindergartners were quite impressed with the "big" first-graders who were so helpful to them, and all of them said that they wanted to be in Mrs. Wright's room next year.

After the children had finished their tour, I asked them how they would feel about doing something similar for the kindergarten class who would be arriving next fall.

"You mean you're going to have *more* kids here? I thought you just taught us," said Daphne.

"Now you know that there is going to be another group here. Remember the recent kindergarten round-up?"

"Yes, but we thought . . . I thought . . . I mean . . ."

"I will remember all of you. You don't have to worry about that. We care about one another, and when we care about people, we don't forget them. But you can't stay with me forever. You are ready to go on and learn more. You don't want to do the same things again. First grade is so exciting! You'll love it, but remember to say hello to me once in a while! But you still haven't answered. Shall we do something for the next kindergarten class like what the first-graders did?" Amid cries of "Yes! Yes!" there was one, Larry, who commented that that would be difficult, since we didn't know who the children would be.

"How about this?" I began, and outlined the plan for creating a mural depicting the various kindergarten activities. The children would put it up on the bulletin board and leave it there. When fall came, the new students would see some work done by "big" kindergartners telling them what to expect. The children loved the idea, and so did I. One of my pet peeves has always been that I begin the school year without any artwork from children on the walls—now there will be.

Self-selected reading has been highly successful this year. We're up to eight minutes a day as a class. However, some children continue reading after the timer rings. Mandy told me that she enjoys the idea of everyone reading at the same time.

I have found that I can do Think Links almost without thinking. It seems very easy to me now to examine a book for which one of the thinking processes can be highlighted and then to talk my way through the book. I have also found that by varying the kinds of materials I read—magazine articles with animal facts, books about other cultures, poems, and stories—I have thoroughly covered all of the thinking processes by this time. By now I have begun asking the children at several points to tell me what they are thinking and what caused them to have that thought. Even Chip and Alex are doing well with this now.

I did decide to risk making a whole meal at school, and it actually came off well! I had considered an early lunch for them to prepare, but I decided after one of our book sessions that nothing would do but to fix breakfast. The impetus for this decision, as you might have guessed, was Dr. Seuss's *Green Eggs and Ham*! The room was set up in stations for the big event. There was the measuring and mixing area, the scrambled eggs area, the toast area, the juice and milk area, and the cleanup area. Five children were in each of the areas, with clearly defined responsibilities.

The scrambled egg recipe was quite easy, although it did involve some high-level counting skills. For each person to be served, they measured and mixed: 1 egg, 1 tbsp. milk, and 2 tsp. diced ham. When it was all mixed together, they added the special ingredient: 1/2 tsp. blue food coloring! (We had quite a discussion about what color we should add to the yellow eggs.) The eggs were cooked in three electric skillets at the scrambled eggs area. Many cries of "Yuk!" and "Gross!" were heard and brought others to the scrambled eggs area to exclaim anew at the mess they saw before them.

Meanwhile, the people in "juice and milk" were pouring out servings into paper cups, and the people in "toast" were making four slices at a time. After the toast came out of the appliance, they used a plastic glass and pressed the top into the slice of toast, cutting out a circle. They made two heaps of toast: circles and slices with holes. The cleanup people, who would not have anything to do until after the breakfast was over, came to the toast area and placed one circle and one slice on each one of the paper plates. They carried the plates to "scrambled eggs," where a spoonful of green eggs and ham was put into the hole of the bread slice. They got their beverages and then their plates, and we all ate heartily! I didn't think Chip would ever stop eating, and I was sure that Daisy wouldn't, though she informed us that she had a huge breakfast before arriving at school. Even Mort seemed to show a flicker of interest—I suppose because it was not our normal routine (he seems so bored by routine).

My routine, lately, has involved sorting out materials and tossing away some of the accumulation. In doing so, I came across my very tattered copy of the critical knowings. I looked over the list yet again and thought back over all the activities I had been led to do using those seven factors as my guideline. I did indeed have children using shared book experiences and lots of writing. They dictated all sorts of language experiences to me. I read to them and talked with them a lot. Many of the activities, such as writing, fulfilled several of my goals at the same time. I wonder if it is possible to delineate all of the learnings that occurred in this room this year, or is there such an interaction of children, needs, and knowings that it would not be possible to construct two-dimensionally? I think I'll leave that one for contemplation at my beach retreat this summer!

As I look back across the year, I guess I am proudest of what Manuel has accomplished. I just never would have believed that he would have learned to listen, speak, read, write, and apparently think as much English as he has. He has a ways to go, but he is definitely on the road to academic success. It makes me realize how much more he could have accomplished had we had an ESL teacher to work with him regularly each week. The combination of a literacy-rich kindergarten *and* a good ESL classroom would have ensured a speedy transition to English proficiency for Manuel. I know Mr. Topps is trying to get an ESL teacher for us in the future, but the number of children who need such a service is lower at our school than at several others in the district. I'll be sure to speak with Manuel's first-grade teacher about him at the beginning of next year.

THE CURRICULUM COMMITTEE MEETING

Miss Launch sat at the large oval table, trying to restrain herself from tapping her pencil on the tabletop. She had been sitting at this same table every week for the last three months. Miss Launch had been very quiet during these meetings, feeling that, as a relative newcomer to the district, she should allow those who had been with the school system longer to do most of the talking.

As nearly as she could tell, this group of kindergarten teachers, all of those who taught in the school system, were divided into three distinct camps. Miss Launch felt sorry for Sue Port, the curriculum supervisor, who had to chair the meetings. She had always found Ms. Port very facilitative and helpful. But these meetings must surely be a strain on her good nature!

"All right, people," interrupted Ms. Port, "let's try to get some consensus on this matter. Let me summarize what we have all agreed on." There was general laughter around the room, since they all knew that this would be a short summary.

"Our kindergarten curriculum guide is 15 years old, and although it has some good aspects to it, it seems that some of the information and guidelines are outdated. It also seems that the guide is better the longer you have taught! This indicates to us that the guide is not very helpful to beginning teachers, since more experienced teachers have to fill in with materials and knowledge they already possess—not a problem for them, but it surely is to some others. The feeling among many of you is that you like the, shall we say, vagueness of the present guide because it allows a lot of freedom for individual teaching styles. But there is no choice, which is what I've been trying to get through to you these past many weeks; we are mandated by the school board to produce a new kindergarten curriculum guide by the end of the summer. Frankly, I'm getting worried! I see three factions in this group. Let me outline them for you so that we can try to bring this together today.

"We have one group of teachers who would like us to purchase one or more of the kits on the market. This group argues that the kits are complete with materials, teacher's guide, and objectives. I brought a few examples of kits today so that we could examine them more closely.

"Another group seems to want to develop a new curriculum guide that will be a kind of super-teacher's manual and to meet through the summer over salad lunches to put together the materials you'll need for the first few weeks. We would then meet regularly during the school year to produce additional materials and to add to the teacher's manual based on the actual teaching done with it.

"The third group is inclined to forget the whole thing." She paused as laughter interrupted. "But knowing we can't, they would like us to add a couple of things to the old guide and continue to ignore it and teach as they have always done."

"Wow," thought Miss Launch, "she's not pulling any punches today."

"That's not quite fair," spoke up the most vocal member of the third group. "We have been teaching for a long time, and nobody seems to have complained about what we've been doing. Why change now just to be changing? I know for sure that I can do a better job with the children I teach than if you made me use one of those kits over there! Those kits don't contain all the aspects that I deal with in my program."

"You know, Kay," said Ms. Port, "you just might be able to pull off the greatest program in the world. However, much as I'd like to think it, this school system just is not filled with Kay Longs. What about some of our teachers who just got out of college? What about teachers like Helen Launch who came to this school system from another, very different one? Don't we owe those people a chance to share in your expertise?

"One problem we face is that we have to have some consistency within our school system so that kindergarten means essentially the same thing no matter where one goes. Why, even within the same school I've noted great differences, substantive differences, in the kindergarten program. Another fact to face is that the instruction in kindergarten should help to facilitate the child's beginning reading and writing experiences, not hinder them. If we have some common goals toward which we are all working, then we should be facilitating beginning reading and writing. Right now, we only hope we are. We have some ideas about specific teaching emphases based on our experiences with the spring kindergarten screening we do. However, I've always felt *that* information is somewhat suspect because the situation in which the children are assessed is so strange to them. They are taken into a big room, the cafeteria or gym, and meet with many different people to perform many different tasks. You all know how hard it is to get a five-year-old to perform on command! So we know if they can see or hear, but I wonder how much valid information we get on their academic knowledge.

"I'm open to suggestion as to where we go from here. Yes, Helen, is that your hand I see?"

"Well, I've kept rather quiet through all of these discussions, but I wonder if I might be able to offer, just as a starting point, the guidelines I used to help me teach this year. Maybe we could look at the kits up there using these objectives, so that at least we would all be talking about the same things."

With Ms. Port's encouragement, Miss Launch put the seven critical knowings on the chalkboard in the room and then sat down and discussed each of them briefly. She noticed murmurs and nods of agreement among teachers from all three factions. No one could argue against any of them, because they did seem to be essential to beginning reading and writing success. However, the discussion turned lively when they began to examine the kits, using the knowings as guidelines!

"Hey, where are all the books? If we are to encourage children to read and listen to a variety of materials, and to immerse them in books so that they develop a desire to learn to read, then we're going to need more books than the five they have in this kit. Five books is an insult! Why put in any?"

"Look how flimsy all this stuff is! My kids would have these thin cardboard pictures destroyed in a week, even though they're pretty careful. And those puppets! Do you believe they are trying to pawn those off for classroom use? I give them three days!"

"Speaking of the pictures, just look at them closely. What's that a picture of? A dog? A beagle? A puppy? Pet? Stuffed animal? It's really hard to tell. The pictures are small and not very clear—too much distraction in them."

"Listen to this manual, you guys. This whole kit as well as the other two really hit phonics hard! But the instruction is too hard for my students, and they need a lot more repetition than these kits provide for. It says here we can 'add additional materials' from our own sources, if necessary. I thought this was supposed to be complete!"

These comments continued for some minutes as the teachers found that, even with their aura of professionalism, the kits were not complete sets of materials that would make teaching a breeze for the school year. More important, they didn't even come close to providing for all the learnings that adherence to Miss Launch's seven knowings called for. Ultimately, it was clear to Ms. Port that the consensus had indeed been found. Though much discussion about the details of pulling off the new curriculum guide remained to be gone through, basically the teachers agreed that Miss Launch's seven knowings should be the core of the new curriculum guide. They realized that they could produce their own curriculum, which would be much more complete than the kits they could purchase for the same money.

Helen and Sue left the room together, the last of the group to trail out. "Thank you for your help today," said Sue. "I think they see now that good learning and teaching can't be totally packaged, nor can it exist without structure. That was the breakthrough today. You've left your mark on this school system. I'm glad you're one of us!"

Miss Launch waved to the departing back of the smiling Ms. Port, marveling at what she had just said. "Me? I left a mark? I'm just trying to teach all the kids the best way I know how."

CHILDREN'S BOOKS/MATERIALS CITED

Alphabetics, by Suse MacDonald, Bradbury Press, 1986.
The All-Around Pumpkin Book, by M. Cuyler, Scholastic, 1980.
Brown Bear, Brown Bear, What Do You See? by Bill Martin, Holt, Rinehart, & Winston, 1970.
Frederick, by Leo Lionni, Knopf/Pantheon, 1970.
Green Eggs and Ham, by Dr. Seuss, Random House, 1960.
Hailstones and Halibut Bones, by Mary O'Neill, Doubleday, 1990.
The Hungry Thing, by J. B. Slepian & A. G. Seidler, Scholastic, 1971.
Mushroom in the Rain, by Mirra Ginsburg, Scholastic, 1974.
The Napping House, by A. Wood, Harcourt Brace Jovanovich, 1986.
Swimmy, by Leo Lionni, Knopf Books for Young Readers, 1970.
The Taming of the C.A.N.D.Y. Monster, by V. Lansky, Book Peddlers, 1978.
The Timbertoes ABC Alphabet, by Highlights for Children, Boyds Mills Press, 1997.
Where the Wild Things Are, by Maurice Sendak, HarperCollins, 1963.

Mrs. Wright: First Grade

THE PARENT MEETING

Rita Wright sat in her first-grade classroom, awaiting the arrival of the parents for their orientation meeting. She remembered how nervous she had been at her first parent meeting years ago, and although there was still a little nervous flutter in her stomach, she had learned to approach these meetings with confidence. "The parents all want the best for their children," she reminded herself, "and I have learned so much since that first year about how to teach them." Mrs. Wright felt particularly confident and excited about this year because last year she had phased in a four-block approach to reading and writing (Cunningham, Hall, & Sigmon, 1999) that had resulted in accelerated progress for her top and her bottom students. She had worked out the "bugs" in this balanced approach and was beginning this year with a clear sense of how she would organize and what she might accomplish. Tonight, she hoped to explain to the parents, in simple terms, what this four-block approach was and how it would benefit all their children.

As parents began to arrive, Mrs. Wright rose to greet them and make sure they all put on name tags. She recognized several parents whose older children she had taught and chatted with them for a minute about how these children were doing. As parents introduced themselves and put on their name tags, she found herself noticing how like and unlike some of their children they were. Daphne's grandmother was there, and Mrs. Wright understood where Daphne got her nurturing, caretaking ways. Chip's grandfather came and he, just like Chip, was clean and presentable but dressed in old, threadbare clothes. Mike's father came and paced around restlessly, and Mrs. Wright could picture his constantly-in-motion son. Betty and Roberta's mother came, and Mrs. Wright could account for Betty's neat, orderly, pleasing style. She wondered if Roberta took after her father! These twins' differences had reaffirmed Mrs. Wright's belief that children come with their own personalities and do not all learn in the same way.

When everyone appeared to be there—Paul, Butch, and Alexander, three of her students she was most concerned about, had no parent or other relative present—Mrs. Wright began the meeting.

"I am just delighted that you took time out from your hectic schedules to be here tonight. School has been in session only a week, but your children and I are already hard at work here in our classroom. My goal is that all your children will learn to read and write and do math and learn more about the world in which we live. Accomplishing this with a diverse class of 25 children will take all our best efforts. Your making the effort to be here tonight lets me know that your children and the school have your support, and I will do my very best to teach all your children and keep you informed of their progress.

"Many of you know that summer before last, we had a two-day retreat to really spend some extended time talking about what we believe and how to make our instruction consistent with out beliefs. Out of that meeting came this list of 12 guiding principles, which all the teachers at Merritt try to follow. I would like each of you to have a copy of this and as I talk, I will try to remember to point out how our classroom program reflects each of these principles." Mrs. Wright passed out the following statement of 12 principles.

At Merritt Elementary, we believe that all children can learn to read and write. We hold high expectations of every child. To make these expectations a reality, we all agree to have our instruction reflect 12 guiding principles:

1. Provide a balanced literacy program.
2. Make instruction multilevel.
3. Use language as the foundation for reading and writing.
4. Teach reading and writing as thinking.
5. Use feelings to create avid readers and writers.
6. Connect reading and writing to all subject areas.
7. Read aloud to students daily.
8. Schedule daily self-selected reading.
9. Have students write every day.
10. Teach the decoding and spelling strategies reading and writing require.
11. Use observation to assess learning and plan instruction.
12. Inform parents of expectations and progress.

"I would like you to look at our schedule, which is posted on this chart," Mrs. Wright continued. "When I explain to you what happens during each of these blocks of time, I think you will understand all we have to accomplish and how hard we will be working each day."

Here is the schedule for Mrs. Wright's first-grade class:

8:30–8:45	Morning Meeting/Planning for the day
8:45–9:20	Writing Block
9:20–9:50	Working with Words Block
9:50–10:10	Break/Recess
10:10–10:45	Guided Reading Block
10:45–11:30	Math
11:30–12:00	Lunch
12:00–12:15	Rest/Quiet Time
12:15–1:00	Science or Social Studies Unit
1:00–1:30	Specials—P. E., Music, Library
1:30–2:00	Teacher Read-Aloud/Self-Selected Reading Block
2:00–2:15	Summary/Review/Prepare to go home
2:15–2:45/3:00	Centers

Pointing to each of the time slots, Mrs. Wright explained what happened in each of these and what they were intended to accomplish.

"Although some children are in the room earlier, we start our official day at 8:30. The children check in when they arrive and indicate their lunch choices, so we don't waste time with attendance. In the first 15 minutes, I try to accomplish a number of goals. We always do some activities with our calendar, such as determining what day and month it is, and counting the number of days to certain special days. This may seem simple enough to you, but many first-grade children are still unsure of important time concepts like days of the week, months, and seasons. We then look at our daily schedule, and we move the hands of this big clock to show what time we will do each activity. If there are any changes in our normal schedule, I point these out to the children and write them on a note that I attach to our schedule. Starting out each morning by orienting ourselves in this way helps the children have a real sense of orderliness and allays any fears they might have that we might forget one of the important parts of the day like recess or lunch or centers. It also gives us lots of opportunities to use math in real situations as we count days, months, and so on and work with the important first-grade math concept of telling time. We usually end this opening meeting by singing a favorite song, reciting a favorite rhyme, and doing a favorite finger play.

"At 8:45, we begin Writers' Workshop. Daily writing is a very important part of how children learn to write, and writing is also a major way in which children become readers. Each day, I do a minilesson in which I write something while the children watch me write. Then the children write. Right now, we are in what I call the 'driting' stage. The children both draw and write, often intermixing the two. I model this for them by drawing something each day and writing a little something to go with my drawing. Here is the driting I did this morning." Mrs. Wright displayed the large piece of drawing paper on which she had created her drawing and word labels. Parents chuckled when they saw her artwork!

"As you can tell, my drawing skills are limited, but I try to turn this disadvantage into an advantage. My children never tell me that they can't draw. They know that they can all do as well as—and many better than—I do.

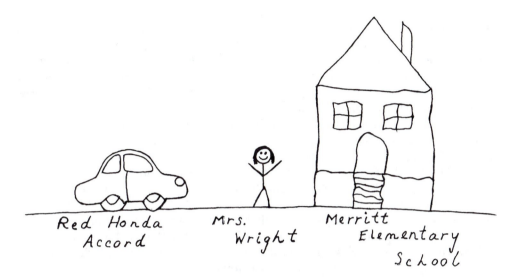

Red Honda
Accord

Mrs.
Wright

Merritt
Elementary
School

"After I draw and write a few words and tell the children about my driting, they all get a piece of drawing paper and they 'drite' something they want to tell about. I go around and encourage them, but I don't spell or write words for them. If they want to write a word, I encourage them to put down all the letters they hear, and write it just so that they can remember what they want to tell about."

At this point, Mrs. Wright was interrupted by Roberta and Betty's mother, who said, "Mrs. Wright, this is something I have been worrying about. Betty told me that she wouldn't write because she can't spell all the words, and Roberta says that it doesn't matter if you spell them right as long as you know what you are saying. They are always fussing about this when they come home with their driting, and I don't know what to tell them. I always spell words for them at home. How are they going to learn to spell if no one spells words for them?"

Several parents were nodding their heads in agreement, and Mrs. Wright realized she would have to try to convince them that invented spelling was an important part of learning to spell correctly.

"I know that for many of you, letting the children spell words by putting down the letters they hear seems strange. That is certainly not the way things were done when I was in school and not the way I taught just a few years ago. But research has shown that children who are encouraged to put down the letters they hear as they are writing write more and better pieces and become better at sounding out words when they are reading. Think about it. If your child is trying to write *motorcycle* and says *motorcycle* slowly, listening for the sounds in *motorcycle*, he might end up writing 'morsk,' which is not *motorcycle* but does have many of the letters heard in *motorcycle*. The difficulty with teaching children to use phonics to figure out words is not in teaching them the sounds made by letters but in actually getting them to use what they know about letters and sounds when they are reading and writing. Children who invent spell as they write are using the phonics they are learning, and both the research and my experience during the last few years confirm that they write more and become better at figuring out how to read and spell unknown words. I can assure you that your children will not spell *motorcycle* 'morsk' forever. There is a problem with children invent spelling the high-frequency words like *they*, *was*, and *want*, however. Let me finish talking about our Writers' Workshop, and then when we get to our Words block, you will see how we are going to handle that problem."

Mrs. Wright quickly finished talking about Writers' Workshop, saying less than she had intended, realizing that time was marching on and she wasn't even halfway through the morning yet.

"After the children finish their driting, we go around and let each child show and tell about what he or she drew and/or wrote. We will continue in the driting stage for a few more weeks. Meanwhile, during the Words block, children will be learning to read some words, and we will be doing some handwriting instruction. When most of the children know some words and can make most of the letters, we will move to writing on this paper I call half-and-half paper." Mrs. Wright held up a piece of paper with drawing space on the top and writing lines on the bottom. "I will continue to model for the children, but now I will write a sentence or two first and then do a little drawing at the top. When the children do their writing, I will ask them to write a sentence or two or a few words first and then draw. When almost all the children are able to write something readable, we will move to our writing notebooks. In my newsletter to you, I will announce that we are about to graduate to writing notebooks—a very advanced stage—and ask you to send a notebook like this one." Mrs. Wright held up a 70-sheet composition book. "Once the children start writing in their notebooks, we will begin our editing and publishing process. Every three or four weeks, your child will pick one piece to publish. I will work with your child to edit that piece, and at that point we will fix the spelling. Your children will publish in various forms, including these books that they are so proud of. Here is one written by a child who moved unexpectedly last year and left this behind."

Mrs. Wright passed around the book, and she could tell that the parents were impressed and that their fears about spelling were starting to be allayed. She then explained the major goals for the Working with Words block.

"At about 9:20 each morning, we devote approximately 30 minutes to making sure your children are learning to read and spell the most common words and to developing their phonics and spelling skills so that they become increasingly more able to read and spell new words. If you look here above the alphabet letters," Mrs. Wright said, pointing to the space above the chalkboard, "you will see the beginning of our word wall. Currently, as many of you have heard, we are adding the name of one of your children each day. Of course, all your children want their names up first, so to be fair, I have all their names written on different colored paper scraps in this box. Each morning, at the beginning of our Words block, I close my eyes and reach in and pull one out. That child becomes our special child for the day, and the name gets added to the wall. As you can see, Horace, Manuel, Paul, Daphne, and Roberta were the lucky five whose names came out first, but in 20 more days, everyone's name will be up there, and they will all have been special for a day. Perhaps you know that our first social studies unit focuses on the idea that everyone is special and different and that we should celebrate these differences.

"Jumping ahead to our 12:15 to 1:00 slot for social studies or science, I read aloud many books and do other activities during that time to develop the notion that we are all different and special. One thing we do each day is to interview the special child whose name was added to the word wall and do a shared writing chart based on that interview. Once we get all the names up here, we will begin adding those common, hard-to-spell words I mentioned earlier, including *they*, *were*, and *want*. We will add five words each Monday, and we will spend our entire 30 minutes of Words time on Monday working with those five words. We will use them in sentences and have a handwriting lesson on them. On the other days, Tuesday, Wednesday, Thursday, and Friday, we will spend about eight minutes at the beginning of each Words block, practicing how to spell these important words. When the children tell you that they are chanting words and learning to be cheerleaders, they are referring to our daily word wall practice. I pick five words each day, and the children chant them cheerleader style several times and then write them. You will be hearing more about our word wall because it is an important part of our total reading and writing program. Word wall is the main way I have of making sure your children can read and spell what we used to call 'sight words.' When children are writing, they stretch out words and spell them with whatever letters they know, unless it is a word wall word. Your children will get tired of hearing me say, 'If it's on our word wall, we have to spell it correctly!'

"As I said, word wall takes all our 30 minutes of Words block on Monday when we add the five new words, but only about eight minutes on the other days. We devote the remaining 22 minutes to activities that teach phonics and spelling." Mrs. Wright noticed some relieved faces and reminded herself that first-grade parents always need to be reassured that their children are learning phonics. "Currently, we are working with the sounds of the initial letters. If your children told you that *R* is their *running* letter and they ate raisins today because *raisins* begins with an *R*, you know that we are beginning our phonics instruction. The concept that words have beginning, middle, and ending sounds and that letters 'make' these sounds is a very difficult one for young children. I try to make it as concrete as possible by giving them an action and a food for each letter. I have duplicated for you the action and food we are going to do for each letter. One way you could help is by donating one of the foods on the list. We ate raisins today, and tomorrow we will all drink milk as we try to get a handle on the sound of *M*. There is no particular order in which the letters need to be taught, so I try to begin with letters that begin children's names that are already on the wall and to make the first letters taught very different in appearance and sound. By the end of this week, your children should be able to tell you that *R* is the *running* and *raisins* letter and the first letter in Roberta's name, that *M* is the *marching* and *milk* letter and the first letter in Manuel's name, and that D is the *dancing* and *donuts* letter and the first letter in Daphne's name. It is too bad that I don't have children's names for all the beginning letters! Here is a list of the actions and foods that you might use to remind your children when they are reading or writing and can't remember the letter that goes with a particular sound. I have tried to make the foods as healthful as possible. Let me know at the end of the meeting if you would be willing to donate one of these and we will talk about when we will need it." Mrs. Wright handed out the following:

Mrs. Wright's Action and Food List

b	bounce	bananas
c	catch	cookies
d	dance	donuts
f	fall	fish (we will do this on a day when fish is on our lunch menu)
g	gallop	gum (sugarless!)
h	hop	hamburgers (lunch menu)
j	jump	Jell-O
k	kick	Kool-Aid
l	laugh	lemonade
m	march	milk
n	nod	noodles (lunch menu)
p	paint	pizza (lunch menu)
r	run	raisins
s	sit	salad (lunch menu)
t	talk	toast
v	vacuum	vegetables (assorted, raw)
w	walk	watermelon
y	yawn	yogurt
z	zip	zucchini bread
ch	cheer	Cheerios
sh	shiver	sherbet
th	think	three thin things

"We also do many activities during the Words block that focus on the vowel spelling patterns. As you know, the vowels in English have more than one common sound and have different spellings. The *o*, for example, has the sounds you hear in *box* and *boat*. Perhaps you remember that we used to call these the 'short' and 'long' sounds. But *o* in combination with other letters represents many more than just two sounds. Think about *port* and *joy* and *cloud*. Then think about the fact that *boat* and *vote* rhyme but have different spelling patterns. The vowel sound spelled *o-y* in *joy* is spelled *o-i* in *soil*. The sound spelled *o-u* in *cloud* is spelled *o-w* in *cow*."

Mrs. Wright had been writing these words on the board as she said them, and you could tell from looking at the faces of the parents that most of them had never thought about how complicated a spelling system English has.

"The ability to figure out how to read or spell a word you have never seen before is a critical skill in becoming a good independent reader. We will spend most of our Words block every day helping children to learn these spelling patterns and how to use the patterns in words they know to help them figure out how to spell and read new words. Because English is a complex language, this will not happen overnight. We will make charts of rhyming words, and I will include some of these in my newsletters to you. We will also do an activity called Making Words a couple of times a week. The children will be bringing home some Making Words strips and challenging you to see how many words you can make from the letters on the strip. Be sure to encourage and praise them for their growing spelling and phonics skills, and be patient with us. By the end of the year, most of your children will be spelling wall words well and be able to figure out almost any regular one-syllable word."

Mrs. Wright glanced up at the clock and realized she had less than 10 minutes to explain the rest of the day. Quickly, she moved through the other time slots.

"After our Words block, we have our break/recess time. Fortunately, you all know what happens in the 20 minutes. Then we have our guided reading lessons. At this point, we are doing shared reading with Big Books such as these." Mrs. Wright quickly showed them *Mrs. Wishy Washy* and *The Very Hungry Caterpillar*. "We read the book together and do many activities related to the book. In October, we will begin reading in the books in our adopted reading series. These are the books adopted by the school system, and we will read these as well as real books whenever I can get my hands on enough copies."

At this point, Steve's father raised his hand and asked, "How will you do three reading groups in 35 minutes?"

Mrs. Wright hadn't intended to go into this tonight, but the question had been asked. "I won't have three reading groups. Reading groups are another mainstay of our school days that have been seriously questioned in recent years. The children who are put in the bottom group in first grade almost always remain in the bottom group throughout elementary school and almost never reach the point where they can read on grade level. Three groups are also a problem for children in the top group. You wouldn't believe how much difference there is between children in a top reading group. Some are just a little faster and further along than average readers, while others read at second- or third-grade level at the beginning of first grade. For truly top children, just putting them in a book a little above grade level doesn't even begin to meet their needs. The other problem with ability groups is what you pointed out—you can't do three reading groups in 35 minutes. If I were to put your children in three groups, I wouldn't really be meeting the needs of my most advanced readers or of those who need a lot more practice. I also wouldn't be able to give 35 minutes each day to writing, which is an approach to reading, 30 minutes to the Words block, and 30 minutes *here*," Mrs. Wright pointed to the 1:30–2:00 time slot, "to the critically important Teacher Read-Aloud/Self-Selected Reading time. At this time of the year, I usually read to the children for about 20 minutes, and they read to themselves for about 10 minutes, but by February I hope to have that time divided more evenly so that the children are reading books of their own choosing for about 15 minutes each day.

"Having three groups is an attempt to meet the needs of the whole range of diverse children that is found in any classroom. Unfortunately, it doesn't meet the needs very well, and doing three groups takes most of the reading/language arts teaching time. My instruction in reading takes place in all four blocks: the Writing block, the Working with Words block, the Guided Reading block, and the Teacher Read-Aloud/Self-Selected Reading block. These blocks represent the competing methods that people are always arguing about—what is the 'best method.' My experience with the four blocks last year and the experience and research of others who have organized this way show that all children do not learn in the same way. We need a variety of methods going on simultaneously if we are to teach all children successfully. Think about two sisters you have known, born to the same family, growing up in the same house. Have you ever said, 'How can two sisters be so different?'"

At this point, Roberta and Betty's mother piped up with, "Maybe the sisters are even twins—born within minutes of each other!" The group of parents, many of whom knew Betty and Roberta, broke into laughter, and the point that not all children learn in the same way was brought home to everyone.

Mrs. Wright summed up. "If you would look at your list for just a minute, I want to try to show you how the four-block framework allows me to implement all 12 principles. To me a balanced literacy program, number 1 on your list, means first and foremost providing children with many different ways to learn to read and write—something for every personality. Within each block, I make the instruction as multilevel—that's principle number 2—as possible. Writing and Self-Selected Reading are the most multilevel blocks; there is no limit to how high the children can move. The Guided Reading block is the hardest one to make multilevel because whatever we are all going to read has a level—which is too hard for some and too easy for others. I make this block multilevel by not sticking with the same level of material all week and by having the children sometimes read with partners. I also meet with flexible groups that meet for a few days or a week to read a particular story or book. In these groups, the more advanced readers might be reading something challenging together, and the children who need more easy reading might be reading something easy together. Last year was the first year I organized my language and reading instruction into the four blocks, and I have to tell you that the children who would have been in the bottom group made much more progress than in previous years, and that children who would have been in the top group really moved ahead."

Just then Mr. Topps popped his head in the door. A glance at the clock told Mrs. Wright that she was now 10 minutes over and that all the other classes were probably already assembling in the cafeteria for refreshments and the general meeting.

She quickly finished up by saying, "I hope you see that numbers 7, 8, 9, and 10 get daily time and attention in this room. Number 3 is the reason that I focus so much on oral language and listening throughout the entire day. I try to promote thinking—number 4— all day, but I focus on this during Guided Reading when I teach the comprehension strategies and during Writing when I help them learn to think the way writers do. Number 5 is absolutely critical for first-graders. I want them to love books and to love telling their own stories through their writing, and I try to provide enough success so that everyone develops self-confidence. You will see evidence of number 6, the connections we make reading and writing, and science and social studies, in the first newsletter I will send home in a few weeks. This newsletter along with the parent conferences we will be having soon are two of the major ways I meet number 12. I am always observing your children and making records of what they can do and what they need help on. Your children will soon be bringing home books they can read and their own published writing, as well as other samples of what they are doing, so that you too can observe their progress. If I have any particular concerns about any area of your child's development, I will call you, and I trust that you will call me if you have any concerns. Please let me know if you can bring any of the foods on the list. I look forward to seeing you all at parent conference time in eight more weeks and want to remind you that visitors and volunteers are always welcome in this school and in my class."

As the parents left, several offered to send food, and several others said they would love to come and see how "this four-block thing" worked. Mrs. Wright suggested that they wait a few weeks until she and the children could get the routines better established and then just send her a note telling her when they would like to come. She warned them, however, that there were never enough hands to help or ears to listen to children read, and that when they came, she would probably put them right to work!

MONTHLY LOGS

September

Now I know why October is my favorite month—all month long I celebrate my survival of September! My supervising teacher from long-ago student-teaching days used to say, "I could teach first grade until I am 80 if someone would teach the first four weeks for me."

I got my group this year from Miss Launch. They are as ready and eager as a motley crew of six-year-olds can be. And a motley crew they are. I am most worried about Paul. It is a rare day on which Paul doesn't return to his seat, put his head on his desk, and sob. I have tried to contact his parents, but there appears to be no father at home and his mother works odd hours. Miss Grant, the social worker, says his home situation is "not supportive," so I will continue to do what I can for him here. Daisy presents a different set of problems. She doesn't want to do anything and doesn't get along with anyone! Her mother will be in next week for a conference. I hope we can work together to find ways to motivate Daisy. I'd like to say, "Your daughter is a spoiled, selfish child," but I know that won't get us anywhere.

Poor Chip! I have managed to stop most of the taunts and snickers directed at his tattered clothes, but I know Butch and Mort still bother him on the playground. He goes his own way, however, and pays as little attention to them as possible. I do admire the child.

Manuel's English is still not strong, but considering that he didn't speak any when he came last year, he is doing well. The children are all used to helping him understand, and I was surprised to know that they all can speak some Spanish! Miss Launch, apparently, appointed all the children "English teachers" and Manuel their "Spanish teacher." After all my years of teaching, she still amazes me with the clever solutions she comes up with.

Larry, Danielle, Roberta, and Pat are reading quite well. The cumulative portfolios I got from Miss Launch indicate that Larry and Danielle were reading when they came to kindergarten, and that Roberta and Pat learned during the year. Larry has more general knowledge than anyone else. He is always adding some little-known (to the other children) fact to our discussions. The others listen in awe and amazement. Yesterday Hilda said, "Larry, how do you know that?" He responded, "I read it in a book," as if that were the most natural thing in the world, and I guess it is for him.

Alexander has a hard time sometimes dealing with me and the other children. The hearing aid he wears is supposed to give him enough hearing capacity to function normally if he is seated close to you, but his oral language and listening abilities are like those of a four-year-old. Miss Launch says I should have seen him when he came to kindergarten last year. He could hardly talk and wouldn't listen. Apparently, they didn't discover his hearing problem until he was over two years old and had yet to say "mama" or "daddy." I have assigned Steve to be his buddy for the time being and have talked with the children about what an important invention hearing aids are. One hundred years ago, Alexander would not have been able to hear at all! We try to treat Alexander as special and lucky, but he still gets frustrated sometimes and lashes out at us. Once in a while, I think he pretends (or chooses) not to hear—usually when I say, "Time to clean up," or "Where is your paper?" It is hard to know what to do. I want to treat him as normal, but he does need special consideration. Orel Lang, the speech and hearing specialist, will work with Alexander on Wednesdays and Fridays. I will ask him for advice.

We have made good progress this year into our four-block instruction. We are still using drawing paper for our Writers' Workshop, but I think we will move to the half-and-half paper by the middle of October. Almost all the children are adding some letters and words to their drawings now, and Larry, Danielle, Roberta, Pat, and Hilda are often writing sentences along the bottom of their drawing paper. Even the children who are further behind have the idea of what reading and writing are and are adding some labels to their drawings. All but four of the children's names are now up on our word wall, and the children often draw pictures of themselves and other classmates and write the classmates' names next to their pictures. They also draw their pets and usually can spell their pets' names.

We are about finished learning actions and eating foods to go with the letters. Connecting the letter names and sounds with children's names, actions, and foods seems to be really helping all the children. I was reading them one of our many alphabet books before Self-Selected Reading yesterday, and the children were having trouble coming up with the name *porcupine*. Daisy piped up and said, "I don't know what it is but it begins like pizza!"

"And Paul," chimed in Chip.

"And paint," added Butch, acting out the painting action as he said it.

It is truly amazing to me how many different and fascinating alphabet books there are. The children adore the alphabet book *NBA Action From A–Z*, the singable rhymes in *ABC Bunny* by Wanda Gag, and finding the hidden animals in *Alphabeasts: A Hide and Seek Alphabet Book* by Durga Bernhard. I even found two alphabet books that tied in with our I Am Special social studies unit. *Ashanti to Zulu: African Traditions* by Margaret Musgrove allowed us to think about how special each of our heritages and traditions is, and *The Hand Made Alphabet* by Laura Rankin shows children how to finger spell the letters along with some great pictures of objects beginning with those letters.

In addition to interviewing the special child each day and then writing a chart telling what was special about that child, I read them a book almost every day about a child, and we talk about what was special about the child in the book. We also talk about how the same things that make you special can be problems at times. They enjoyed old favorites like *The Hundred Dresses* by Eleanor Estes, as well as some new books including *I Hate English* by Ellen Levine, in which a Chinese girl, Mei Mei, tries to cope with life in a new country, a new school, and a new language. I also read them some books in which animal characters had special characteristics, including *The Biggest Nose* by Kathy Caple, in which an elephant is being teased by her hippo friend about having such a big nose. The elephant feels self-conscious until she realizes that her hippo friend has such a big mouth. My children are very aware of how they are physically different from one another, and talking about the differences is easier sometimes when characters in the book are humorous, lovable animals.

We have read several predictable Big Books during our Guided Reading block, including *Ten, Nine, Eight* by Molly Bang, which portrays beautifully the relationship between an African American girl and her father. In addition to fitting into our I Am Special unit, this counting book tied in with our math. I don't know about the other teachers, but I find it very easy to put into practice the principle that we should connect reading and writing to the other subject areas.

Self-Selected Reading is also off to a good start. I think that is because I didn't take for granted that children knew how to enjoy books before they could actually read them. In the past, I have noticed my children with the fewest literacy experiences at home having great trouble settling down with a book. They would keep picking books up, flipping through them, and putting them back. I didn't mind that they weren't reading the books, but they weren't even really looking at them. This year it occurred to me that maybe they didn't know how you could enjoy a book even when you couldn't read it. I decided that some modeling and direct experience were called for. About the third week of school, as I sat down to read to them before their Self-Selected Reading time, I picked up a copy of *Are You My Mother?*—a book I had already read to them several times and one many of them had at home.

"You know," I began, "there is more than just one way to read a book. Usually, when I read to you, I read by saying all these words." I pointed to the words and read a few pages. "Saying all the words is one way to read, but there is another way to read. Let me show you how my son David used to read *Are You My Mother?* when he was just starting first grade."

I then unzipped my magic bag (this is a big canvas bag I carry around with me all the time. I call it my magic bag because I often keep things hidden in it and surprise the children with them when I pull them out. The children are always asking, "Got anything magic in that bag today?") and pulled out my son's favorite teddy bear and introduced Bare Bear to the class.

"Now, when my son David was just your age, he loved his Bare Bear and he loved *Are You My Mother?* Every night, I would read him two books, and he would always choose *Are You My Mother?* first. After I read to him, I would let him have 10 minutes to look at his books before he had to turn his light out and go to sleep. I would go to the kitchen to clean up the dishes, and I could hear him reading *Are You My Mother?* to Bare Bear. This is how he read it."

I then read *Are You My Mother?* to them the way a young child pretends to read a memorized book. The children watched in amazement. When I finished, I asked them if I had read it the way I usually read to them by saying all the words, and got them to explain that I knew the story so well I could tell it and repeat the familiar parts:

> *"Are you my mother?" the baby bird asked the cow.*
> *"I am not your mother. I am a cow."*

Then I asked, "How many of you have a favorite book at home that someone has read to you over and over again and you can pretend read that book to a little brother or sister or to your favorite stuffed animal?" Several hands went up, and I let the children tell me the title of the book they could pretend read. I then invited them to bring these books the next day and show us how they could pretend to read the book. Betty asked if she could bring her Kitty that she read to. I asked if Kitty was stuffed or alive. Betty looked horrified and said, "Kitty's not alive. I couldn't bring a live cat to school!" Her twin (in name only), Roberta, chimed in with, "I bet I could!"

The next day Betty, Roberta, Harriet, Steve, and Anthony proudly walked in with books and stuffed animals. At Teacher Read-Aloud/Self-Selected Reading time, they "read" their books to their animals and to us. Betty "read" *The Gingerbread Man*, Roberta "read" *Where the Wild Things Are*, Harriet "read" *Goodnight Moon*, Steve "read" *Over in the Meadow*, and Anthony "read" *Where's Spot?* On the following day, several more children brought in their favorite predictable books and "read" them to us. By the end of the week, all my children knew that there were two ways you could read a book. You could say all the words or you could retell the story of a favorite book, making up parts and saying the repeated parts you knew.

Last week, I introduced the third way we read books. Out of my magic bag, I pulled a whole stack of books about airplanes. I explained to the children that when David was their age, he loved airplanes. He wanted to be a pilot when he grew up or the owner of an international airline. He was always checking books about airplanes out of the library, and I bought him many airplane books with great pictures. I then proceeded to show them how David "read" the airplane books, not by saying the words and not by pretending to read them. I showed them that most of the books had a lot of writing and that David would have to be at least 10 or 11 before he could even begin to read these books. There was also too much writing in these books to remember what the book said and pretend you were reading it. David read these books by talking to himself about the pictures. I then went through several of the airplane books with the children, and making no pretense at reading the words, I talked about the pictures as if I were a six-year-old.

"Oh, look at that old airplane. Hard to believe that anyone would fly in something that rickety looking!"

"What a neat fighter jet! I bet that one can go a thousand miles per hour!"

The children joined in and helped me talk about the pictures. After looking at several of the airplane books, I asked the children if any of them had books at home that they couldn't read or pretend read but that had lots of wonderful pictures that they loved to look at and talk to themselves about. Several children volunteered that they had such books, and on the next several days they brought these books in and "read" them to us by talking about the pictures. Mitch brought in some books about trucks. He wants to be a truck driver like his father when he grows up. Steve brought in some books with all different kinds of plants in them. Larry surprised us all by bringing in a bunch of books about different countries and talking about the pictures and where he planned to travel when he was grown up.

"But, Larry," Hilda asked, "you can read! Why don't you just read the books instead of talking to yourself about the pictures?"

"I like the pictures," Larry explained. "That is a lot of words!" he said, pointing to the words on one of the pages.

"Even when you can read," I explained, "there are books you like to enjoy just by looking at them and talking to yourself about the pictures."

Now everyone in my class knows that there are three ways to read books, and the difference at Self-Selected Reading time is incredible. Even Paul, who doesn't participate in much of anything, ponders over the pictures in informational books and sometimes mumbles to himself. Most of my other children are pretend reading some favorite books, and some, of course, are really reading some of the books. While they read, I circulate around, stopping for half a minute to encourage each child. I notice how they are reading their book and join them in whatever kind of reading they are doing. I wish I had realized years ago that some children couldn't settle in with a book because they knew they couldn't read it and that is all they had ever seen anyone do with a book! Now that all the children know three ways to read and that all those ways are acceptable (how could they not be acceptable if geniuses like Larry and my son David did them?), they are all eager readers.

Next month will be a busy month. We will start writing on half-and-half paper, add high-frequency words to our word wall, and begin reading in our reading series. In our social studies/science time, we will do a unit on fall, spend some time discussing Halloween customs, and learn more about families around the world. Good thing October has 31 days!

October

To most first-graders, Halloween is second only to Christmas in generating excitement and distractions. I try to capitalize on their excitement and channel their energies. Our unit at the beginning of the month was on families. We extended the I Am Special unit from September into a Families Are Different and Special unit. The children talked about their families, but I was careful not to ask for too specific information. Fewer than half my class live in a family that contains both the father and the mother they were born to. We defined a family as the people you live with who love you and each other, and we defined an extended family as including all your relatives. We brought in pictures of our families and talked about how families have to work together, do fun things together, and sometimes they don't all get along perfectly. Paul had very little to say during the unit, but he did listen and seemed comforted to know that all families have problems they have to work through.

During Guided Reading, we read the Big Book *Families Are Different* by Nina Pelligrini, which explores all kinds of different families all held together "with a special kind of glue called love." I read aloud to them a number of books that featured various family groups, including *The Mother's Day Mice, A Perfect Father's Day,* and *The Wednesday Surprise,* all by Eve Bunting, who treats the issue of different families with extreme sensitivity. I also read them *Fly Away Home,* Bunting's story of a boy and his dad who live in an airport while looking for a real home.

In addition to our family unit, we spent some of our afternoon science/social studies time on a unit about Weather and the Seasons.

Our Writers' Workshop is moving right along. We are now using half-and-half paper and pencils to write with, instead of drawing paper and crayons. I have made a transparency with lines like the bottom of the handwriting paper and left a little drawing space at the top. Each day, for our minilesson at the beginning of the Writing block, I sit down at the overhead and write two or three sentences and then draw a picture to go with them. Before I write, I think aloud about the topic I might write about:

> "Let's see. What will I write about today? I could write about seeing Anthony and his baby sister at the grocery store last night. She is so cute! I could write about what a time we had yesterday getting George back into his cage after someone left the door open. I know what I'll write about!"

By thinking aloud about a few topics that I don't write about, the children are reminded about some things they may want to write about. I don't write about running into Anthony and his baby sister, but Anthony might. I don't write about trying to recapture our pet gerbil, but many of the children involved in the chase yesterday are reminded of this and they might choose to write about it.

When I do write, I don't say the words as I am writing them. You will be amazed at how closely the children watch me write and how hard they try to figure out and anticipate what I will write when I am not saying it as I write it. I do say a few words aloud, however. Each day in my writing, I stretch out a few words and spell them by putting down the sounds I hear. I tell the children that this is how I used to spell the big words when I was their age. I also remind them that they will need to write many words that aren't on our word wall yet and that they can't spell yet, and that they should put down the letters they hear just as I do when I write the big words in my writing.

I write all kinds of different things. On some days I write something related to what we are learning in science and social studies. Other days, I write about something that happened in our classroom. Sometimes, I write about something special that will happen that day or that week. I tell about children's lost teeth, new baby sisters or brothers, accidents, and upcoming birthdays. The children are always eager to see "what she will write today"! Probably their favorite thing for me to write is what I call the "When I Was Your Age" tales. Here is one I wrote just before Halloween.

When I was your age, I loved Halloween. I went trick or treating dressed as a fairy prinses. My favrit candy was Tootsie Rolls.

The children love my "When I Was Your Age" tales and are always asking me if they are all true. It is a little hard even for me to imagine my middle-aged self going door to door in a fairy princess costume and craving Tootsie Rolls!

I take no more than eight minutes to write and then read aloud my piece to make sure it makes sense. Then the children all get their half-and-half paper and I give them about 15 minutes to write and draw. Some of my more advanced children, including Larry, Pat, Danielle, Steve, and Betty, are writing some fairly lengthy pieces, often taking several days to complete one piece. Other children are just getting a few words down. Paul wouldn't write anything for several days and now seems to be copying the names of the children from the word wall. Alexander is the other one who writes almost nothing. With his hearing loss, I am not sure he can hear any of the sounds in the words he might write. Mostly, he is still drawing. Mike is a surprise! He writes up a storm, putting a letter or two for each word and with no spaces between the words. No one else but Mike can read it, of course, but he draws wonderful monster pictures, and when he shares, he tells all about the monsters, and I guess that is what he is trying to write with his collection of letters. At any rate, the children all love his stories, and I see monster stories being written by other children. It is funny how these writing crazes catch on with six-year-olds. I worry about some of my children who just "go through the motions" during writing time. Mort, particularly, is always sitting there looking pained, and when I ask what he is thinking about writing, he just responds, "I don't really care!"

Finally, all the names are on the word wall, including mine and George's (our gerbil), which the children insisted had to be there. Once we got the names up, I added five words last week—*boy, girl, friend, like, is*—and five more this week—*play, school, good, come, go.* I added these words first because they are some of the words used in the first book in our series, which we began this month, and they are more concrete than the abstract connecting words such as *with, of,* and *they.* They are also words children use a great deal in their writing. I try to make sure that the first words begin with different letters and are different lengths. I use the scraps from the construction paper drawer, write the words with a thick permanent black marker, and then cut around their shape so that the length and shape become quite distinctive. I use only light colors and put easily confused words on different colors. *With* is on blue, so when I get ready to add *will, went,* and *want,* I will make sure I use different colors. The different colors and shapes make for an interesting display and help my children differentiate the confusable words.

On Monday, when I put the new words up, we do a lot with them, count the number of letters, use them in sentences, compare them to other words on the wall, and do a handwriting lesson with them. On the other days, I call out any five words from across the wall—including a name or two each day. I point to each word, and when all their eyes are glued to the word, we clap and chant it three times. Then they write it on handwriting paper as I write it on the board. When they have written all five words, they take out their red checking pens and check each word by making the shape around the word with their red pen. I do the same with my words on the board. Making the shape helps to emphasize which are the tall letters and which go below the line. Most children have written them as best they can, but if they do find something not correct when they are checking, they just go over that part with their red pen. The children are becoming better at their handwriting, but there are still huge differences in their ability to control those pencils and get them to do what they want them to do. I know that handwriting develops with practice, along with maturity and development—especially for my young boys—so I accept whatever they can do, as long as they appear to be making a good effort.

We have actions and food for all the initial consonants and *ch, sh,* and *th.* We are now using the 20 minutes of Words block after word wall to collect rhyming words. I have read them lots of *Hop on Pop* and *The Cat in the Hat* type books, and then we list on a chart a lot of words that rhyme. Our *Cat in the Hat* chart had *a-t* words all lined up with the *at* underlined in each. I do include words that begin with the blends, and we say them slowly, listening for the sounds of both beginning letters.

Our Guided Reading block is going pretty well. We are now halfway through the first book in our reading series. I begin this block with the whole class gathered on the rug and introduce the selection first. We always preview each selection by looking at the pictures and talking about the meaning. As we turn each page, I ask questions such as:

What do you see in the picture?
What do you think is happening?
Why do you think everyone looks so mad?
What is that big brown animal called?

I usually lead them to look through the whole piece with me, and we talk about what we see in the pictures, naming the characters, animals, objects, places, and so on. We predict what might happen next and speculate about what is happening based just on the pictures.

After looking at the pictures one time and focusing only on meaning, we then look through the pages a second time, but this time I write an important word or two for each page on the board. They use what they know about letters and sounds and word length along with the picture on each page to try to figure out the word I have written. These words are not very difficult to figure out when you use all the clues you have. Once they have figured out the word, I have them search the page and put their finger on the word when they find it. This vocabulary introduction works well for the picturable words—*kangaroo, babies, pouch*— but, of course, doesn't work for other words.

I introduce the other words by writing some patterned sentences on the board, using the names of my children and the word I want to draw their attention to. For the word *is,* for example, I wrote these simple sentences:

Mandy *is* a girl. Mitch *is* a boy. George *is* a gerbil.

Because they know each other's names and because they love to have things written about them, they pay close attention and can more easily learn an abstract word like *is.* I then send them on an *is* hunt in the story they are going to read.

They move their fingers along the line of print and try to count how many times they see the word *is.* I introduce a few more high-frequency abstract words in the same way, and these words are likely candidates to be added to the word wall next week.

Next, the children and I read the story. Sometimes we read it together, with everyone chiming in, still sitting there on the rug. After we have read each page, we talk about what we found out and add that to the meaning gained from looking at the pictures. On other days, we don't read it together first, but I send them off to read it with their partners. I have assigned all the children a reading partner, pairing up students who need help with friendly, helpful children who can help them but not do it for them. (I have paired Daphne with Paul and have quietly asked her to just read the story to him and let him read if he wants. She is such a little dear! She leads Paul off somewhere quiet and reads with him the way a mother would to a little child.) The children know that they and their partner should take turns reading pages, and that they should give each other clues when they get to words they don't know:

> "Remember the name of that animal who has the babies in her pouch."

> "It's that little word she used in the sentences about Mandy, Mitch, and George."

After they do partner reading, we gather together again for just a few minutes and talk about the piece, using "what else did we learn from reading the words that we couldn't figure out from just the pictures?"

We usually spend two or three days on each selection. If we partner read the first day, we often read it chorally the second day and then do some comprehension-oriented follow-up such as acting the story out or talking about the order in which things happened or discussing the characters, setting, problem, and solution. I focus on thinking throughout the school day, but I consciously model and have them use the thinking processes—connect, predict, organize, generalize, image, self-monitor, apply and evaluate—as part of my Guided Reading instruction.

So far, the Guided Reading block is going well. Of course, the reading is well below the level of my top readers like Larry, Danielle, and Pat. I would worry about their not being on the level they need to be on if Guided Reading were my total reading program. But my observations of them during the Writing block, the SQUIRT time, and our science/social studies unit time assure me that they are working up to their advanced levels for a large part of the day.

November

Thanksgiving took much of our attention this month. I have always enjoyed all the holidays, and one of the fringe benefits of teaching first grade is that all the traditional holiday songs and activities are fresh and new to the children, and I get into the holiday spirit right along with them. We did many Thanksgiving activities, and I read aloud to them many Thanksgiving stories as well as some nonfiction books describing the first Thanksgiving and the early days of our country.

Our Writers' Workshop is moving along very well. I plan to ask all the parents to send notebooks next month so that we can start writing in our notebooks. I came up with an ingenious plan to limit the amount of time we spend sharing each day. At the beginning of the year, we had time for everyone to share because they were writing just a little and they could show their driting and tell about it. Now that they are writing longer pieces, however, it was taking 20 minutes each day for them all to share. This cut into our Words block time and put us about 10 minutes behind schedule every day. In addition, as what they were sharing got longer, the children were not able to sit and be good listeners for everyone's piece!

I have designated all the children as days of the week. I did this arbitrarily but with an eye to having some of the most prolific and reluctant writers spread across the days. Each day, we end the writing block with an Author's Chair, and the designated children get to sit in the rocking chair and read one piece they have written since the last time they shared. After they share their piece, they call on one person to tell them something they liked about their piece. This is working out quite well. With the exception of Paul, the children are all eager to read on their special day. The listeners listen better when they are listening to only five authors.

I have also extended this "Day of the Week" idea to other areas. The children whose day it is pass out and pick up things whenever that service is needed. They lead the line and get to do whatever other special things need doing. This has certainly cut down on the "But I never get to do . . ." and the occasional "You always let her do everything!"

I am also using these designations to do my anecdotal records on children. Last year, we moved to a report card/conference system that really stresses using observation and reading and writing samples to monitor and demonstrate progress. I have an anecdotal record sheet for each child, and I was walking around with 25 sheets on my clipboard and never able to pull out the right sheet at the right moment. Now, each morning I put on my clipboard only the sheets for the children whose day it is. I begin writing comments when they share in the Author's Chair, and then I glance at their writing, which they hand to me after they read. I continue to note how they do with our Words block activities, and I make sure to have them read a little bit to me during our Guided Reading block. During Self-Selected Reading, I have the children come on their designated day and read to me—in whichever of the three ways we read—two pages from a book they select. I write down the title of the book, which way they are reading it, and a comment about their comprehension, enjoyment, fluency, and so on. Since I carry around these sheets with me anyway, I am making some notes about their math skills, their contributions during our science/social studies unit time, and a note about what they choose to do during center time. By the time I got to report cards and conferences this month, I had a great deal of information about each and every child. This "Day of the Week" system is so simple, I can't figure out why I didn't think of it earlier.

We now have 30 words on our word wall in addition to the names. The children are continuing to respond well to our daily look, chant, and write practice, and they are obviously using the word wall when they are writing. As I write each day, in addition to modeling the invented spelling of a few big words, I also model looking up at the word wall and finding a word there that I need in my writing. As I do that, I think aloud, "If it's on our word wall, I have to spell it correctly!"

In addition to our word wall, which has high-frequency words, I am doing content boards related to our science or social studies theme. Along with pictures, I put important words children might need in their writing. Our Thanksgiving

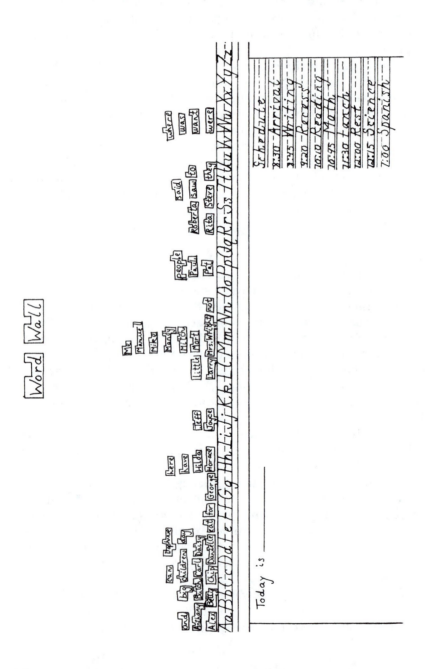

board has Thanksgiving pictures and the words *Thanksgiving, thankful, turkey, feast, Pilgrims, Indians, corn,* and *food.* Between the high-frequency words now on our wall and the content words, every child is doing some writing. Last week Alexander wrote:

> I like Thanksgiving. It is fun. I have a feast. I eat good food.

While this is hardly an award-winning piece, for Alexander, who still has not learned how you separate words into sounds, his ability to write something is remarkable. He is pleased with himself, too, and I think he now has a strategy for writing. With the word wall, the content boards, and their growing awareness of letter-sound patterns, all my children can and do write.

We are continuing to work on rhyming words, and our room is now filled with charts of rhymes. In addition, I have come up with a little activity that helps them apply their knowledge of initial letters and sounds. To prepare for this activity, I write four or five sentences using my children's names in each and cover up an important word in each sentence. Here are the sentences I used this week. (The food word in each sentence is covered with two sticky notes so that the children cannot read it.)

> Butch likes to eat hamburgers.
> Mitch likes to eat cheeseburgers.
> Paul likes to eat spaghetti.
> Mrs. Wright likes to eat lasagna.
> George likes to eat carrots.

The children see the sentences when they first come in the morning, and they immediately begin trying to guess the words hidden under the sticky notes. (I put these high up on the board so they can't peek under!) Once we finish our daily word wall activity, we begin to guess what each person likes to eat. I write several possibilities they suggest on the board, and then we observe that "the word can be lots of different foods when you can't see any letters." I then remove the sticky note that covers the first letter or letters (all letters before the vowel). We then cross out any guesses that don't begin correctly, observing that the guesses made sense but didn't begin with the right letters. Next, we guess some more things that both make sense and begin with the revealed letters, and then we reveal the whole word.

We do sentences like this one or two days a week, and my children are becoming very good at realizing that when you come to a word you don't know, you can make a really good guess if you think of something that makes sense and starts with the right letters. We call this activity "Guess the Covered Word," and the children love it!

We are reading in the second book of our adopted series now. Before beginning this book, I had the children I was most worried about—Paul, Mike, Alexander, Mitch, Daisy, Mort, and Chip—read a few pages in the first selection to me. I took an oral reading record as they were doing this, and then I had them retell what they remembered. Using the 90 percent word accuracy criteria, Mort and Chip just made it. Alexander, Mitch, and Jeff were less than 90 percent but better than 80 percent. All five of them had good comprehension, although it was hard to tell with Mort because he was so bored by the whole process, he didn't tell me much! Paul, Mike, and Daisy, however, were not even close. They are reading with us in the second book, but I am doing some individual work with them, rereading the first book. I have scheduled each of them for 10 minutes with me. Paul is always here when I come to open up the room, so I have my 10 minutes with him first thing. I take Mike during the after-lunch quiet time because Mike can't sit quietly under any circumstances, and I read with Daisy for 10 minutes during centers.

I am doing repeated readings with them with the book we have already read and discussed. Each day, when it is time to read with one of them, we set the timer for 10 minutes, and beginning on the first page each day, we see how far we can read in 10 minutes. They read to me, and if they miss or don't know a word, I help them. Then I model fluent reading of the page, and they read it fluently, without error, before going on to the next page. We continue reading until they get stuck; then I help them, model fluent reading, and have them reread the page. When the timer signals the end of the 10 minutes, we note down the page on which we stopped. On the first day, Mike got to page 5 in 10 minutes. Starting again on page 1 the next day, he got to page 9. On the third day, he got to page 15. When he got to page 20, I stopped beginning on the first page each day but did back up about 10 pages, beginning with the story that began on page 10.

This is working exceptionally well for Mike. He is much less distractible when I have just him to focus on, and he loves trying to beat the clock and seeing the progress he is making on his pages-read chart. Daisy is making some progress, but she doesn't particularly like giving up 10 minutes of her center time, so she is not always very cooperative. Paul is sporadic. Some days, he does quite well, and other days, he won't read at all. I try to talk to him and assure him that he is making progress, and I give him a hug and tell him I love him. Some mornings, if he can't read, I just rock him and talk to him the way you would a crying two-year-old. I have yet to see his mother, but Miss Grant tells me the home situation is pitiful—whatever that means! I have referred him for psychological evaluation, but I don't know what they will tell me that will help. It just isn't right that children should be so emotionally upset and we can do so little for them! I have always found this the most frustrating thing about teaching first grade.

December

Finally—two weeks' vacation! Am I ever ready for it after this month. Every year I forget what a fevered state my little ones get into as they await the big day. Of course, much of what we do this month is related to the holidays. This year we celebrated Christmas, Hanukkah, and Kwanzaa! Many of my read-aloud books were holiday connected, including *A Picture Book of Hanukkah* by David Adler, *My First Kwanzaa Book* by Deborah Newton Chocolate, and *Happy Christmas, Gemma* by Sarah Hayes. Joyce's mother came and talked to us about the Kwanzaa celebrations they were taking part in. Mort's mom came and talked to us about their Hanukkah customs. I thought Mort might perk up with his mother here, but he was his typical, uninterested, "Who cares?" self. I talked briefly with his mother about his apathy, and she says he is the same way at home and she doesn't know how to motivate him either!

Our Writing and Words blocks are moving along nicely. Of course, I put some holiday boards up in our room with words attached to them, enabling the children to write their letters to Santa, and so forth. Butch and Hilda insist that there is no such thing as Santa, and they tease some of the others about this. Yesterday, Butch had Rita in tears, so I decided to try to call a halt to it. I told them that I didn't know for sure that there was a Santa Claus, but that someone always left presents under my tree. Larry refuses to comment on the subject, but he wears a knowing look.

We did manage to finish the second book in our reading series this month, and again I had the children who are borderline read to me a few pages from the third book. All but Daisy, Paul, Mike, and Chip could read with at least 90 percent word accuracy. Mort read well, but I couldn't get him to tell me enough to be sure his comprehension is adequate. Chip was close enough and tries hard enough that I think he will be okay. I had Daisy, Paul, and Mike read to me the first selection in the second book—the one we just finished. Daisy and Mike read it with better than 90 percent word accuracy. Paul didn't meet the criteria, but he could read some, and he told me what was happening in the story and seemed to enjoy it. I plan to continue my 10-minute timed repeated readings with Paul, Daisy, and Mike in the second book and to make sure they have helpful partners or are included in a group with me during our Guided Reading time.

I did get the psychological report back on Paul. He doesn't qualify for anything! His IQ is well below average but not low enough for him to be classified EMH. Of course, his IQ is too low for him to be classified as learning disabled. Although he has many emotional problems, he is not severely enough disturbed to meet the criteria for the emotionally disturbed class. The report recommended that he be given individualized instruction on his level and that adjustments be made for his slow learning rate and his periods of inattention. I will continue to work with him, but it is frustrating that more can't be done. So often with a child like Paul, you know he needs help, but he doesn't fit anywhere! Thank goodness for Daphne. She loves being his partner, and when I tried to rotate partners more, she quietly told me, "He reads a little with me, and I think I am helping him. Can't I still be his partner?"

Our afternoon Teacher Read-Aloud/Self-Selected Reading time is going exceptionally well. For many years now, I have suggested to parents that if they wanted to send me a holiday gift, they could donate an "easy-to-read" book to our classroom library. I have stressed that I didn't expect a gift, but that if they wanted to buy something I would really appreciate, we could never have too many copies of the *Clifford* books; *One Fish, Two Fish, Red Fish, Blue Fish; Robert the Rose Horse;* or *The Gingerbread Man.* By now I have multiple copies of many of these easy-to-read classics. This month, I began reading them to the children. As I read, I made a tape of the reading. I signaled the children, and they clapped their hands when it was time to turn each page. They also joined me in saying any repeated refrains— "Run, run, as fast as you can. You can't catch me. I'm the gingerbread man!"

Once I had read this book and made the tape, I pulled out my many copies of the book and put them in the Self-Selected Reading crates. The next day, I read another easy-to-read favorite of which I had multiple copies, making the tape with the children's help. Again, I added multiple copies to the crates. By the end of the week, I had read aloud and made tapes of five easy-to-read books of which I had multiple copies. These books are all out for the children now, and many children are amazed to find that they can really read them. I overheard Roberta remark that she was reading these books, not just pretend reading! That, of course, was my plan. By now most of them know enough to really read some of these old favorites, and they are delighted with their newfound ability. It is one thing to be able to read in a "schoolbook," but a real book that you can buy in a store or get through the book club—that's reading!

Of course, I put the tape I made, along with a copy of the book, in our listening center. Each day from 2:15 to 2:45/3:00 (children leave on buses at staggered times), we have our center time. I started this many years ago when I realized that things would go well in our classroom for almost all day and then fall apart in the last 30 minutes. It was almost always during this last half hour that arguments would occur between the children, and I often found myself losing my composure and yelling at someone. Yelling is not my style, and after the children left, I would feel terrible and berate myself for not handling the situation better. "We were having such a nice day," I would think, "until it all fell apart at the end!"

After many years of teaching, I decided that neither the children nor I could give learning the kind of attention required by any subject after 2:15. I had been doing some center activities in the morning on certain days, and I just decided to pretend the day ended at 2:15—get the children all ready to go, notes distributed, book bags on desks, and so forth, and then children could go to the centers. This is a very nice way to end the day. The children all look forward to it, and because they get to choose what they want to do and don't have to attend to me or each other, there is almost no fussing or squabbling. (Mike does still have some problem during center time, but I give him one warning and then send him back to his seat, and he is learning some self-control.) I enjoy this time because I get to circulate and talk with the children individually, a luxury that I seldom have at any other time when I try to keep up with 25 children.

Some centers stay with us all the time, and some centers change as we work on different projects. We have a center board in our room, and the number of clothespins there indicates how many children can go to each center at one time. Each day at 2:15, the children choose their centers. We do this by days of the week. On Thursday, the Thursday children go first to claim their clothespins, followed by the Wednesday, Tuesday, Monday, and Friday children. The Friday children who choose last on Thursday don't complain, though, because they know that they will choose first on Friday. Children can change centers if there is a clothespin available indicating space in the center they want to go to.

This month, the two most popular centers have been the art center and the writing center. In the art center, I put old greeting cards and the materials for making greeting cards. The writing center has, among other things, stationery on which to write to Santa and catalogues of many of the items on their wish lists. I

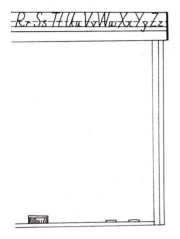

was delighted to see many of the children going off to find a copy of one of their favorite books so that they could copy its title on their list. They aren't taking any chances when it comes to someone knowing exactly which book they are hoping to find among their holiday presents. They want to spell it right!

January

January is always one of my very favorite teaching months, and this year has been no exception. The fall is wonderfully exciting, with all the big holidays, but exhausting, too, as I get to know a new class of children and get them smoothly into reading and writing and the routines they need to follow. But when we come back after the holidays, they and I are rested, eager, and ready to move!

Over the break, I pulled out my list of guiding principles again, and I think I am doing very well with most of them. I definitely think that doing all four blocks every day gives children many avenues to literacy and provides them with a balanced literacy program. My Writing, Self-Selected Reading, and Words blocks are very multilevel. Guided Reading still worries me—not so much about Larry and the other exceptional readers, because they enjoy what we read and like helping their partners, but I think we need some easier reading for Paul, Manuel, and the others who aren't quite where they should be. I decided to split up my week between grade-level guided reading and easier selections. I do have lots of sets of easy-reading books that I am going to use for Guided Reading on Thursdays and Fridays. I gave myself an "A" for teaching in ways that reflect the principle that language is the foundation of reading and writing and for emphasizing thinking. We always preview selections, connecting what we know and predicting what will happen or what we will learn. We do a lot of talking and acting out of what we read, and I am always asking the children what they think about the selections we read during Guided Reading. Language and thinking are readily apparent during our Writing block each day, and of course we do a lot of discussing and listening and concept development during our science and social studies units.

Number 6 is one I am going to work more on for the remainder of the year. I do try to get the children motivated and excited about reading and writing. Choice is a big part of motivation, and they choose what they want to write about and the piece they are going to publish, as well as what they read during Self-Selected Reading. They do choose their centers in the afternoon. I am going to try to find some places where I can give them more choices. I know that success plays a big part of how you feel about activities, and making the blocks as multilevel as possible helps provide success, but I need to do more to show my struggling students that they are growing and learning. My schedule means that I read aloud to them daily, and that they have daily time for Self-Selected Reading and writing. I definitely teach decoding and spelling, but I see them applying their phonics knowledge more when writing than when they are reading. I am going to work on getting them to use what they know as they are reading. I think having two days of easier reading each week during Guided Reading will help here, because children apply their phonics more when they only need to figure out a few words.

Assessment is always hard, but I do most of my assessment by observing what the children can actually do. I had the children pick some writing samples they wanted me to share with their parents during parent conferences this month, and they each made a tape recording of a book they liked and could read well. Next month, I am going to start being more systematic in what I do with each child during our weekly Self-Selected Reading conference and see if I can use this time to both encourage them in their reading and see what strategies they are using.

I think I do a good job of communicating my expectations to parents. The newsletter I send home every two weeks lets them know what we are working on and gives them suggestions for home activities that will support what we are doing here. Parents come in and help and visit whenever they want to. The conferences we hold at report card time allow me to talk to them about their child's individual progress. Unfortunately, the parents of the children I worry most about—Paul, Daisy, Butch are seldom seen or heard from.

We did a science unit on animals this month. Children love animals, and we took a trip to the zoo. This was a major adventure because the zoo is two hours away. The bus rolled out of our parking lot here at 8:00 and we returned about 6:00. I always do this trip on a Friday so that I have the weekend to recover. It was worth it, however. Most of my children had never seen any animals except for pets and some farm animals. Tigers, lions, bears, kangaroos, and penguins were just pictures in books and images from TV! Of course, we did a lot of research and reading and looking at videos before we went, and since we have come back, many of the children have started writing about various animals.

Our Writers' Workshop is moving along quite well. The children are all writing in their notebooks now. On Fridays, I let them select one piece they have written and draw a picture to go with it, but on the rest of the days, they are spending their full 15 minutes writing. I still do a minilesson each morning, but I am writing slightly longer pieces, just as they are. I have begun our editing checklist. As I was getting ready to write one morning, I told the children that now that they were all real writers—writing in their writing notebooks every day—they would need to learn how to help each other edit their pieces. We talked about editors and publishing books and how every book that I had read to them or that they had read had been written by an author, but the author had an editor's help to make the book as exciting and easy to read as possible. I told them a little about publishing companies and how books got published and the many different people who are involved in the publishing of a book. I then wrote on a half sheet of chart paper:

OUR EDITOR'S CHECKLIST

1. Do all the sentences make sense?

I explained to the children that one thing editors always read for is to make sure that all the sentences make sense. Sometimes, writers leave out words or forget to finish a sentence, and then the sentences don't make sense. "Each day, after I write my piece, you can be my editors and help me decide if all my sentences make sense." I then wrote a piece and purposely left out a few words. The children, who were, as always, reading along as I wrote and often anticipating my next word, noticed my mistakes immediately. When I finished writing, I said, "Now let's read my piece together and see if all my sentences make sense." The children and I read one sentence at a time, and when we got to the sentences where I had left a word out, we decided that the sentence didn't make sense because my mind had gotten ahead of my marker and I had left out some words. I wrote the words in with a different-colored marker and thanked the children for their good editing help. I then had a child come and draw a happy face on my paper, because although my sentences didn't all make sense when I first wrote them, I checked for that and fixed them.

After I wrote my piece, the children all went off to their own writing. As they wrote, I circulated around and "encouraged" them. I don't tell them what to write, but I do engage them in conversations about what is happening in their worlds and remind them of some of the possibilities. I don't spell words for them, but I do help them stretch words out and put down the sound they hear.

When the 15 minutes of allotted writing time is up, I point to the Editor's Checklist we have just begun. "Be your own editor now. Read your paper and see if all your sentences make sense. If you didn't finish a sentence or left a word out, take your red pen and fix it." I watch as the children do their best to see if their sentences make sense, and I notice a few writing something with their red pens. After just a minute, I say, "Good. Now, use your red pen to draw yourself a little happy face to show you checked your sentences for making sense."

Every day after that when I write, I leave a word or two out or don't finish a sentence. The children delight in being my editor and helping me make all my sentences make sense. Every day, when their writing time is up, I point to the checklist and they read their own sentences for sense. They don't find every problem, but they all know what they are trying to do, and I have noticed almost everyone picking up the red pen and glancing up at the checklist as soon as I ring the bell to signal the end of writing time. I am about to add to our checklist a second thing to read for. I will add:

2. Do all the sentences start with capital letters?

Once I add that, I will begin some sentences with lowercase letters and let them help me edit for sentences both making sense and beginning with capital letters. Of course, they will read their own piece for these two things also. We will then be to the "two–happy-face" editing stage.

Our writing is going so well that next month we are going to start publishing some pieces. I hope that by the end of February all my writers will be published authors!

The Words block is going well. I add five high-frequency words each week to our word wall. We do about eight minutes of looking, chanting, and writing practice each day. Many of my children are learning to spell these words. Some children still have to find them to write them, but they have all learned to read them.

I continue to do some work with rhyming words, and one day a week, I do the Guess the Covered Word activity they enjoy so much. I also began this month our Making Words lessons (Cunningham & Hall, 1997). I usually do two Making Words lessons each week. For the first five lessons, I gave the children only one vowel. Here is how the very first Making Words lesson went.

The letters for this first lesson were *u, k, n, r, s,* and *t.* I have made letter cards with the lowercase letter on one side and the capital letter on the other side for all the letters. The vowel letters are written with a permanent red marker and stored in large red plastic cups, one for each vowel. The consonants are written with a blue marker and stored in blue plastic cups. That morning, I appointed some of my early arriving children "holder stuffers." I put the cups containing the letters needed and a stack of holders on the back table. I then showed the holder stuffers how to take one letter from each cup and put it in a holder. (The holders are made by cutting file folders in half and folding up and stapling the bottom inch.) At the beginning of the lesson, I handed each child a holder, and they had all the letters needed. Tomorrow morning, I recruited some early arrivals to unstuff the holders.

I began the lesson by making sure the children had and could name all their letters. I held up the *u* card from the pocket chart and had them hold up their *u.* I told them that the *u* was red because it was the vowel, that every word needed at least one vowel, and that because their only vowel today was the *u,* they would need it for every word. I then held up the other letters, named each, and had the children hold up and name theirs. I told them that we would use these letters to make lots of words, and that at the end of the lesson, we would make a word that used all six letters. I then wrote a 2 on the board and told them that the first word would use only two letters. I asked them to take two letters and make *us.* I had them say the word *us* and watched as they decided how to spell *us*. I then asked Mike, who had made *us* correctly with his little letters, to come up and make it with the pocket chart letters. I then put the word *us,* which I had written on an index card, along the top of the pocket chart.

Next, I crossed out the 2 on the board and wrote a 3. I had the children hold up three fingers and told them that the next word would take three letters. I asked them to take three letters and make *run*. Again, I watched and sent someone who had made it correctly to make it with the pocket chart letters. I placed the word *run* next to *us* along the top of the pocket chart. "Change the first letter in *run* and you can change your *run* into *sun*." They made two more three-letter words, *nut* and *rut,* and then I crossed out the 3, wrote a 4 on the board, and said, "If you add a letter to *rut* you can change your *rut* into *ruts.* After it rains, my driveway has lots of ruts in it."

Once a child had come and made *ruts* with the big letters, I said, "Now, this is a real magic trick. Don't take any of the letters in *ruts* out of your holder and don't add any. Just change around where the letters are, and you can change your *ruts* into *rust.* Say *rust.* When we leave things made of metal out in the rain, they might rust." The children seemed amazed to discover that just changing the position of those last two letters could change *ruts* to *rust*!

We then made two more four-letter words, *tusk* and *stun.*

I crossed out the 4, wrote a 5, and said, "Now we are going to make a five-letter word. Take five letters and make *trunk*. We have been studying about animals, and we know that an elephant has a trunk. Say *trunk* slowly and listen to where you hear all those letters."

At the beginning of the lesson, when we were making *us* and *run* and changing *run* to *sun*, I had been monitoring my struggling children and sending them to make the word with the pocket chart letters, but the lesson had now moved to a challenging stage, and I was watching to see how Danielle and Pat were going to spell *trunk*. Pat got it spelled correctly, and as she did so, she also realized what word you could make with all the letters. "If you put the *s* on *trunk*, you have *trunks*," she exclaimed. "That's exactly right," I said. I then had her make *trunk* with the pocket chart letters, asked everyone to make sure they had made it right with their little letters, and let her show how adding the *s* made the word *trunks*. I asked the children if the word *trunks* was in any way connected to our animals unit. They quickly realized that we had seen elephants at the zoo and been amazed at the size of their trunks. Larry pointed out that trunks were also large suitcases for packing things, and Butch reminded us that cars have trunks.

Next, I had the children close their folders with the word *trunks* still in them and directed their attention to the words on index cards I had been placing along the top of the pocket chart. I had them read the words with me and talk about what we changed to make them:

us	run	ruts	trunk	trunks
sun	rust			
nut	tusk			
Crut	stun			

I then had them sort out the rhyming words:

run	rut
sun	nut
stun	

The final step in any Making Words lesson is the most important step—Transfer. Children need to see how noticing rhymes and spelling patterns help them to decode and spell new words. For this step, I took a blank index card and wrote the word *shut* on it.

"What if you were reading and you came to this word?" I asked as I was writing *shut* on the card. Don't say this word yet, if you know it," I warned, "but who can go put this word with the rhyming words that would help you figure it out?"

Manuel went up to the pocket chart and put *shut* under *nut* and *rut,* and we said all three rhyming words, making *shut* rhyme with *nut* and *rut.*

I then wrote another rhyming word—*bun*—and Roberta put *bun* under *sun, run,* and *stun,* and we pronounced *bun* to rhyme with the others.

Thinking of rhyming words can help you figure out how to spell words too, I said, as I picked up a third blank index card. What if Steve were writing about building a "hut" in the woods. Which words rhyme with *hut*?" The children decided that *hut* rhymed with *nut, rut,* and *shut* and would be spelled "h-u-t." We then used *run, sun, stun,* and *bun* to help us decide how Joyce could spell *spun* if she were writing about Rumpelstiltskin.

That afternoon when the children were getting ready to go home, I gave them a take-home sheet. The sheet had the letters *u k n r s t* along the top and boxes for words. Most children immediately recognized that these were the letters they had used to make words. "For homework," I said, "take this sheet home and cut the letters apart and see if you can fill these boxes with words. Don't tell anyone else the secret word—the word that can be made with all the letters—but see if they can figure it out." I could tell that the children were going to enjoy seeing if they could stump their parents. I overheard Roberta warning Betty, "She told us not to tell, and you'd better not!"

We did several other lessons this month with just one vowel. From the letters *i, g, n, p, r,* and *s,* we made the words *in, pin, pig, rip, rips, nips, spin, pins, sing, ring,* and *spring.* From the rhymes we sorted, we decoded the new words *bring* and *chin* and figured out how you would spell *string* and *fin.* From the letters *o, g, n, r, s,* and *t,* we made *so, no, go, got, rot, not, song, sort, rots, snort,* and *strong* and used the rhymes to decode and spell *spot, long, trot,* and *shot.* From the letters *e, d, p, n, s,* and *s,* we made *Ed, Ned, end, pen, den, pens, dens, send, spend,* and *spends.* The transfer words were *then, bend, lend,* and *men.* From the letters *a, h, l, p, s,* and *s,* we made *Al, pal, lap, sap, has, ash, pass, pals, slap, slaps,* and *splash.* The transfer words were *trap, mash, clap,* and *smash.*

The children enjoy manipulating the letters to make words. Even Paul can successfully make the easier words in the lesson. Stretching out the words as we make them and sorting out the rhymes and saying the rhyming words to figure out the transfer words provide excellent phonemic awareness practice for children like Manuel, Paul, and Alexander, who still need it. My whiz kids love trying to

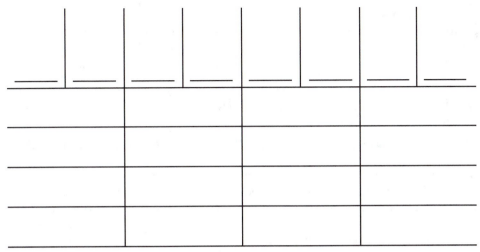

The letters you need to "Make Words" tonight are at the top of the page. Write capitals on the back. Then, cut the letters apart and see how many words you can make. Write the words in the blanks.

From *Month-by-Month Phonics for Second Grade,* p. 148. Material appears courtesy of Carson-Dellosa Publishing Company, Inc.

figure out the word that can be made with all the letters. Using the rhymes to decode and spell new words helps children apply what they are learning about letters and sounds Making Words is truly a multilevel activity. In one 20-minute lesson, there is something for everyone! The parents tell me that their children love bringing home their Making Words sheets and often stumping them about what word can be made with all the letters.

February

In addition to all the Valentine's Day excitement, we have done units this month on African Americans in celebration of Black History Month, and we have learned about our nation's presidents, including Abraham Lincoln and George Washington. I read several biographies to them, including *If You Grew Up with Abraham Lincoln* by Ann McGovern, *If You Grew Up with George Washington* by Ruth Belov Gross, and *A Picture Book of Martin Luther King* by David Adler. We have talked about biographies and autobiographies. The children are fascinated with the idea of autobiographies and with it being such a huge word!

I have modeled how you write biographies during some of my minilessons, and last week, when I wrote a "When I Was Your Age" tale telling about my first-grade boyfriend and the valentine I made for him, Larry observed, "If these 'When I Was Your Age' stories are true, you are really writing your autobiography!" I had never really thought about that before, but I had to admit that I was at least writing the six-year-old part of my autobiography. At any rate, many of the children are into writing biographies and autobiographies.

We have published one set of books, and the children are thrilled. Before we began, I showed them the book made last year by Jonathan, a boy in my room who moved and forgot to take his book. I read the book to them, beginning with the dedication page ("Dedicated to Mrs. Wright and all the people in my class"), reading the story about a soccer match between Jonathan's team and his cousin's team, talking about the illustrations that Jonathan had done to accompany his writing, and ending with the "About the Author" page on which I had written:

> *Jonathan Marr is seven years old and is in the first grade at Merritt Elementary School. He loves to read and write and play soccer. This book tells the true story of his soccer team's biggest victory!*

I then explained how Jonathan and my other first-graders last year had made the books. "They couldn't all make books at once," I explained, "because, as you know, books need editors and you can help each other edit, but I will be the editor-in-chief who approves final copy." No editor-in-chief could have 25 authors in the publishing stage at the same time! Because we had talked a lot about publishing companies and how books got published, the children knew that a book takes a lot of work after the first draft is written.

I explained how I had helped Jonathan's class and would help their class so that everyone would publish a book by the end of the month, but only one-third of the class would be publishing at a time. I then showed them the blank books that some parents had helped me assemble. The books were spiral-bound, with covers made from half sheets of construction paper. Inside each book were half sheets of paper. The first page of each book had a place for the title, author, and date. The second page said "Dedicated to" and had several lines on which the author could write the dedication. The last page said "About the Author" and had lines on which I would write something about each of them. The middle pages all had two writing lines at the bottom and the top half blank for the illustration. I showed the children that the parents had made books with 8, 12, 16, and 20 pages and reminded them that some books were much shorter and some books much longer than others. We counted the pages in Jonathan's book and realized that he had published a 12-page book! "Most of your books will probably be 12 pages, too," I remarked, "but some may be shorter and some longer." I could see by the looks on Larry's, Steve's, and Roberta's faces that they already had long books in mind.

I then explained to the children how we would go about getting everyone a published book by the end of the month. I had arbitrarily divided the class into thirds, making sure to put my weakest writers—Paul, Daisy, and Alexander—in different thirds, and my best writers—Larry, Hilda, and Pat—also in different thirds. I wanted Paul, Daisy, and Alexander in different cycles because I knew they would each require a lot of individual attention, and I wanted Larry, Hilda, and Pat in different cycles so they could help me edit. I showed them the list, and there were some grumblings from children who were not going to be first, but I told them that everyone would have their turn and that those publishing later would have more time to work on a really good first draft. Roberta chimed in and said, "I don't care if I'm in the last group. I need the time because I am going to write a really long book."

Finally, I explained how we would make each book. The children who were in the first group had to decide by tomorrow which first draft they wanted to make into a book. We would work together to help each writer revise—make the meaning clear and the book as interesting and exciting as possible. Then children would work with partners to do a first editing. I would do a final editing, and the children would copy their piece into their book and do the illustrations. "By the end of the month, if we all work hard together, you will all have a published book like Jonathan's."

It was easier said than done, but we did do it! For the rest of the month, we continued beginning Writers' Workshop with my minilesson and ending it with the children whose day it was sharing in the Author's Chair, but during the 15 to 20 minutes of writing time, two-thirds of the class were writing in their notebooks while I helped the other third edit and publish.

On the first publishing day, I sat down with Paul, Daphne, Pat, Rita, Horace, Danielle, Jeff, and Mike. I had each person read the piece he or she wanted to publish, and after they read, I and the other children made comments. As in Author's Chair sharing, we always began by telling the writer one thing we liked. Next, however, I modeled helping the author make the piece as clear and exciting as possible by comments such as, "Daphne, I loved your story about your grandmother, and I know she will love reading this book. You say she is very nice to you. Tell me some of the nice things she does."

Daphne had many examples of her grandmother's love and caring, and I suggested that she address these in her story. I told her to write these on another sheet of paper and then, when we edited, we would figure out where they should be inserted.

As each child read, I tried to listen for anything that was unclear or something that could be added to make the book more interesting and I suggested this. I also invited the suggestions of the other writers, and some of them had good comments. In the time we had that first day, five of the eight children read their first-draft pieces and listened to our comments on meaning. We finished this on the second day. I knew that Paul would not share his with the group, so I got him to tell me ahead of time what he wanted to publish, and then I explained this to the group. They were very supportive and said Paul's book about George, our gerbil, was going to be terrific! On the third day, the children worked on adding or changing anything they wanted to do based on our comments. They then chose someone to help them read their piece for the two things on our Editor's Checklist: Do all the sentences make sense, and do they all begin with capital letters?

While they did this, I worked with Paul. I explained that I wanted him to have a great book about George the gerbil, and I got him to tell me what he wanted to say. I then wrote his sentences on a clean sheet of paper and let him choose an 8-page book. I had him read his simple sentences to me several times and made sure he understood that he would copy them in his book and then illustrate them. I asked him who he wanted to dedicate the book to and helped him write *My Mom* on the "Dedicated to" page.

By the fourth day, Paul was working on his book, and I was ready to play editor-in-chief for my other writers. I talked with them first and helped them decide how many pages they needed in their book and about how much would go on each page. They wrote the page number on their first draft in red pen above what they thought would fit on each page. I told them that the sentences wouldn't all fit exactly on each page, and that it would be fine for sentences to go over to the next page. By knowing approximately what was going on each page, the children could begin their illustrations while I was helping each child edit. For the next three days, I worked with each child individually to edit his or her piece. I helped them fix up sentences that didn't make sense. I inserted needed punctuation and wrote the correct spelling of words above their invented spelling. After my editing, they copied their writing into their books and did their illustrations.

Seven days after I began with this first group, I had the second group sitting with me and reading their chosen piece so that we could give them feedback on their message. Children from the first group finished up their illustrations and then went back to their writing notebook first-draft writing. I helped Alexander, who was in this group, just as I had helped Paul, and he got a nice book written about his dog.

By the time I got to the final third, they were ready to go. The children who had already published had shared their books when it was their day in the Author's Chair, and the last third had a better idea than the others about what they were trying to accomplish. They worked hard, and by the very last day in February, all 25 of my children were published authors. I have put their published books in special baskets in our classroom reading center, and these are very popular choices for reading during Self-Selected Reading.

The children are already asking me when they can do another book! We are going to take a few weeks just for first drafts at the beginning of March, and then we will begin another book publishing cycle. This is a lot of work, but the pride they take in their books and their clear sense that they are all real writers now makes it worth all the time and trouble.

Work in the other blocks has also moved along this month. We now have 65 words on the wall, besides our names. We continue to do work with rhyming patterns, Guess the Covered Word, and Making Words lessons.

We are now reading in the fourth book of our reading series for some of our Guided Reading lessons. On Thursdays and Fridays, however, I am using easier books. Some weeks, if the easier book ties in with our comprehension strategy of the topic of what we read earlier in the week, we all read in the same easier selection. I partner up the children and remind them of how we help partners when they come to words they don't know by giving them clues instead of just telling them the word. Other weeks, I have three or four different titles, and following through on my decision to give children choices whenever possible, I let them make a first and second choice and then form flexible groups to read the book. I spend some time during Guided Reading meeting with the groups and coaching them to use their decoding strategies. I meet with all the children across the week but spend more time with the children—Paul, Daisy, Mike, Chip, Alexander, Mort, Jeff, Carl, Butch, Manuel, and Alex—who need the most coaching. The groups change from week to week, and I never put all my struggling readers together in one group, but I often include more of them together—along with some good reading models—and give these groups more of my time.

Their burgeoning independent reading ability is really showing up during our afternoon Read-Aloud/Self-Selected Reading time. Currently, I am reading to them for 15 minutes, and they are reading on their own for the remaining 15 minutes. Even Mike is getting to the point where he actually settles down and reads most days. Now if I could just find something to motivate Mort and captivate Daisy!

March

We did a science unit on weather this month. We read two terrific Big Books, *What Will the Weather Be Like Today?* by Paul Rogers and *Caps, Hats, Socks, and Mittens* by Louisa Borden. I also read many other books to them. Their two favorites were both about snow—*The Snowy Day* by Ezra Jack Keats and *White Snow, Bright Snow* by Alvin Tresselt. We are up to the three–happy-face stage of our Editor's Checklist with the addition of:

3. Do all the sentences have ending punc (. ? !)?

Now in my writing, I make all three kinds of mistakes—but just one or two total in any one piece. On some days, I leave a word out, resulting in a sentence that doesn't make sense. Other days, I begin one of my sentences without a capital and stick a capital right in the middle of a word. I might write four or five sentences and forget the ending "punc" on one of them. The children are getting good at seeing my mistakes and helping me edit. At the end of their writing time each day, I remind them to read their sentences for sense, beginning capitals, and ending punctuation and to give themselves three happy faces.

We are halfway through our second book publishing cycle. The third that had to wait until last to make their first books went first this time, and the first third has to wait until last. This publishing has gone much more smoothly because we all learned so much the first time through. They are producing some really terrific books. We should be able to get one more publishing cycle in, and then they will all have three published books to take home for the summer.

My children are getting so fast at chanting and writing their five words each day that I have added an "on the back" activity. After they have written the five called-out words on the front and checked them by tracing around them, I have them turn their papers over and we do an activity on the back. At least one day a week, I have them write their word wall word with an ending. I always preface this with "Sometimes when you're writing, . . ." because I really stress that the word wall is not there just so we can chant and write the words during our daily word wall practice but to help us when we are writing.

Last Tuesday, I had called out the five words: *play, go, come, give,* and *want.* When they turned their papers over, I said, "Lots of times when you are writing, you need to write a word that is on our wall but you need to add an ending. What if you were writing *I was playing baseball.* How would you spell *playing*?" I got them to tell me that you would spell *playing p-l-a-y-i-n-g* and then to write it on their papers. I continued, having them write *wanting, going, coming,* and *giving,* making sure they told me about dropping the *e* before adding *ing* before writing the last two.

On Wednesday, I called out the five words: *house, look, thing, those,* and *saw.* When they turned their papers over, I said, "Lots of times when you are writing, you need to spell a word that is not on our word wall, but if you can think of a word that is on our word wall that rhymes with the word you want to write, you might be able to use that word to help you spell your word. What if you were writing a story about a mouse; which word from the wall will help you spell *mouse?* I had the children tell me that "since *house* is spelled *h-o-u-s-e, mouse* is probably spelled *m-o-u-s-e.*" They wrote *mouse* on the back of their papers, and I continued in the same manner. What if you were writing about a crook? A rose? Some string? A house of straw? For each word, I had them tell me the word wall word that rhymed and how that might help them spell the word they needed, and then I had them spell it aloud before writing it. These on-the-back activities are taking only about two minutes each and are giving me a lot of good spelling practice beyond just the word wall words.

We are finishing the fourth book in our reading series and have continued our small-group reading of multiple copies of easier books on Thursdays and Fridays. This is working out remarkably well, and I plan to continue this through April and May. Many of my children are rereading during Self-Selected Reading the books we read during Guided Reading, as well as their old favorites that we earlier made tapes of. I forget from year to year what absolute delight first-graders take in being able to "really read!" And how much they enjoy reading books again and again, for the sheer pleasure of doing it!

This month, I have made a special effort to get my children actually using the letter-sound knowledge they have when they are reading. When they write, they have to represent the word in some way, so they do use their letter-sound knowledge to spell words. But getting them to look at the letters and use what they know to figure out a word in reading is harder.

I do several things to help them learn to apply their phonics skills. One thing I do is to model for them how I would decode an unknown word. Of course, I do this during Guided Reading, but I also do it during the afternoon science and social studies time as I am introducing words needed in our units.

This month our science unit was on weather. I wrote sentences on the board one at a time, underlining the words I wanted to introduce. I told the students that the underlined words were words they didn't know, but that if they used the letter sounds they knew and made sure the words made sense, they would be able to figure them out.

I read the first sentence and stopped when I got to the underlined word, *hot.* I then thought aloud, "Hmm, if I didn't know this word, how could I figure it out? I know that *h* usually has the sound it has in *hamburger* and *house.* I know that *n-o-t* spells *not* and *l-o-t* spells *lot. H-o-t* should be a rhyming word—*hot!* Yes, hot makes sense because it is a kind of weather."

I then had children read the other sentences, led them to figure out the underlined words, and helped them to explain how they might have figured it out. *Cold* was decoded based on the rhyming word *old.* The children knew the words *rain* and *sun* and pronounced "rainy" and "sunny" so that they sounded right in the sentence. *Storms* was decoded because "it starts with *st,* has *ms* at the end, and

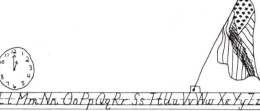

AaBbCcDdEeFfGgHhIiJjKkLlMmNnOoPpQqRrSsTtUuVvWwXxYyZz

Today is ————————

Sometimes the weather is <u>hot</u>.
Sometimes the weather is <u>cold</u>.
Some days are <u>rainy</u>.
Some days are <u>sunny</u>.
Some days we have bad <u>storms</u>.
On <u>stormy</u> days, we see
<u>lightning</u> and hear <u>thunder</u>.

makes sense because storms are bad." *Stormy* was difficult, but when I pointed out how *rain* and *sun* became *rainy* and *sunny,* most of the children understood it. *Lightning* was decoded because "you see lightning on stormy days, and it has *light* as the first part." *Thunder* "begins with *th* and then has *un* like *fun* and *run* and ends like *her,* and you hear thunder in storms."

Next, I had the children read part of the weather chapter in their science books. I told them that there would be several new words they would have to figure out and reminded them of what they could do when they came to a word they didn't know. After they had read, I let several children write words on the board that they had figured out in their reading and explain how they had figured them out.

On the following morning, I gave each child a yellow index card and asked all of the children to try to find a word somewhere in their reading that day that they didn't know. They should write that word on the yellow card and then use the card to mark the page on which they found the word. At the end of the day, each child who found a word came to the board, wrote that word on the board, read the sentence in which the child had found the word, and tried to explain how he or she had figured it out. The children really seemed to like doing this, so I designated Wednesdays as official "word-busting" days. Every Wednesday the children get their yellow cards and are on the lookout for one new word they can figure out. I hope their enthusiasm stays high.

April

All year I have been concerned with providing direct experiences to promote concept development and increase the depth and breadth of my children's meaning vocabulary store. I try to constantly remind myself that language really is the foundation of reading and writing. Adding words and concepts to their oral and listening vocabularies increases the number of words they can make sense of while reading and use in their own writing. Whenever possible, I bring real objects into the classroom and encourage them to bring objects in. We not only name each object, but we also describe and classify it and decide which attributes it shares with other objects and how it is different from other objects. Often these objects relate to the science or social studies unit we are studying, and in addition to talking about these objects, we write about them in shared writing charts. I also use many videos, picture books, and pictures to provide the students with visual experience with words and concepts for which we don't have real objects readily available. Years ago, I started a picture file for one of my methods courses, and I have added to it ever since. Currently my picture file categories include: food, animals, plants, clothes, occupations, vehicles, holidays, city life, South America, Asia, Africa, United States, famous people, tools and utensils, and a huge and disorderly miscellaneous category. I have laminated most of the pictures I have collected, and I find my picture file an invaluable resource in concept and meaning vocabulary development.

I also do many categorization activities with my children to help them clarify and extend meanings for words. One I particularly enjoy doing is a list, group, and label lesson originated by Taba (1967) for use in the social studies curricula. To do a list, group, and label lesson, you begin by asking children a question that will elicit many responses. Last week, as we were beginning our science unit on nutrition, I asked the children to list all the foods they could think of. As they named various foods, I wrote these food words on the board. From time to time, I stopped to read what was already listed on the board and encouraged them to think of more foods. Finally, when we had filled almost the whole board, I said, "Let's just have Mike, Roberta, and Horace tell me their foods, since they have their hands up. We will then have the whole board full of food." I then reread the whole list, letting the children read along with me if they desired. I then left the list on the board for the next day.

On the following afternoon, I pointed to our list of foods and told the children that I was going to read the list again and that this time they should listen and think, "Are there any foods on the list that seem to go together in some way?" I then read the entire list and asked if anyone had a group of foods that seemed to go together.

Mitch said that cake, cookies, chocolate pie, ice cream, and gingerbread went together. I wrote these five on a sheet of chart paper and asked him why he had put these foods together. He said, "Because you eat them all after the meal." I then asked him if he could think of a name or label for his group. He hesitated a moment and then said, "Desserts."

Steve put mushrooms, grapes, berries, rhubarb, and nuts together. I listed these five foods on the chart paper and asked him why he had put those particular foods together. He said it was because they all grew wild. I then asked him if he could give a name or label to that group. After some hesitation, he said, "Things That Grow Wild."

Chip put peanuts, chocolate candy, hamburgers, potato chips, soda, oranges, and tomatoes together. I listed them and in response to my "why" question, he said, "Because they are my favorite things to eat." When I asked him to give a name or label to this group, he couldn't. I said that that was fine, that we couldn't always think of names for groups, and went on to the next child.

While doing these lessons, I accept every child's response. During the listing process, everyone usually contributes something, but I call on the children with smaller vocabularies first, so that they have a chance to contribute. I usually save the grouping and labeling steps for the next day, so that the lessons don't take more than 25 minutes. When we form groups, each child who wants to organize a group tells me why those particular things are grouped together and then attempts to give a label to that group. This labeling step is difficult for many of my children, and if they can't do it, I simply accept that and go on to the next volunteer.

As you can see, the children have different categories and different reasons for grouping things together. Therefore, no child is allowed to add anything to another child's group. I also write the name of the child who labeled a group under that group. Objects from the list can be used over and over again as different children make groups. The children enjoy these lessons, and I can see that they have had an effect on their vocabulary and categorization skills.

We are through with our second book publishing cycle, and everyone is going to publish one more book in May. The children are even more excited about this last book, and those children who have been in the second publishing third each time have already informed me that it is their turn to be first. I have added the fourth and final thing to our Editor's Checklist:

4. Do all the people and place names and I start with a capital?

I continue to write during the minilesson each day and the children help me fix my piece using the four items on the checklist. I have been amazed at how well all my children are writing. When I think back to my early teaching days, when I thought that children had to be able to read well before they could write independently, I am appalled! It is perfectly clear that with word wall and content board support, plus encouragement and modeling of stretching out words to spell them, all children can write, and for many of them, writing is their major avenue to reading. I consider all four blocks—Writing, Words, Guided Reading, and Teacher Read-Aloud/Self-Selected Reading—equally important, but I must admit that Writing is the block in which many of my lowest and highest achievers seem to make the most progress. I guess Writing is the most multilevel block.

We now have 110 high-frequency words on the word wall, in addition to the names. I am not going to add any more words this year because I want to use May to really help them consolidate their knowledge of these critical words. I will, however, continue the daily practice with the words. On Mondays we are making up sentences, using only words on the wall or on our content word boards. This is quite a challenging task, but the children are enjoying it. After they make up the sentence, I locate all the words, and we all write the sentence. We are trying to make up big "fancy" sentences, and they are very clever at combining the words.

Here are the three sentences they composed last Monday using the word wall and our nutrition board. (The underlined words are attached to our nutrition board. The others are on the word wall.)

> *Vegetables* are very very good for you.
> People should not eat too much *junk food*.
> People should eat some *cereals* and *grains*.

I am continuing to do an "on-the-back" activity after we chant, write, and check five words on the front. In addition to adding endings to our wall words and spelling rhyming words, we have written some compound words, including *boyfriend, girlfriend, playhouse, without, cannot, someone, something, somewhere, everything, seesaw.* The children are very impressed with their ability to spell such big words! I am also occasionally having them put the five words they wrote on the front in alphabetical order on the back as we begin to learn some alphabetizing/dictionary skills.

We are continuing to do Making Words lessons at least twice a week. Whenever possible, I tie these into our science/social studies units or what we are reading during Guided Reading. This month we did three lessons in which the last word connected to nutrition. From the letters *a, o, c, r, r, s,* and *t,* we made the words *car, cat, rat, rot, cot, coat, cost, star, oats, coats, coast, roast, actor,* and *carrots.* We then sorted out the rhyming words and used them to decode *toast* and *flat* and to spell *pot* and *chat.* From the letters *a, e, o, g, n, r,* and *s,* we made *an, on, Ron, ran, rag, sag, gas, nose, rose, sore, snore,* and *oranges.* The transfer words we decoded and spelled were *core, nag, score* and *chose.*

The word that no one could figure out was the word that can be made from the letters *a, a, e, o, l, m,* and *t.* They noticed immediately that they had more red letters—vowels—than blue letters and this had never happened before. I began by having them take three letters and make *eat.* Then I told them that they could just change their letters around and that, like magic, these same three letters could spell *ate.* When they had accomplished that trick, I told them that the same three letters in different places would spell the word *tea.* While they were still marveling at three words they knew spelled with the same three letters, I had them add a letter to *tea* and turn it into *team,* and then move the same four letters around to spell *tame, meat,* and *mate.* After changing *mate* to *late* and *late* to *lame,* I had them move the letters in *lame* around to spell *meal* and then *male.* The children are really getting the idea that where you put letters makes a big difference in what word you spell, and this lesson with so many "turn-around" words made a big impression on them. Next, they made *mole* and *motel,* and then, since no one had figured out the word that could be made with all the letters (and most of my children were convinced that there was no such word!), I got to show them how all their letters could be used to spell *oatmeal.* They hate it when I stump them like this, and I don't get to do it very often. (They did love taking home their Making Words Homework sheet that night, however, and stumping all their parents.) Of course, we finished the lesson with some transfer words, *crate, cheat, game,* and *blame.* Most of my children's spelling is beginning to reflect what we do as we make words, sort out the rhymes, and use the rhyming words to decode and spell new words. Many of them realize that you often need letters you can't hear, and they are using rhyming words they know to figure out vowel patterns.

We are reading in the final book of our adopted series now along with books in sharing groups on Thursday and Friday. I had each of them come and read to me a few pages of a selection toward the end of their first reader, and all but Paul, Daisy, Mike, Butch, and Alexander met or exceeded the 90 percent word identification criteria I use when I make oral reading records of their reading. I then had these five read to me from a middle-first-grade-level book they had not read before, and all but Paul were successful with that. While I would love to have them all reading at or above grade level at the end of the year, I know that not everyone can accomplish that in one year's time. I am delighted that Daisy, Mike, and Alexander have moved as far as they have, and even Paul is not a nonreader. When he is having an "alert" day, he can read early first-grade material independently.

I have as I planned put a bit more structure into my weekly conferences with children during Self-Selected Reading. While, I still allow them to "pretend read" familiar stories and "picture read" informational books, I ask them to bring to our weekly conference a book in which they can read most of the words. I also ask them to choose two pages that they want to read to me at the beginning of the conference. As they read, I observe whether or not they are correctly reading almost all the words, and I notice the strategies they use to figure out an unknown word. I also notice their self-correction strategies. When they have read the two pages to me, I point out what I have seen:

> "You have chosen a good book that you can read very well. I was very proud of the way you went back and reread this sentence when you realized that it didn't sound right and something must be wrong. You used the letters in the word you knew and the ideas from the rest of the sentence to help you figure out the word."

If a child has brought a book that is much too hard, we talk about how that child could read that book—pretend reading or picture reading—and then I steer the child toward books in which they can read almost all the words. I show that child how to read the first page or two and put one finger down for each word he can't figure out. "If you get all five fingers down on two pages, that book is too hard for you to read and bring to our conference. You need to find an easier one." I help the child find a suitable book to bring to our conference next week.

Some children—especially Mort and Daisy—seem to just grab any easy book. I try to steer them toward some books they haven't read yet and would like and that would be on their level but a little bit challenging. I have made a rule for everyone that you have to bring a different book each week after Mort brought the same easy book three weeks in a row! Does he think I don't notice or does he not care?

During the conference, I make anecdotal notes about what each child read and how well they were reading. I note their use of picture clues, attempts to figure out unknown words, fluency, self-correction, and other reading strategies. I always ask them what they liked about the book they were reading and sometimes I suggest another book that they might like. I try to make the conference more of a conversation than an "inquisition," but at the same time I do ask some questions that will let me know how well they are comprehending. Depending on the child and the book, I might ask two or three questions such as:

> Why did you choose this book?
> What did you like about this book?
> What was your favorite part?
> Who was your favorite character?
> Did the book have any pictures you really liked?
> What was the most interesting thing you learned in this book?
> What was the funniest (saddest, most surprising, silliest, strangest) part of this book?
> Can you tell me what happened at the beginning, middle, and end of your story?

What new facts did you learn about penguins (or whatever topic we have
    been learning about) from this book?
Is your book a fiction (made-up) book or nonfiction (informational) book?
What do you think will happen next?
How did the author let you know that the main character was scared?
Did you learn anything from this book that you can use in your own writing?

I am just delighted that all my children see themselves as readers and writers!
That is one of the main benefits of not putting them in fixed ability groups and
giving them multiple opportunities to read and write. The discouraged, de-
feated attitude that has taken hold by this time in the year for children in the bottom group is not evident in my struggling readers. I just hope they can make
more progress next month, and I am going to do my best to encourage their parents to take them to the library and read with them this summer. I know Mike's
mother will try. I am not sure about Butch's, Alexander's, or Daisy's parents,
and I have yet to meet Paul's mother. I am also going to encourage Chip's and
Carl's parents to make library trips and books a regular part of their summer.
They are right on grade level now, but they probably won't be if they don't look
at a book for three months!

May

Well, the year is almost over. Just one more week of school for the children and
lots of report writing and finishing up for me. I always feel a little sad during the
last weeks of school—so much yet undone. All in all, this has been an exceptionally good year. The children have all learned to read and write and do math, and I
know they know a lot more about the world we live in than they did when they
entered this classroom in September.

    We finished the year with a social studies unit on friends and a science
unit on water. I like to do the friends unit at the end of the year because by now
the children have so many friends here at school, and they also have friends in
their neighborhoods and in the places they will visit this summer. We talk about
what it means to be a friend and how most of us have friends who have moved
away or whom we see only at certain times of the year. We locate on the map
the places they will visit this summer, as well as places some of their friends
have moved to. I modeled writing letters to some friends during my minilessons, and I did a few "When I Was Your Age" tales, in which I wrote about
my friends when I was in first grade. Of course, I read them some books about
friends and reread some of their old favorite *Frog and Toad* and *George and
Martha* stories.

    Our water unit was, as always, a lot of fun. Many of the children will vaca-
tion near some kind of water this summer, and the rest will spend some time at the
community pool. We did lots of experiments with water, learned about water pollution and the need for water conservation, and realized how critical and huge a
part water plays in our everyday lives. We read books about the ocean and other

bodies of water and enjoyed some of the Jerry Pallotta alphabet books, including *The Ocean Alphabet Book* and *The Underwater Alphabet Book.* By far, the children's favorite book this month was *The Magic School Bus at the Waterworks.* Like the other books in Joanna Cole and Bruce Degan's science series, this book finds Mrs. Frizzle and her class taking an incredible journey—this time right through the town's waterworks. The children marveled at what they found on this journey. They remarked longingly, "Wouldn't it be wonderful if we could really go inside things like they can on *The Magic School Bus.*"

Fortunately, Ms. Maverick's class had foreseen the popularity of *The Magic School Bus* books and had ordered many copies of each title for their annual end-of-the-year book fair. My class was one of the first to go, and they bought up all the copies of *The Magic School Bus at the Waterworks* and a lot of the other titles. This book fair is a super idea, but I worry about the children who can't scrape together any money. Paul surprised me by bringing five dollars, which he spent with great care. Daisy had money but wouldn't spend it. The others teased her, saying that she was probably going to spend it all on candy! Chip was the only one who didn't bring any money, but I had anticipated that and had hired him to stay after school for several nights and help me do some of the end-of-the-year packing up, and then I paid him with books he had selected.

Last week, we had an experience in here! Sue Port came and asked me if I would spend a half day with all the first-grade teachers in the school system and explain to them my four-block approach to reading and writing. I protested that I couldn't possibly explain this in just a few hours' time, but she persisted. Then she had this brainstorm. "How about if I send our central office media person to make some videotapes of what is happening in here? That way, you could show them what is happening, and the teachers would really understand what a lively, varied day the children have and how well they are all reading and writing." Before I could convince her that I didn't want someone in my room taping everything we did during these last hectic days, she had bustled off to "set it up"!

The next morning Miss Media arrived, and she stayed for three days! Of course, the children were beside themselves on the first day, and I didn't think we would get any good tape. But on the second and third days, they settled down and started ignoring the camera—as did I—and although I haven't looked at it all yet, I do think we will have some parts that really show what is happening and how well the children are reading and writing. On the third day, Miss Media had each child bring a book he or she wanted to read and the last book he or she authored, and each child read a few pages of the favorite book and the entire authored book for the camera. This part we watched together as a class, and the children all did remarkably well. The books Danielle, Pat, and Larry read parts of were chapter books usually read by fourth-graders. Mike's authored collection of monster stories is extraordinarily clever! Even Paul had one of the *Sunshine* readers he enjoyed reading and could read the book he wrote. I hate to admit it, but Sue was right. I am going to pick portions to show each block, as well as the children reading and writing. That all my children are reading and writing better than anyone could expect them to is undeniable when you see them doing it. Although I don't enjoy talking to groups of my peers, particularly other teachers I work with, I think I might actually look forward to this presentation!

THE FIRST-GRADE MEETING

Sue Port called the meeting to order and introduced Mrs. Wright. "To most of you, Rita Wright needs no introduction. Rita has taught at Merritt Elementary School for more years than she likes to admit to. Rita has served on and, at times, chaired your grade-level curriculum committees. Rita is, and has been for many years, an outstanding first-grade teacher who uses all means at her disposal to get children off to a terrific start. Last year, Rita began implementing what she calls her four-block approach to reading and writing. She had read about this approach to organizing beginning reading instruction, and the idea that children do not all learn in the same way and that multiple methods were needed if all children were going to succeed was one she had believed in for many years. Another part of this organizational plan she agreed with was not putting children in fixed reading groups. Reading groups have been our major way of dealing with the differences children at entering literacy levels bring with them to school, but the effectiveness of reading groups has been seriously questioned in recent years. I don't want to take any more of Rita's precious time because, knowing Rita, I am sure she has this planned down to the minute, but I do want you to know that I have been impressed with what I have seen in Rita's classroom in the past two years, and it is at my insistence that she is here to share with you today."

The assembled teachers clapped in a restrained, polite way as Rita rose to speak. The anticipation she had felt earlier began to turn to anxiety as she looked out at the somewhat skeptical faces of some of her colleagues. She began by telling them that she felt a little uneasy talking to them about first grade. She knew most of them and knew that they were all terrific first-grade teachers.

"If you had asked me two years ago to honestly tell you how good a job I thought I was doing as a first-grade teacher, I would have told you that there were things I would like to change—mostly things about some of the kids." Some teachers nodded and laughed in agreement, and Mrs. Wright began to relax a little. "But all in all, I thought I was doing as well as anyone could, considering the wide range of children we have at Merritt and the lack of home support many of the children we teach today have. Two years ago this summer, however, I read an article by Cunningham, Hall, & Defee (1998), which Sue has had duplicated for you to take with you, and I got excited by what I read. A lot of what was in their article I was already doing, but the teachers who developed the four-block approach had put components together in what looked to me like a very workable, practical way. Last year, I tried out some of the parts of this approach, and this year, I jumped in feet first! I am the same teacher, teaching in the same school, teaching the same variety of children, using the same materials, working as hard as I always work, and my children—particularly the ones who came least prepared and the ones who came already reading—are reading and writing much better than they have in all the other years. Since there are no other changes except for this new way of dividing up my time and organizing my day, I have to assume that this approach is just better suited to the varied needs of my children. Let me begin at the end and show you some of my children reading and writing."

Mrs. Wright switched on the VCR and there on camera was Chip. Chip read a few pages from a *Curious George* book he had selected and then read and showed the illustrations of his last published book. Daisy was next to read, followed by Alexander, Mike, and finally Paul. When these five children had all read from selected books and their own published books, Mrs. Wright paused the tape and said, "Now I know that many of you are thinking these children are not unusually good readers and writers for the end of first grade, but these are my five lowest children. Chip can almost read on grade level. Daisy, Alexander, and Mike are on a good solid middle of first grade level, and Paul is my lowest, but he can read easy books independently, and he can read the three books he has authored."

Mrs. Wright could tell that most of the teachers were looking at this reading and writing of these five children differently when they realized they were the below-level readers. Mrs. Wright then fast-forwarded through the rest of the class reading and writing, stopping once or twice so that the teachers knew that these children all read easily at first-grade level or above. She showed the tape at normal speed once again while Larry, Danielle, Pat, and Steve read aloud. All four of these children had chosen to read a couple of pages of chapter books usually read by fourth- or fifth-graders. The published books they shared also demonstrated writing abilities way beyond that of average first-graders.

When she stopped the tape, the teachers were all abuzz, talking to each other. Mrs. Wright mouthed a "thank you" to Sue for insisting on the three days of taping and on having all the children read for the tape. The teachers now had all kinds of questions:

> Was Mrs. Wright sure that this was a normal class at the beginning of the year?
> How far had she taken those last four students in their reading series?
> How could a student like Paul write a book like the one he wrote?
> Wasn't there a single child who was still a virtual nonreader/nonwriter?

Mrs. Wright laughed at this question and said, "I didn't hide any children or ask any of their parents to keep them home when the visitors came, as I hear used to happen in the old days."

Mrs. Wright then showed the teachers her daily schedule and showed clips of each of the four blocks. As she went through, she reminded the teachers that they were seeing the last few days of school, and that although she had done all four blocks from the beginning of school, what she and the children did in those blocks looked quite different in September and even in February from what they were seeing at the end of May.

She showed some tape of the Writing block and of her minilesson in which she wrote while the children watched. The teachers expressed amazement that she didn't say the words while she was writing them, but she had them focus on the children, and it was obvious that the children were all trying their best to read what she was writing. She also pointed out to the teachers that in her minilesson, she always looked for a word or two on the word wall, looked pleased to find it there, and commented, "If it's on our word wall, we have to spell it correctly."

When she got to the point where she spelled a couple of big words, stretching out the words and writing down the letters you could hear, she could tell from the shaking heads that some teachers didn't think a teacher should ever spell a word wrong. Leaving out some ending punctuation and capital letters did not please some either. As soon as Mrs. Wright finished writing, she pointed to the Editor's Checklist:

EDITOR'S CHECKLIST

Do all the sentences make sense?
Do all the sentences start with capital letters?
Do all the sentences have . ? or ! at the end?
Do all the people and place names and I start with a capital?

She took a different-colored marker, and the children helped her read for each item on the checklist and fix each and then draw a happy face. In addition she asked them which words she had stretched out to spell, and she underlined these, remarking that she would have to find the correct spelling for these words if this were the piece she chose to publish.

Next, the tape showed the children writing. Most children were writing in their notebooks, but a few were finishing up the copying and illustrating of their final first-grade published books. When Mrs. Wright rang the bell to signal the end of the writing time, five children lined up and read their chosen piece in the Author's Chair. Each child who read chose one child from the audience to tell something he or she liked about the piece.

Mrs. Wright stopped the tape, and there were a slew of questions!

How did she get them started writing?
Did she give them a topic for writing?
How did they know how to choose a topic?
How did she have time to help them all edit and publish?
Who made all the blank books?

Mrs. Wright tried to answer the questions, and then Sue Port jumped in to announce that it was time for a break, and that after the break, she wanted Mrs. Wright to show tapes of the other blocks. "I know that you all still have questions about the writing, and you will have questions about the other blocks, but we will have only an hour left, and I want you to get an overview of all four blocks. When we end this afternoon, I am going to ask you to write down the questions you still have, and then I will see what we can plan before the start of the next school year to help provide answers to your questions."

The teachers talked to each other and asked Mrs. Wright individual questions throughout the break, and Mrs. Wright was amazed at their enthusiasm. After the break, she did a whirlwind tour of the other blocks. She showed the word wall and explained about putting the names up one each day and having one child be the special child for the day. She told them how she had added five high-frequency words each week and explained that they took all the Monday Words time to work with and practice handwriting with the five new words. On the other days, five words were reviewed. The teachers watched the children clap and chant and write the words and then get out their red pens to trace around and check them. Then the children turned their papers over and Mrs. Wright led them to use their word wall words to spell rhyming words on the back. The tape then focused on their content board, which at this point had pictures of water and water words, and Mrs. Wright explained that between the word wall and the content boards, even children like Alexander, who still couldn't hear sounds in words very well, were able to write.

Next they watched a Making Words lesson in which the children used the letters *a, e, h, l, s,* and *w* to make the words *we, he, she, sea, was, saw, law, slaw, heal, seal, sale,* and *leash.* The teachers were amazed when Mrs. Wright got to the end of the lesson and asked, "Has anyone figured out what word we can make with all these letters?" At least a dozen hands went up from children who (unlike many of the teachers watching) had figured out that these letters could spell *whales*—an animal they were studying about as part of their water unit. Mrs. Wright then led the children to sort the words into patterns and they used the rhyming words to decode and spell *claw, steal, meal* and *thaw.*

The teachers again had all kinds of questions about the word wall and Making Words lesson, but Sue insisted that they write down their questions and pushed Mrs. Wright forward to show some of the Guided Reading block. Mrs. Wright showed part of Wednesday's lesson in which they were all reading in partners from the adopted reader, as well as part of Thursday's lesson in which they were reading in small groups in the easier books.

Finally, Mrs. Wright showed just a little snippet of Thursday's Teacher Read-Aloud/Self-Selected Reading block. The teachers were all amazed at the ability of all the children to sit and sustain their reading for 15 minutes as Mrs. Wright conferenced with the Thursday children.

The meeting was running a few minutes over, and Mrs. Wright knew that many of the teachers had to rush off to pick up their own children from day care. She summed up, however, by telling the teachers what she had learned during the last two years.

"Remember in your education courses, when you were taking an essay exam, no matter what the question was, you knew you should always get the words *individual differences* in the answer somewhere if you wanted an A?" The teachers all chuckled and Mrs. Wright knew they had all had this universal experience.

"Well, what I learned is that individual differences are really true—not just something we should give lip service to. The differences in the levels are the obvious ones, but there are also differences in the way children learn and respond—personality differences, I guess you would call them. This year, I taught two twins—born within minutes of each other, raised in the same environment—and the two girls are as different as night and day! Not different in their ability—they are both smart girls—but different in how they approach things, in the amount of structure or freedom they need, for example."

The nods of the teachers assured Mrs. Wright that all the teachers knew these learning style/personality differences were a reality of teaching. "The four blocks—Writing, Words, Guided Reading, and Teacher Read-Aloud/Self-Selected Reading—are like four roads, four ways to get there. The reason I think my children—particularly the children on either end—are reading and writing so much better is that regardless of how they learn best, that method is present in our classroom for some consistent part of every day. The four blocks represent different ways children learn, and within each block there are a variety of levels on which children can operate. I don't have time to discuss this now, but the multilevel concept is critical when you have the differences we always have at Merritt. The Writing and Self-Selected Reading time are naturally multilevel, but I have had to work to make the Words block and the Guided Reading block multilevel."

Sue hurriedly brought the meeting to a close, thanking Mrs. Wright and reminding the teachers to pick up their articles and leave their questions with her. Some teachers hurried off, but many others stayed and talked until late in the afternoon. Mrs. Wright could sense their genuine interest, and she reminded herself that most teachers work hard and want the very best for their children. "It's not that we don't care enough or that we don't do enough. It's just that the differences in learning style and entering level make it so complex to get it all organized," she assured them.

As the teachers left, many of them exchanged phone numbers and agreed to meet for a few potluck lunches over the summer and make plans for next year. Sue was beaming as she walked Rita to her car. "You see," she said, "those teachers know a good thing when they see it, and next year, I will arrange for them to come and visit your class and you can be their support as they move into this. Now aren't you glad I made you do this and sent Miss Media to tape for three days in your class?" Mrs. Wright smiled and said, "I'm glad it went well, and I'm glad they are enthusiastic, but I am going to have to decide how I feel about the rest of it." Sue assured her that she would be there to help and that Rita would love her new leadership role.

REFERENCES

Cunningham, P. M., & Hall, D. P. (1997). *Month-by-Month Phonics for First Grade.* Greensboro, NC: Carson-Dellosa.

Cunningham, P. M., Hall, D. P., & Sigmon, C. M. (1999). *The Teacher's Guide to the Four Blocks.* Greensboro, NC: Carson-Dellosa

Cunningham, P. M., Hall, D. P., & Defee, M. (1998). Nonability grouped, multilevel instruction: Eight years later. *The Reading Teacher, 51*, 652–664.

Taba, H. (1967). *Teachers' handbook for elementary social studies.* Palo Alto, CA: Addison-Wesley.

Children's Books/Materials Cited

ABC Bunny, by W. Gag, Putnam, 1978.

Alphabeasts: A Hide and Seek Alphabet Book, by Durga Bernhard, Holiday, 1992.

Are You My Mother? by P. D. Eastman, Random House, 1960.

Ashanti to Zulu: African Traditions, by M. Musgrove, Puffin Books, 1980.

The Biggest Nose, by K. Caple, Houghton Mifflin, 1985.

Caps, Hats, Socks, and Mittens, by L. Borden, Scholastic, 1989.

The Cat in the Hat, by Dr. Seuss, Random House, 1987.

Clifford books, by N. Bridwell, Scholastic, various dates.

Curious George books, by M. Rey & H. A. Rey, Houghton Mifflin, various dates.

Families Are Different, by N. Pelligrini, Scholastic, 1992.

Fly Away Home, by E. Bunting, Houghton Mifflin, 1993.

Frog and Toad books, by A. Lobel, HarperCollins, various dates.

George and Martha books, by J. Marshall, Sandpiper, various dates.

The Gingerbread Man, by K. Schmidt, Scholastic, 1986.

Goodnight Moon, by M. W. Brown, Holt, Rinehart, & Winston, 1969.

The Hand Made Alphabet, by L. Rankin, Dial, 1991.

Happy Christmas, Gemma, by S. Hayes, Morrow, 1992.

Hop on Pop, by Dr. Seuss, Random House, 1987.

The Hundred Dresses, by E. Estes, Scholastic, 1980.

I Hate English, by E. Levine, Scholastic, 1989.

If You Grew Up with Abraham Lincoln, by A. McGovern, Scholastic, 1992.

If You Grew Up with George Washington, by R. B. Gross, Scholastic, 1993.

The Magic School Bus at the Waterworks, by J. Cole & B. Degan, Scholastic, 1988.

The Mother's Day Mice, by E. Bunting, Ticknor & Fields, 1988.

Mrs. Wishy Washy, by J. Cowley, Wright, 1989.

My First Kwanzaa Book, by D. N. Chocolate, Cartwheel, 1990.

NBA Action From A–Z, by J. Preller, Scholastic, 1997.

The Ocean Alphabet Book, by J. Pallotta, Charlesbridge Publishers, 1989.

One Fish, Two Fish, Red Fish, Blue Fish, by Dr. Seuss, Random House, 1987.

Over in the Meadow, by O. A. Wadsworth, Scholastic, 1990.

A Perfect Father's Day, by E. Bunting, Houghton Mifflin, 1993.

A Picture Book of Hanukkah, by D. Adler, Holiday, 1982.

A Picture Book of Martin Luther King, by D. Adler, Holiday, 1989.

Robert the Rose Horse, by J. Heilbroner, Random House, 1962.

The Snowy Day, by E. J. Keats, Puffin Books, 1976.

Sunshine and *Story Box* books, Wright Group, various dates.

Ten, Nine, Eight, by M. Bang, Morrow, 1991.
The Underwater Alphabet Book, by J. Pallotta, Charlesbridge Publishers, 1991.
The Very Hungry Caterpillar, by E. Carle, Putnam, 1986.
The Wednesday Surprise, by E. Bunting, Houghton Mifflin, 1990.
What Will the Weather Be Like Today? by P. Rogers, Scholastic, 1992.
Where the Wild Things Are, by M. Sendak, HarperCollins, 1988.
Where's Spot? by E. Hill, Putnam, 1987.
White Snow, Bright Snow, by A. Tresselt, Morrow, 1988.

Miss Nouveau:
Second Grade

THE PARENT MEETING

Norma Nouveau arrived at the school two hours before her 7:30 P.M. parent meeting was scheduled to begin. Frankly, she was nervous and dreaded having to face all the parents in a large group. But at least, she thought, Mr. Topps would be there to help. He had generously offered to come to her meeting in case she needed help answering questions about schoolwide policies she might not even know about yet.

She was looking over her new bulletin board when Mr. Topps arrived at 7:15 p.m. He told her that it was lovely and that the fall theme she had chosen brightened the room. She didn't tell Mr. Topps that she had been working on that bulletin board for two weeks, sometimes until 2:00 A.M. She wanted him and the parents to think that she was efficient and organized.

Miss Nouveau had made name tags for all of the parents to wear. That way she could easily identify each parent, and she would know from the leftover name tags who had been unable to attend. When all of the parents were seated, Mr. Topps, as had been agreed earlier, introduced her to the group.

"As you all know," he began, "I am Mr. Topps, the principal. I especially wanted to come this evening to introduce your child's teacher to you. Miss Nouveau comes to us this year as a first-year teacher. She did exceptionally well both at the university and during her student teaching, so that when this position opened up last spring, I was delighted to have her among the applicants for the job. I know that you will be as happy with her as we are. If there is anything that you would like either of us to do, do not hesitate to call. Now, let's hear from Miss Nouveau."

"Thank you, Mr. Topps. This is an exciting moment for me. All my life I have dreamed of being an elementary school teacher. Tonight, I want to explain to you the kind of program that I have planned for this school year and how my instruction will meet these guiding principles." As Miss Nouveau said this, she pointed to a poster on which were printed the 12 guiding principles the Merritt faculty had come up with two years earlier.

At Merritt Elementary, we believe that all children can learn to read and write. We hold high expectations of every child. To make these expectations a reality, we all agree to have our instruction reflect 12 guiding principles:

1. Provide a balanced literacy program.
2. Make instruction multilevel.
3. Use language as the foundation for reading and writing.
4. Teach reading and writing as thinking.
5. Use feelings to create avid readers and writers.
6. Connect reading and writing to all subject areas.
7. Read aloud to students daily.
8. Schedule daily self-selected reading.
9. Have students write every day.
10. Teach the decoding and spelling strategies reading and writing require.
11. Use observation to assess learning and plan instruction.
12. Inform parents of expectations and progress.

"I wasn't here, of course, when the faculty decided on these, but I learned about them during our new-teacher orientation, and they look pretty basic and simple to me."

Miss Nouveau went down the list of beliefs and explained each in a way that showed she didn't think that meeting these was going to be any big deal.

"Of course, I will provide a balanced program, and I will make it multilevel by putting your children in the right reading group. I will be using the reading series adopted by the school system." Miss Nouveau held up her copy of the teacher's manual. "It explains here how the series is based on language, how the comprehension lessons help the children learn to think, and how important developing reading interests and attitudes are. Of course, we will be reading and writing in the content areas because we will use these science and social studies books." Miss Nouveau pointed to the science and social studies texts displayed on the table.

"I will read aloud to the children after lunch every day, and then they will have their Self-Selected Reading time. There are lots of writing activities in the manual for the reading series, so they will write every day, and of course I will teach the phonics lessons that go with every selection. There are assessment ideas here, too, and of course, I will be reporting to you with our reports cards and in our parent conferences. All in all, I don't think it will be difficult—even for a novice like me—to do all the things the Merritt faculty is committed to." Miss Nouveau, relieved that *that* was over, hurried on to a topic she knew more about.

"You know that physical factors are quite important in determining how well your children do in school. You can be most helpful in seeing to it that your children get to bed by 8:30 at night, that they come to school after having had a nutritious breakfast, and that they play out in the fresh air for a while every day after school. I intend to emphasize these basic health habits with the children this year. We will be studying nutrition, the value of recreation, and the importance of adequate rest. Starting on Monday, I am going to ask you to send a snack to school with your child. We will have snack time every morning in order to help keep the energy level of the children high. The school nurse will test vision and hearing in October, and if there are any problems, I will be in touch with you."

Miss Nouveau looked at her watch and saw that what she had planned to take 30 minutes had consumed only 15 minutes of time, so she asked Mr. Topps if there was anything he would like to add. There was not. The time had come for the part of the meeting that she had been dreading. She turned back to the parents and asked, "Are there any questions?"

All over the room, hands shot up. She called on Mrs. Moore first.

"How did you determine which reading group each child should be in?"

Miss Nouveau proudly explained that she had already assessed each child's reading using the Informal Reading Inventory that accompanied the reading series.

Mrs. Penn raised her hand to ask, "Why are you using *this* particular series?"

Mr. Topps intervened. "If I may, I would like to answer that one, Miss Nouveau, since the decision was made before you were hired. You see, Mrs. Penn, the teachers in this school met together last spring and selected this series from among the six state-approved adoptions. Most of the teachers at that meeting believed that this series allowed for the most flexibility while still retaining the structure and sequential development of skills that is a strong point of the basal reader approach."

Another hand went up, and Miss Nouveau called upon Mr. Tomâs. "When the kids aren't with you, how will they know what to do? Won't they just waste time and not do their work?"

"I will make sure they have plenty to do to keep them busy and out of trouble. They will complete the worksheets that come with the reading book, and they will do other work in the centers I am setting up. I will make sure they all make good use of their independent working time."

Mrs. Penn glanced over at Mr. Topps for his reaction. Had he pressed his fingertips to his forehead because of a headache?

There were many more questions, but Mr. Topps told the parents that it was time for them to adjourn to the cafeteria for the schoolwide meeting. He assured them that Miss Nouveau would be an excellent teacher and that he would work closely with her, as he would with any first-year teacher.

Miss Nouveau thanked them for coming. She started to gather up some of her materials when she noticed Mrs. Penn at her elbow.

"Miss Nouveau, I just want to offer to help you in any way that I can. I used to be a teacher, so I think that I might be of some help to you. *Please* feel free to call on me. I really enjoy helping out, and I know what a difficult task you have."

"Oh, thank you, but I'm sure that won't be necessary. I think that I have things pretty much under control now. But I do appreciate your offer. I will call for help if I need it."

"Fine. Good evening. It was lovely meeting with you this evening."

Mrs. Penn and Mrs. Middleman left the room together. They were talking quietly, but Miss Nouveau heard some of what was said.

> Mrs. Middleman: She's going to find out that meeting those 12 principles is easier said than done. But she is smart, and she seems to love the children, and she will learn a lot with Mr. Topps' help. She also did a lovely bulletin board. My, she certainly is creative.
>
> Mrs. Penn: Yes, she is. But you know, I always like to see the children's work up on the bulletin board. It's not as pretty or tidy, but there's something wonderful about your own child's work displayed. Mrs. Wright did so much of that last year.

Miss Nouveau was crestfallen. All of that work, and they would rather see things that the children had done! "Maybe I should think about having the children do something to put up. Oh, but it will be so messy!"

MONTHLY LOGS

September

My major premise is wrong! I thought that all children loved to read or that at the very least they were eager to learn. How wrong! How wrong! I just can't understand it. Butch sits in his seat (sometimes) just waiting out the day. If I ask him to do one of the assignments, he just looks at me and asks, "Why?"

"So that when you grow up you'll be able to read. You need to be a good reader to get a job."

"Oh yeah," he replied. "Well, my dad, he don't read so good, but he makes two hundred bucks a week!" That sounds like a great deal of money to a seven-year-old, but if only he knew!

One of the most frightening aspects of this teaching business is the weight of responsibility one feels. I was so excited to have my own classroom assigned to me and spent a lot of time here this summer getting my room ready for the first days of school. But the full realization of the responsibility didn't hit me until I saw the first children come into the room—my room—*our* room.

I fervently hope that I will never again live through a day like the first day of school. The children were quite well behaved (I suppose the novelty of returning to school), and I had prepared an excess of material for them, just in case. I had enough for two days—so I thought! By noon, I had used up everything I had planned for the first day. They worked so much more quickly than I ever imagined! By lunch time I was rattled. What to do? That afternoon I used up the next day's lessons!

Another horrible feeling of incompetence came when I realized that I had to put these children into reading groups. How many *is* a group? Grouping had been talked about in my undergraduate reading course, but I now realized I really didn't have a well-defined idea of how to go about it.

I gave all the children the IRI that accompanies the series. It wasn't easy to get it done because the other children were so noisy and interrupted me so often. I think also that it was too much to try to do it all in two days. Next year (if I am alive and teaching!), I will spread it out across a week so that the children have to work independently for only a little while.

By the time of the parent meeting, I did have my groups formed, though that had not been as easy as I felt it would be. Larry gives every indication of being an extremely bright child, yet when I was scoring his IRI, I was amazed at the number of errors he made in oral reading. Instead of "He could not get the car to start," Larry read, "He couldn't get the car started." Yet with all of those errors, his comprehension remained high! As a matter of fact, he did amazingly well, answering every question correctly and completely. I put him into the middle group anyway, because the requirements for the IRI include both oral reading and comprehension. But he is clearly the best reader in the class. I think I will move him to the top group and see how he does.

Daisy and Mike didn't really meet the 95 percent oral reading accuracy criterion for the first-grade book that I am planning to use with my low group, but I didn't think I could manage another group so I put them there. Paul wouldn't read for me! I pleaded, threatened, and bribed, but he just sat there. I put him in the lowest group, but I don't know where he belongs. He won't read aloud or do his workbook. He is not mean and behaves; he just won't do anything. I must ask Mrs. Wright about him.

Once I had the children assigned to reading groups, I let them choose a group name. For some of the groups this took a long time, but eventually all three groups were named. The top group (all girls until I move Larry in) chose to be butterflies. The middle group are astronauts, and the bottom group (all boys except for Daisy) chose monsters. I tried to get them to change the name, but Mike, the leader in the group, said I told them they could choose and they chose monsters. I just hope that no one thinks that *I* named them! (They certainly chose a descriptive name!)

I work with each group for 30 minutes. They spend the time they are not with me working on their worksheets at their desks or completing the activities I have put in the centers. At least, that is what they are supposed to do! Many of them are just not independent workers. They wander around the room and fool around. Daisy draws pictures. Paul just sits and stares, except when he is crying because Butch and Mike are picking on him. Even Roberta, who is very smart, often doesn't get her work done. I don't know what to do about this. I try to make sure they have plenty to do, and I have kept the ones who didn't have their work in the "done" box in for recess a few days. But I don't think I am supposed to do this—they need fresh air and exercise. I also don't get any break at all when I keep them here, because I can't go off and leave this crew alone! I asked them if they behaved this way for Mrs. Wright last year and was informed by Mike and Butch that Mrs. Wright didn't give them all this dumb boring work to do!

I am also having problems getting it all graded and back to them to take home on Friday. Last Thursday, I ended up throwing one set of papers away in my home trashcan because I just had to go to bed and I couldn't send them home ungraded. So far, no one seems to have missed it. Creating work to keep them busy at their desks and in centers so that I can work with groups and getting them to do it and getting it graded is the biggest problem I have and is consuming most of my time and energy. There must be a better way, but I can't figure out what it is. I will have to ask someone—but I hate to admit I am having trouble with something that should be so simple.

Except for reading-group time, the rest of the day goes relatively smoothly. When I am right there with them during math, science, and social studies, they behave pretty well, and I even have taught some pretty good lessons. They and I enjoy the reading aloud I do right after lunch every day, and they are settling down pretty well with their books for Self-Selected Reading. Even Paul seems to enjoy looking at the books, and Mike is happy if he can have books with monsters in them. I have been reading as they read—to provide a good model—but now that they are in the habit of reading, I think I might take that time to grade some of that morning's papers.

October

If only I can survive until January! I student taught during the winter last year, and if we can only get to January, I'll know what to do. Why did everything look so easy when my supervising teacher did it? Either I am doing something wrong, or else I have a really rough group of children. I always wanted to teach second grade because the children are still so cute and they already know how to read. That seemed like the perfect grade to me, but how different it really is. Some of them can hardly read, and some of them are definitely not in the "cute" category.

This class makes me wonder about the first-grade experience that they had. Whenever I walk by Mrs. Wright's classroom, it *appears* that she has good discipline, but I wonder if she does really. If she had good control of her class, how could a class like this one be giving me so much trouble? I know that Mrs. Wright is an excellent teacher—listening to the reading of Pat and Rita convinces me of that—but perhaps she is just not a disciplinarian. Well, whatever the reason, I've really had to crack down on these kids. I had to close the centers because they were just going from place to place and not getting their assignments done there. Now, I have to find twice as much to keep them busy at their seats. I have put a handwriting assignment on the board for them to copy, but some of them finish it in no time and others just "slop it out" or don't do it. I have also given them some dot-to-dot sheets to complete and color. They seem to like these, but I worry about what they are learning from this. All of them already know their numbers in order, and I know that coloring doesn't make you a better reader. The worksheets that I give them with their reader are on their level, except for Paul, Daisy, and Mike, who probably can't read them, and Larry, Pat, and Hilda, for whom they are much too easy. But the other assignments that I have to give everyone to keep them busy now that centers are closed are a real problem. I know that the seatwork should require reading and writing if it is going to move them along in reading and writing, but what can I give everyone when they range from Paul to Larry?

Even Self-Selected Reading is not going as well as it did. The children are still attentive and seem to enjoy it when I read to them. This month, I read them several informational books by Gail Gibbons, *Halloween* and *The Reasons for Seasons*, which tie into our unit on seasons and holidays. They also enjoyed *Spider Storch's Teacher Torture*, an easy but funny chapter book. Some of the children are settling in well during Self-Selected Reading, but others, particularly the struggling readers along with Roberta and Mitch, are talking, fooling around, passing notes, and generally not reading. I hope it is not because I quit modeling reading and started grading papers, but I fear it may be. I may be giving them too long to read now—15 minutes seems like an eternity to my children who don't like to read.

Mr. Topps came in to observe me this month for his first formal observation. He let me choose what I wanted him to observe, and of course, I chose math. We do math first thing in the morning, and I am always prepared and ready to go. The children are quite attentive then, too, and I am a good math teacher, if I do say so myself. I began my lesson with some real-world mental math problems. Then we reviewed addition facts with a fast-paced fun game, and then they worked with partners, using manipulatives to solve some regrouping problems. We then checked our work together to end the lesson.

The good news was that Mr. Topps was most impressed and wrote me a wonderful evaluation. The bad news was that he wants to observe reading—my worst subject! I think I will have him observe a lesson with the butterflies, since they read well. I just have to make the others behave. Perhaps they will if he is here.

November

So much has changed this month that I don't know quite where to begin. Mr. Topps came as scheduled and observed me during reading time. I had promised the class a special popcorn party if they were all working quietly when he was there. (I felt guilty about this, but I was desperate to have things go well!) I began my lesson with the butterflies by building prior knowledge and introducing vocabulary, and then I had them take turns reading the pages aloud. They read quite well, and after each child read, I asked the others some questions to make sure they were comprehending. It took a long time to read the story, and the children who had already read got restless at the end, but comparatively, the lesson went well and the children at their seats behaved. (I didn't know whether to feel good or bad about that, since it does prove they can sit and do their work when they want to.) At the end of the lesson, Mr. Topps said he had enjoyed being here and asked me to meet with him that afternoon to talk about the lesson.

He left and the class exploded! Mike was shouting and Daisy was running around yelling. "Popcorn, popcorn, bring out the popcorn!" I was appalled. I didn't even want to give them the popcorn, but they had done what I asked, so I knew I had to. That afternoon, while we were all eating popcorn, Mr. Topps came back! "Mr. Topps," said Roberta, "come help us eat the popcorn we earned by behaving while you were watching Miss Nouveau teach!" Mr. Topps looked surprised for just a moment and then smiled and graciously accepted the popcorn offer. I wanted to disappear! I can't ever remember having been that mortified!

When the children left, Mr. Topps consoled me. "You aren't the first teacher who has ever promised the children a reward for good behavior," he assured me. "Now, let's forget about your bribe and focus on why you felt you had to make it. Your math lesson went wonderfully. Did you bribe them for that one too?" I cringed at the word "bribe" but I knew that was what I had done.

"Oh, no," I replied, "I am a good math teacher—and pretty good at science and social studies too. It is just reading that is so awful." Now that my guard was down, I poured out my soul to him. I told him how I had closed the centers and how I had to give them things to keep them busy that I knew were not helping them be better readers and writers and how Paul, Daisy, and Mike belonged in their own group and I couldn't possibly do another group. By the time I got around to telling him about how even Self-Selected Reading was falling apart, I was in tears.

Mr. Topps handed me his handkerchief (he is such an old-fashioned man in many ways), and after I had cried it all out, I felt much better. He then explained that reading is the hardest subject to make multilevel, and that what to do with the ones your aren't working with so that you can work with groups is the hardest management problem most teachers face.

"Let's not try to solve every problem right now, but let's begin with the easy ones—your centers and Self-Selected Reading. Tomorrow, I want you to observe Mrs. Wright during her Self-Selected Reading time and center time. I will come and teach your class for you while you do this, and then we will talk again."

At 1:30 promptly the next day, Mr. Topps took over my class and I went next door to observe the "venerable" Mrs. Wright. She read aloud to the children for about 15 minutes. After reminding them that it was the Tuesday people's day to conference with her, she dismissed them to their reading. I noticed that they had crates of books on their tables, and that they all went eagerly to read. I went around and listened in on the children reading, and although some were picture reading and others were pretending they could read the book, most were actually reading the words and doing a remarkably good job. I also observed what Mrs. Wright did. She spent only two minutes with each child, but the children seemed to know just what to do, and they got a lot done in the two minutes. "This is certainly a more responsible bunch than the bunch she sent me," I thought.

At 2:00, Mrs. Wright prepared the children to go home, and then children went to the centers. She dismissed them to centers by their "days of the week." The Tuesday children picked a center first and slotted their card into that center. Next, the Wednesday people picked, Thursday people, etc. Each center had a limit on how many children could go there, so the Friday and Monday people didn't get their first choice, but I see how they wouldn't mind because they would pick first on their day. "Ingenious," I thought and vowed then and there to have my children designated by days of the week by tomorrow.

As the children were working in centers, I noticed Mrs. Wright reading some very easy books individually for 10 minutes each with two of the children I had noticed were not yet reading many words during the Self-Selected Reading time. She accomplished a great deal in that 10 minutes alone with each child, and I realized that was what Paul, Daisy, and Mike needed. "But where could I find the 10 minutes?"

I also noticed something else about the centers. The things the children were doing there were not anything Mrs. Wright had to check or grade. Children were painting and drawing in the Art center, listening to books on tape in the Listening Center, writing or enjoying an animated book in the Computer Center, watching and playing with George the gerbil, Tom the turtle, and Louise the lizard in the Pet Center. The children were talking, but they were using quiet voices instead of yelling like mine do. Once, when things got a little rowdy, Mrs. Wright informed two boys that they were on warning and would have to return to their desks if she saw any more "roughhousing."

After the children left, I was so excited and had so many questions for her that I forgot all about Mr. Topps in my room and stayed talking to Mrs. Wright. He came into her room, however, and we all three had a good talk.

I stayed until almost midnight, getting ready for the next day. When the children arrived, they found "transformed" centers. No more activities in each center to complete and put in the done box, but more open-ended activities that allowed the children to explore and didn't require grading! I sat down with them, and we had a heart-to-heart talk. I told them about all the things I had seen in Mrs. Wright's room. They all joined in and told me about how they got to pick first on their day and how it was their job to prepare for their conference by picking two pages to read to Mrs. Wright and tell here why they chose the book. They talked about their favorite centers, and Daisy explained that you had to use a quiet voice and not bother other people or you lost your place in the art center and had to sit at your desk while someone else painted at your easel!

I then bragged on them, telling them all the good things Mrs. Wright had told me they had learned to do. "I am sorry I didn't know you were grown up enough to prepare for conferences or work independently on what you chose to do in centers," I explained. "But now I know, and there are going to be some changes here. Next, I showed them a chart on which I had listed their days. I followed Mrs. Wright's suggestions about spreading out the rowdy ones and the strugglers so they didn't all clump up on one day. Here is the chart I worked out:

MONDAY	TUESDAY	WEDNESDAY	THURSDAY	FRIDAY
Mike	Daisy	Paul	Butch	Alexander
Chip	Horace	Daphne	Betty	Mort
Steve	Alex	Jeff	Manuel	Mandy
Mitch	Larry	Anthony	Joyce	Pat
Rita	Hilda	Roberta	Danielle	Carl

"We are going to have our center time for 30 minutes while I am working with groups," I explained. "Astronauts will go to centers for the first 30 minutes, while butterflies do their work to prepare to meet with me and I meet with monsters." (Why did I let them choose their name? I cringe every time I say that!) I then let Daphne, Jeff, and Anthony, the Wednesday astronauts, have first pick of centers—followed by Manuel and Joyce, the Thursday astronauts, and then the others. They took their card and slotted into their desired center, and I let them go to their centers. I then took a few minutes to explain the seatwork the butterflies needed to do during this first half hour. "Your center time is next," I explained. "I will collect your work as you choose your centers. It doesn't have to be perfect, but it does have to show that you tried if you are going to get to go to centers."

With the astronauts in centers and the butterflies working at their desks, I sat down with Paul's group. ("They might call themselves monsters," I thought, "but I don't have to!") I did my lesson with them, and then I showed them what they needed to do in the next 30 minutes to earn their center time. "I will collect your work before you go to centers," I explained. "It doesn't have to be perfect, but you do have to work quietly and show that you are making a good effort."

I then dismissed Paul's group to their desks, helped the astronauts get the centers ready for the next group, and let the butterflies pick their center—by days of the week and after handing me their morning work, which I looked at just enough to see there was something there that showed some effort! Amazingly, everyone—even Roberta—had their work and it was all "acceptably" done. "This might really work," I began to think.

As the butterflies worked in the centers and Paul's group worked at their desks, I began my lesson with the astronauts. Mr. Topps had told me that there was no reason to have my middle or top group read the whole selection aloud while they were with me.

"Do your before-reading set-up just as you have been doing, then read the first two pages to them to get them into the selection, and then send them to their seats to finish reading it. Give them a short writing assignment that goes along with your purpose—just a few sentences—to complete and bring back the following day. On the second day, after they have read it silently, you can let them do some oral reading—but not the whole selection—just a few sentences or a paragraph on each page to read specific things you ask them to read for. Then assign them their workbook activities to do in preparation for group on the third day."

I dismissed the astronauts to their work, helped the butterflies put their centers back in order, and then called Paul's group for their center time. Amazingly, everyone—even Mike, Daisy, and Paul—appeared to have made an effort to do their work. I let them choose their centers and met with the astronauts. Once again, I did the prereading activities with them—introduced vocabulary, looked at all the pictures and made predictions, read the first two pages to them, and let them know the purpose for reading the selection by telling them what they would do tomorrow when they came back to talk about and reread parts of the selection orally.

So far, this is working quite well. I was afraid the children would get back into their bad behaviors after the novelty wore off, but for the most part, they seem to really want to go to the centers they choose. Daisy, especially, is putting much more effort into her work. That girl loves to paint and is quite an artist! I have had to withhold center privileges one day for Roberta, Mitch, Alexander, and Butch, and two days for Mort and Mike, but most days, they do their work with an acceptable effort and behave well enough that they earn their center time.

I am also checking their work with them when they come to group, now that I don't have to spend all that time sitting and listening to them read the whole selection aloud. I still worry that they may not be reading it all, but they do seem to, and they are able to do the comprehension and activities I have them do, so I guess I do not have to hear everyone read aloud every day. I am still reading the selection with Paul's group, but I am having them do some echo reading and choral reading so that they all get more reading practice. I have not found a time to work with Paul, Daisy, and Mike individually, but I know that is what they need, so I am going to look again at my schedule and see what I can come up with.

I moved Self-Selected Reading time back to 10 minutes and began conferencing with them on their day, just as Mrs. Wright does. It is amazing how much of a difference this makes. Mike still has trouble settling in, so I have given him his own crate of books and sat him at the table with me while I conference. He spends more time listening to my conferences with the children than he does reading, but he does read some, and he is not acting up and ruining things for everyone.

December

I have tried, up to this point, to write in my journal at the end of each week so that I could keep up with what was happening, but since my chat with Mr. Topps, so many things have been happening that the weeks rushed by until the holidays gave me a chance to sit down at home and continue my journal. I am so excited by the changes that I have made and the ones I am going to make!

After my afternoon visit to Mrs. Wright helped me so much, Mr. Topps hired a sub for me so that I could spend a full day this month in Mrs. Wright's classroom and another full day with Mrs. Wise. Was that ever enlightening! I saw how Mrs. Wright made her guided-reading block multilevel by reading two selections each week and by using various partnerships to support children. Mrs. Wise makes hers multilevel by choosing books on different levels tied together by topic, author, or genre. I might try one of those ways next year, but for now I think I need to stick with my groups. The problem, of course, is that it takes 90 minutes for me to meet with all three groups, and I don't have time to do writing or a word wall. I could see in both classrooms how important the writing was and how the word wall supports that writing, so I made up my mind to look at my schedule and see how I could possibly fit them in.

After my visits, Sue Port came to visit. She is the reading supervisor for the system, and I knew her from our new-teacher orientation. She visited during reading, and was I ever glad that things were going better than they had earlier. That afternoon, we had a conference and she commented on how "organized" and efficient everything was and how all the children seemed "happily engaged." I thanked her and told her that things were better and that Mrs. Wright and Mr.

Topps had been my saviors. I told her, however, about wanting to find 10 minutes each day to do a word wall and 30 minutes for a daily writing time, but I still thought I had to meet my reading groups every day—particularly now that they were going more smoothly.

"Let's see your current schedule," she said. "There must be a way!" Together, we looked at my schedule and decided that if I cut math from 60 minutes to 45 minutes and cut my unit time back to 50 minutes, I could find the 40 minutes I needed.

"I think 45 minutes for math in second grade is enough," Miss Port mused, "but you need more time for science and social studies. What if you met with your groups on four days and took Friday mornings for some intensive work on your science or social studies unit?"

"That would be all right for my butterflies," I responded. "They do the first reading at their seats now, and that is saving a lot of group time for the word and comprehension lessons they need. Maybe I could get done what I need to with the astronauts—particularly if I did word wall every day to work with the high-frequency words and I didn't have to worry about that during group time. But Paul's group needs all the teaching they can get. I am reading two selections every week with their group now—one at the level of Carl, Chip, Butch, and Alexander and a second easier one that is on level for Daisy and Mike and Paul when he is having an alert day. I can't possibly get it all done with them in four days!"

We talked some more and decided that on Friday, I would do a whole-class listening comprehension or writing lesson on something related to our unit topic. Then I would give the butterflies and astronauts something to work on—a web or other graphic organizer to complete—something to write—or a similar follow-up activity while I met with Paul's group. I could then meet back with everyone together again and follow up what the children had worked on.

"That would give you back your 90 minutes of science or social studies time, and you could still work with Paul's group every day."

"You're a genius," I said as I practically hugged her. "I don't know why I couldn't have thought of that. I used to think of myself as a creative problem solver, but this year, I just can't see beyond my nose."

"Well, my dear," Ms. Port replied, "when we are under a lot of pressure and feeling anxious, we just don't think very well. That is often the sad dilemma of the beginning teacher. That's why you need people like Mr. Topps and Mrs. Wright—and me—to help you think through these problems. In a few years, you will be the expert helping another beginning teacher solve the inevitable first-year problems."

"Now, the biggest problem I have is finding time to read with Paul, Daisy, and Mike," I told her. "I conference with them during Self-Selected Reading, and I am including a selection for their group every week that is closer to their instructional level, but if I could sit down with them for 10 minutes a day and coach them individually in material on their level, I could really move them. The year is half over, and as much as I hate to admit it, they haven't moved very far in their reading."

"You mean, we need to find another 30 minutes?" she responded. "Well, let's look again at your schedule. The children come back from specials and get ready to go home. What do you do between 2:45 and 3:00 when different children are leaving on the buses?"

"The children are finishing up work or something in one of the centers. I guess I could work with one of them then but not all three. I could take turns, but then they would only get 10 minutes every third day, and I don't believe that will be enough."

As I was saying this, I was picturing Roberta and Betty leaving at 3:00 every day when the car riders were dismissed. I remembered that it was their mother, Mrs. Penn, who had told me that she was a teacher and volunteered to help at our original parent meeting. (I also remembered my cavalier "Thanks but no thanks" response. Could I have been so naïve that I thought I wouldn't need help, or was I just afraid that she would know more than I did?)

"I have an idea," I said. I then told Ms. Port about Mrs. Penn's offer. "If she is driving over to pick the twins up anyway, maybe she would come 20 minutes early. I could work with one of them every third day, and she could work with them on the two intervening days, and they would get 10 minutes of individual help every day."

"Brilliant!" responded Sue. "Let's go and call her right now."

We did, and she said she would be delighted to help, and we made plans to begin as soon as school resumed in January. Here is the schedule I will be following from the first day back in January.

I was quite eager for the holidays to begin! Not, as originally, so that I could escape from here, but so that I could have some uninterrupted time to plan how I would begin the new year. I want to work out the specifics of my new schedule and look through the books I got at the faculty Christmas party. Each teacher was to bring an "idea" book for another teacher. Mrs. Wise drew my name, and she gave me an excellent book that explains how to do story drama to improve listening and reading comprehension and one on writing. I also got two unexpected presents. Mrs. Wright gave me a timer. She says it is her most valuable teaching resource. I can see why she says that, having watched her teach. Mr. Topps also gave me an unexpected gift—a copy of the latest best-seller. "This book is totally worthless," he announced, "and your homework over the break is to relax and not think about school long enough to read this." Never in my wildest dreams did I think I would ever have a principal like Mr. Topps! This is what he wrote in his Christmas card:

> Dear Norma,
>
> As you take a well-deserved rest, I just wanted to tell you how glad we are that you have joined our faculty this year. I know you are discouraged at times, but almost all new teachers have a similar experience. Teaching is at once the most challenging and most rewarding profession there is. I appreciate your willingness to take counsel and to try suggestions. You have improved so much in how you teach reading that teachers with many years' experience could benefit from watching you!
>
> Merry Christmas!
> Tip Topps

Maybe, just maybe, I'm going to be a good teacher someday after all!

	Monday	Tuesday	Wednesday	Thursday	Friday
8:30–8:50	Group Meeting and Planning for the Day				
8:50–9:00	Word Wall				
9:00–9:30	Writing				
9:30–10:00	Paul's Group Astronauts-Centers Butterflies-Seatwork	Same as Monday	Same as Monday	Same as Monday	Science or SS Unit Comprehension or Writing Lesson
10:00–10:30	Astronauts Butterflies-Centers Paul's Group -Seatwork	Same as Monday	Same as Monday	Same as Monday	Children work on Unit Topic while I meet with Paul's group.
10:30–10:50	Break/Recess				
10:50–11:20	Butterflies Paul's Group -Centers Astronauts-Seatwork	Same as Monday	Same as Monday	Same as Monday	Science or SS Unit Follow-up
11:20–12:05	Math				
12:05–12:40	Lunch				
12:40–1:10	Teacher Read-Aloud Self-Selected Reading				
1:10–2:00	Science or Social Studies Unit				
2:00–2:30	P. E.	Music	P. E.	Art	P. E.
2:30–2:45/3:00	Children prepare to go home, finish up work and things in centers. Mrs. Penn and I work 10 minutes each with Mike, Paul, and Daisy				

January

I always thought that if I could survive until January, I could make it. This turns out to be true but not for the reasons I had thought. I student taught last year starting in January, and I figured when I got to January, I could pull out my student-teaching lesson plans. I did pull them out, but they weren't very relevant to this class. Many of my children read much better than the children in the class in which I student taught, and then there are always Mike, Paul, and Daisy! Besides, the children in my student-teaching classroom had had an excellent teacher prior to January, and these children have had me. I'm getting better, however. Those visits to Mrs. Wright's and Mrs. Wise's classrooms and my several long chats with Mr. Topps and Ms. Port have really helped. I now have a new schedule that I have posted, and each morning, first thing, the children and I look at the schedule and decide who is going to be where doing what when. I couldn't possibly keep on schedule, however, were it not for the timer Mrs. Wright gave me for Christmas. I carry it around with me and use it to keep my groups to 25 minutes, to see who can get their old places cleaned up and get to their new places in the 5-minute transition time, and to time Self-Selected Reading and snack time. It is so much a part of me, I feel as if I am missing something when I leave for home and do not have it in my hand.

I have begun letting the middle and top groups work on their workbook pages in partners—two children working together to come up with their best responses. We then go over these responses together when they come to the group. During reading group, we check the pages and analyze why an answer is right or wrong. I also have them explain the reasoning behind their answers. It helps children who haven't understood something to hear the thinking of others who came up with the right answer. Usually, I let each child choose a workbook partner—or choose to work alone. I stress that I am letting them work together because "two heads are better than one." Consequently, I expect to see better—more thorough and thoughtful—responses when they put two of their brilliant heads together. When I see sloppy, "thrown together" work or when I look up and see the partners not working well or quietly, I withdraw their partner privilege. I have had to do this several times with Roberta and Hilda and with Mitch and Jeff. They do not appreciate being sent to their desks to work alone while many of the others are working together, but they do understand why they have lost the privilege. With both the centers and the partners, I have to be consistent in expecting good behavior and withdrawing privileges to make them work.

I would like the children in Paul's group to work with partners, but they are all so difficult to get along with. I guess I could try and at least give them a chance. Even if two of them could partner up and work well and quietly, they would help each other, and those two would learn more. I am going to give it a try and see what happens!

Once in a while, I have children come to the reading group who I suspect haven't read the selection. I try to encourage them to do it, and I don't let them participate in our group's activities if they indicate by their responses to comprehension questions or in oral reading that they haven't read the story silently.

Last week, I had to send Roberta to her seat during group time to read a story she hadn't read. When I questioned her about it, she protested, "It was a dumb sissie story." I told her I was sorry she didn't like it but that she had a responsibility to come prepared. I then sent her to her seat to read the story while I did some story dramatization with her group. Roberta, who loves to act in stories, was furious, but she hasn't come to reading group unprepared since. I have also had some trouble with Alex's not reading the selections, and I have had him sit with me in the group area while I meet with Paul's group and read the selection there. He is very unhappy about this, especially since the rest of his group is having center time.

We have increased our Self-Selected Reading time to 12 minutes. I am continuing to conference with the children and am amazed at how much I can learn about their reading interests and strategies in just two to three minutes. The children all seem to enjoy the conference, and I enjoy the little bit of individual time I have with each of them. I now know that Rita, Pat, Larry, and Hilda can read well above the level of the book I have their group in. Mr. Topps says I shouldn't worry about this because they will get their instructional-level reading during Self-Selected Reading time and they get comprehension instruction and knowledge building from my guided reading instruction.

"One of the major reasons we insist on having daily Self-Selected Reading time in every classroom is to make sure that every child has time each day to read material they choose that is on their level. If you look only at what you are doing during guided reading, you can't meet the needs of every child, but if you consider all the reading and writing they do, you can," Mr. Topps explained with certainty and passion.

One afternoon, when I was talking with Mrs. Wise, I ended up telling her my latest "Mike story." She said that after hearing about Mike all year, she was considering retiring a year early so that she wouldn't have to spend her last teaching year with Mike! I was horrified to think that someone like Mrs. Wise would worry about discipline and told her so. She responded, "You are going to worry about discipline for as long as you teach. I have to run out early this afternoon and haven't helped you much with your problems. Why don't you come over and have dinner with me tomorrow night. We can have a long, uninterrupted chat then." Of course I accepted. We had a lovely, relaxed dinner during which she steered me away from school topics whenever I brought them up. As we were stacking the dishes, she told me that she knew I wanted to discuss school but that her own philosophy of life prevented her from doing so. "We live with school so much of our lives as it is that I force myself to forget it, or at least not discuss it, during dinner. There are so many disturbing things about school that they can ruin your digestion!"

I could hardly believe that this woman with all those years of teaching experience could still have troubles in school! That made me feel better.

After dinner, though, we did talk. I was getting ready to do some publishing with the children and couldn't figure out how to organize it. I had seen children publishing in her room, but they were in all different stages and I couldn't figure out how they knew what to do. She explained her system to me.

"I have a list for the children to sign up on when they have three good first drafts. Good is a relative term, but I do quickly glance at their three pieces to make sure they have made a good effort (for them) on all three. I then form a cooperative revising group of all the children ready to publish. Each child reads his or her piece to the group and calls on group members to suggest ways to make it better. I act as recorder, writing down the suggestions for each writer. Next, the children go off to make whatever revisions they think are needed. When they have done this, they pick a friend to help them edit for the things on the checklist. Then they come to me for a final editing, before going off to publish the final draft. This works well for most of the children. I give more help to my struggling writers, often telling them I will be their friend to help them do the first editing because their piece often needs more than any of my children could handle."

"I can see that this takes a lot of structure organizing, and independence. Do you think my children are mature enough to handle that?" I asked.

"I'm not sure, but you could also try Mrs. Wright's system. I think she works with a third of the class each week to revise a piece—dividing the struggling writers and advanced writers among the thirds. Your children were used to that from last year, so perhaps that is the way for you to go. Mrs. Wright should be starting her publishing cycles about now. Ask her to tell you exactly how she does it and then pick the one that seems right for you."

We talked about discipline, too, and particularly about Mike. Mrs. Wise seems to think I am handling him about as well as he can be handled. "Make sure he knows the rules. Withdraw privileges as necessary. Keep giving him chances to be responsible and show him he will not get the best of you," she advised. "Some children are difficult, and we must continue to be firm and fair with them. No system will work for everyone, but it sounds as if what you are doing is working quite well for most of your children most of the time. You are having a good year for a first-year teacher."

As I was trying to absorb the fact that Mrs. Wise seemed to have such faith in me, the doorbell rang. Mrs. Wise went to answer it and I gathered up my things. Mrs. Wise then returned with her neighbor, a new doctoral student at the university. She introduced me to Horatio Flame, who said, "Just call me Red." We chatted for quite a while and I got home much later than I usually do on a school night. As I was driving home ,I realized that we had talked for over an hour about things other than teaching. What a wonderful feeling! Red seems like a really nice guy. I wonder why he just happened to drop in like that. Surely, it was just a coincidence that he came while I was there.

February

This month, I read them *Miss Nelson Is Missing* and *Miss Nelson Is Back* by Harry Allard. After reading the books, we discussed them, and I had to admit to feeling like Miss Nelson sometimes. "I wonder if there is a Viola Swamp living anywhere in this area," I mused aloud. "Don't get any ideas, Miss Nouveau," Horace pleaded. "We're being much better than we were! Aren't we?" Carl asked. "There aren't really mean teachers like Viola Swamp," Roberta declared.

The book clearly made an impression on them, and I have been tempted to buy a black wig! Rita found another Miss Nelson book—*Miss Nelson Has a Field Day*—at the public library and brought it in to read. Many of the children are now reading the Miss Nelson books on their own during Self-Selected Reading time.

At 8:50, we do our daily words on the wall practice. I do it exactly the way I saw Mrs. Wright doing it. Each Monday, I add five new words. I choose the words by looking for the words they commonly misspell in their writing. Each day, I call out five of the words from the wall, and they chant them and then write them. I have them check the words themselves, just like Mrs. Wright, but some—Butch, Mike, Mort, Alexander, Daisy—don't check them very carefully. "It doesn't matter," I heard Mort say. "She doesn't grade them." I have told them that not everything needs a grade, but a few of them won't put forth the effort required unless there is some consequence, a grade or a withdrawal of privilege.

It was Red (who knows nothing about teaching, thank goodness) who came up with the brilliant idea. "Why not have five checkers in a box," he suggested one night as I was telling him my problem while he was, as usual, whomping me at checkers, "four red ones and one black one. When the children have finished and exchanged and checked their words, let one child close her eyes and pick a checker. If a red checker comes out, this was only for practice. If the black one comes out, however, this was 'the real thing' and you can collect them, verify that they are correctly checked, and record them in your grade book." I told Red he would be a wonderful teacher, he is so creative, but he declares he hasn't "the stomach for it."

At any rate, we now use his checkers system. It is super! All the children, including Mike, put forth their best efforts each day because they never know when it will count. They love to have the black checker come out because, if they try, they can do well and they want the perfect score. I am going to try this system during math when we practice addition and subtraction facts. Each day, we will have a five-minute timed practice, check papers, and then see if it counts or not by having a blindfolded child select a checker. This will give the children the practice they need without putting an impossible grading burden on me.

Our morning writing time is one of the best parts of our day. I asked my children about the books they published last year, and the next day, many of them proudly brought in their books to show me. Even Paul, who rarely brings anything from or says anything about home, brought three books he had published. He even read them to me, with fluency and confidence! That afternoon, I asked Mrs. Wright how children like Paul could write books, and she explained about how she divided the class into thirds for publishing purposes and put one of the three lowest children in each third. She then explained how she did the editing and publishing and how she let Paul tell her what he meant to write and she wrote it for him to copy into his book. I am beginning to understand why everyone thinks Mrs. Wright is such a savvy lady.

I have gotten all the children to bring in writing notebooks, and we are writing each day. I do a minilesson as Mrs. Wright does and try to write about varied topics. Mike was the one who asked me to write a "When I Was Your Age" tale. When I admitted that I didn't know what that was, the class was amazed. They told me all about when Mrs. Wright was in the first grade, how she liked to dress up as a fairy princess at Halloween, and about her boyfriend in first grade. I must have looked a bit incredulous because Betty quickly explained that Mrs. Wright never really told them if the tales were all true or some were made up. Harriet volunteered that if they were true, Mrs. Wright was writing part of her autobiography. The children all nodded, and I was once again amazed at how much they knew.

So I wrote my first "When I Was Your Age" tale!

When I was in the second grade, I loved school. My teacher's name was Mrs. Hope, and I thought she was the most beautiful lady in the world. I only got in trouble once, and that was when Billy Higginbopper kept teasing me because I was so tall and skinny and had so many freckles. I didn't mean to knock him down, but I was so mad. When he fell, he hurt his arm and had to go to the hospital. It was a terrible, no good, very bad day!

"Is that really true?" they all asked, when I had finished. I just smiled and sent them off to do their writing.

We have begun the Editor's Checklist again. Mrs. Wright suggested that I add the items to check for gradually and remind the children to read their papers for each thing when their writing time was up. We have the first three items that they learned last year, and I will add the final review item next month. I will try to add a few new ones before the end of the year.

We have just begun publishing, and I hope that by the end of the year, the children will all have a couple of books they wrote in second grade to add to their first-grade collection. I am so grateful to Mr. Topps for arranging for my visits to Mrs. Wright and Mrs. Wise. I can't imagine that all that "know-how" was right here in this very building and I might never have realized it!

March

We had parent-teacher conferences early in March. Everyone except Paul and Jeff had a parent or other relative come. I was so much more at ease because I knew I was doing a better job. I wasn't on the defensive waiting for them to ask me something I didn't know or expecting them to attack me for something I wasn't doing. Rather, I was relaxed (relatively!) and we had good conversations about their children. Most of the parents expressed their pleasure at what I was doing with their children. I think this may have been a reflection of how relieved they were that things have gotten much better as the year has gone on. Mike's mother is quite worried about him and says she can hardly handle him at home. I told her that he is making some progress and seems to be able to learn when he settles down long enough. I suggested that she read some easy-to-read books at home with Mike each night and let him chime in when he knows a word. She said she would try but that she practically had to "rope" him to get him settled down long enough to eat, never mind anything else. When she left, I thought, "I shall be more patient with Mike. I imagine that that woman must deal with his energy for as many waking hours as I do each day, and all day on Saturdays, Sundays, and holidays."

Many parents expressed their pleasure with the writing their children were doing. Mandy's mother declared that Mandy has decided to become a writer and keeps a writing notebook at home in which she writes faithfully. She told me that the children liked writing each day and especially like my pulling the popsicle sticks out of the hat to see which children get to read their stories. (This was Red's solution to the problem of everyone wanting to read and not enough time.) When the timer signals the end of the 15-minute writing time, the children who wish to read their piece put the popsicle stick with their name on it in a special container. I pull the popsicle sticks out and those children whose names come out get to read their pieces. The children love the drama of wondering whose stick will come out and are very good listeners because they know we will get to pull more sticks in the allotted time if I don't have to interrupt constantly and ask them to be good listeners.

Thanks to Ms. Port, I have now learned how to get Paul's group to read silently. When I called her a month or so ago and told her that the silent reading just wouldn't work for my six poorest readers, she told me she would get back to me. One day a few weeks later, she arrived at my room after school and taught me how to teach a comprehension strategy lesson. Students like Mike, Daisy, and Paul have to have a very particular kind of comprehension lesson if they are to learn how to read silently with understanding.

She went on to explain the seven steps of a comprehension strategy lesson and gave lots of examples so I could plan and teach one myself. She suggested that I try it with my top two groups first before using it with my bottom two groups. "They will like and profit from it, too," she said.

Even the first comprehension strategy lesson I taught to Paul's group went surprisingly well. The third one was truly wonderful. It went like this. I started out by introducing the strategy I was going to teach to them that day (Step 1). I had chosen to teach them *to follow the sequence of a story.* Remembering some warnings that Ms. Port had given, I did not rush this introduction. We spent enough time here for the students to connect with the concept of *story sequence.* I told them that most stories would be hard to understand and impossible to enjoy if we confused the order in which the main actions take place. Their faces revealed that my telling had failed to impress them. So I told them the story of "The Three Billy Goats Gruff." I had the biggest billy goat cross the bridge first and kill the troll; then I had the middle billy goat start to cross the bridge. Daisy seemed to wake up. "No, no, Miss Nouveau, that's not right. You can't have the biggest billy goat cross first! That messes up the whole story."

Then I started to tell them the story of "The Three Bears." When I started out with the part where the bears returned home to find their house in disarray, everyone protested. I had prepared sentence strips, each of which had a major event from the story. I laid them out in front of Paul's group on the table and let them take turns organizing the strips into the right order. Even Paul took a turn, although Daisy tried to tell him what to do at each decision point. I put a stop to that. They were all able to organize correctly the events of this simple, familiar story. I then told them again how important getting things in the right order was to understanding and enjoying a story. They were with me now. I told them that as stories get harder, it gets more difficult to figure out which things happen first, next, and last. I told them that grown-ups who are good readers follow or monitor the order in which actions happen in a story, and if they become confused about the order, they reread and think until their confusion is ended. I told them that I wanted them to learn to follow the order in which things happen in every story they read or hear.

I then attempted to prepare them to understand the particular story I had chosen to use with them to teach them the comprehension strategy of following story sequence (Step 2). The story was in the easier book that I use with Paul's group. It is a modern retelling of the Aesop's fable "The Wind and the Sun." To complete this step, I followed the teacher's manual suggestions for teaching general background knowledge and specific passage vocabulary. These suggestions helped the students to call up what they already knew, as well as to learn new background information.

Following Step 2, I set a purpose for reading that clearly reflected the comprehension strategy I was teaching (Step 3). Before the lesson, I had determined what I thought were the five major events of "The Wind and the Sun":

> The wind blew the boy's hat off.
> The wind blew the boy's balloon into a tree.
> The wind gave up trying to get the boy to take off his jacket.
> The sun made the boy hot.
> The boy took off his jacket.

I had written these five major events on sentence strips and put them in the pocket chart in a random order. I read the five events aloud once and then had them read them with me. Next, I explained that all events happened in the story they were about to read, but that they were not in the right order. I explained to them that when they finished reading, they would have to close their books, and then we would decide as a group how to put these events in the right order.

I set the timer for 10 minutes, plenty of time for them to read the story, and then walked around the room, checking in with the butterflies at their seats and the astronauts in the centers. Paul's group sat in the group area and read the story. It wasn't exactly silent because some of these children still need to hear themselves read. But they were reading, and I could see them glancing up at the events on the chart, thinking about the sequence. Ms. Port had told me they would read to themselves if I gave them enough preparation before reading and if I gave them only one clear purpose for reading, but it still had to happen for me to believe it.

I returned to the group before the timer sounded. Carl and Mike had finished reading, and I whispered to them about which events they though happened first, second, etc., and had them go back and find places in the story that let them know the correct order.

When the timer sounded, Paul was still reading. I asked them all to close their books, telling Paul he could finish the story when he returned to his seat but we needed his help now to get the events in the right order.

They then attempted to put the events in order as a group (Step 5). We had no trouble figuring out what happened first, second, and last, but Daisy and Mike disagreed about which event was third and which was fourth. I then asked everyone to open their books and see if they could find some parts to read aloud which would tell us the correct order. When that dispute was settled, they all closed their books again. We then read together the five events, now in the correct order in the pocket chart, and decided they had done an excellent job of reading to themselves to figure out the sequence in a story. Their pride in their accomplishment was evident on the faces of every one of them!

We then talked about the story, how they liked it, which part they liked best, what was funny about it, etc. (Step 6). Regardless of the specific comprehension purpose for reading, it is also important to have children give their personal responses to anything they have read, and this evaluation is what you are supposed to accomplish in Step 6.

At this point in the lesson, I had them turn to two pages in the workbook that had sequence as the focus (Step 7). One page had another selection for them to read, and on the other pages were the events—but not in the correct order. We read the events together, and the children understood exactly what they were to do—read the story and put the events in the correct order. I reminded them that I would collect and look at their workbook pages before they went to centers, and that we would talk about and check the order tomorrow at the beginning of our group time. I sent them to their seats to complete the pages. For the first time this year, they went without complaining about either the lesson or the assignment.

I have done several other comprehension lessons with them since that first one, and they are learning to read to themselves and think about whatever purpose I set. I usually introduce a strategy first with the easier book and then do it with the selection in the harder book. For the harder book, we usually read it together, stopping to talk about each page because Paul, Daisy, and Mike cannot yet read at this level on their own. It is clearly good for everyone to learn a new strategy while working in something easier. In fact, I am going to have the astronauts read some selections in an easier book and use these to introduce strategies, and then I'll have them read for the same purpose in their instructional-level book.

I have read many books aloud this month. I have discovered that there is a veritable treasure trove of informational books that build important science and social studies concepts. This month our science unit was on planets and our solar system. We read several wonderful books by Jeanne Bendick, including *The Planets: Neighbors in Space, The Sun: Our Very Own Star,* and *The Stars: Lights in the Night Sky.* Steve brought in a marvelous book, *The Magic School Bus Lost in the Solar System,* by Joanna Cole. As soon as the children saw it, they started chattering about Miss Frizzle's trip to the waterworks. When they discovered that I didn't know any of the Magic School Bus books, they insisted on going to Mrs. Wright's room right then and there and borrowing *The Magic School Bus at the Waterworks,* which we read and enjoyed again. It is amazing what a lasting effect a truly great informational book has on their retention of information!

In social studies, as part of our continuing study of communities, we are doing a unit on Native Americans. Again there are many wonderful, sensitive books that portray how different groups of Native Americans live today and lived in the past. The children especially enjoyed Ann McGovern's *If You Lived with the Sioux Indians* and Mary Perrine's *Nannabah's Friend*. I even found a book that connected up to both the science and social studies units. *They Dance in the Sky* by Jean Guard and Ray Williamson recounts the myths and stories told about the constellations by various Native American tribes.

Red, who is working to put himself through his doctoral program, has offered to come to school early next month to show the children the musical instruments that he plays. He is the leader of a band that he calls "Red and the Flamers." I know that Mike and many of the others will be enthralled with his presentation as well as his personality, which matches his gorgeous, curly auburn hair. I realize how busy he is and am delighted he is willing to talk to the class.

April

Red's appearance was enormously successful! We discussed bands, and I was amazed at how knowledgeable these young children are about music groups. Mike was fascinated with the drums. Red had brought an amplifier along as well, and we caught Butch just in time; he had plugged in the electric guitar and was ready to strum—full blast!

After Red left, I had the children tell me about his visit, and I wrote what they told me on chart paper. We read it over together, cut apart some of the sentences, and relocated them in the correct order of occurrence. Here is what they came up with.

Mr. Flame of "Red and the Flamers" came to our class. (Alex)
It was really cool, man! (Mike)
He showed a variety of instruments. (Larry)
Some of us danced when he played. (Rita)
I almost played the electric guitar. (Butch)
He asked Miss Nouveau for an aspirin before he left. (Mandy)

I have begun doing some imitative reading with Paul, Daisy, and Mike. Imitative reading is a fancy name for having the children read a story enough times so that they can read it easily and fluently, "like a good reader." One day, Ms. Port was visiting our school. That afternoon, she popped into my room with some easy-to-read books and tapes. She then explained to me how I could let Paul, Daisy, and Mike each pick one of these easy-to-read books and listen to it during part of their seatwork time. Each child was to listen to the book until he or she could read the book without the aid of the tape recording. Then that child would read the book to me, and assuming that the child could indeed read the book well, that child could choose another book-tape combination.

So far, so good! Paul has read two of the easy-to-read books. He listens to them at his signed-up time each day and then will often come in first thing in the morning or stay a little late in the afternoon to listen to them. Daisy is not happy with me, however. She listens to the book-tape one time and then comes to read it to me. Of course, she can't, and I send her back with instructions to listen to it at least two more times before she comes to read to me again. Mike's mother has bought him a tape recorder, and he takes his book-tape home every night. Even he seems pleased that he can easily read, cover-to-cover, four books and seems motivated to read more. Imitative reading is an important addition to my reading instruction for Paul, Daisy, and Mike. I think that by listening to the tape of the easy-to-read book often enough, they get to the point where they can easily identify the words and anticipate what is coming next, and they have, probably for the first time, the experience of reading like a good reader. Combined with the 10 minutes of easy-reading coaching they get each afternoon with me or Mrs. Penn, all three children are starting to read more fluently and confidently.

This month the children got into mysteries. I started them off, I guess, by reading *Nate the Great* by Marjorie Weinman Sharmot, *Encyclopedia Brown Sets the Pace* by Donald Sobol, and *Two Bad Ants* by Chris Van Allsburg. The children quickly began finding mysteries, including more *Nate the Great* and *Encyclopedia Brown* mysteries and the reissued *Boxcar Mysteries* series. Now almost everyone is into the mystery craze, and several children, including Hilda and Butch, have declared their intention to be detectives or spies when they grow up.

I read them books related to our science unit on plants, including a beautifully illustrated plant alphabet book, *Allison's Zinnia* by Anita Lobel. I even found some books to integrate with math this month. We are doing a unit on counting and big numbers, and the children were fascinated by David Schwartz's *How Much Is a Million?* and Mitsumasa Anno's *Anno's Counting Book* and *Anno's Mysterious Multiplying Jar.*

We have finished our first publishing cycle, and although it did not go as smoothly as Mrs. Wright had made it sound, we did it and the children all have books they are very proud of. Mrs. Wright was so pleased when I showed her the books that she brought her first-graders over and we had an authors' party. We put the children together into mixed groups of first- and second-graders and let them read their books to each other. My children all behaved very well and seemed determined to be more "mature" than the first-graders. I was amazed to see how little the first-graders are and how well they can write. My children have not gone as far in writing this year as those first-graders have, but knowing what I know now, at the beginning of next year I should be able to pick up right where Mrs. Wright left off. The first-graders seemed delighted to be "up in second grade." As many of them left, they gave me a hug and said, "See you next year!" The true rewards of teaching!

May

I can't believe this year is coming to an end. We have had a busy last month. I wanted the children to have two published books from second grade, so we did another publishing cycle. This one was easier!

I read them some of the *Amelia Bedelia* books, which appealed greatly to their seven-year-old silliness. That got them started on lots of other word-play, joke, and riddle books. We also read books connected to our final combined science/social studies unit on the environment and what various communities can do to help clean up and maintain a healthy environment. After reading *The Empty Lot* by Dale Fife, we took a walking field trip to a nearby empty lot and discovered that our empty lot was also teeming with animal life. The children also loved *When the Woods Hum* by Joanne Ryder and *The Great Kopak Tree* by Lynne Cherry.

We are now up to 16 minutes of Self-Selected Reading time! I never thought last fall that I would be here in May, and I probably wouldn't have been if Mr. Topps and the others hadn't helped me isolate my problems and correct them. I certainly never thought that I would see my class sitting still and reading attentively for 16 straight minutes and liking it. In some ways it has been a long year, but in others it has been too short. How I wish I could have begun my current reading program earlier!

Anticipating next year and the first day of school (it just has to be better!), I asked the children to think back over the year and all of the things we have done. I wrote their comments on the chalkboard and we filled it in no time. I had no idea that we had done so many things or that the children could remember them.

The next instructions that I gave them were to pretend that they were their own desk. As the desk, they were to write a letter to whoever would be sitting in that seat next year. They were to give the new second-graders an idea about what to expect during the new school year. We would leave the letters in the desks and surprise the new children with them in the fall. The children seemed excited about the project and eagerly began to write. Here is a copy of the letter that Roberta wrote:

> *Hi, Kid,*
>
> *You're pretty lucky to be starting second grade already. And boy, will you have fun. Especially sitting at this desk. This is where Roberta Marie Smith sat last year, and she had fun. This year you will learn to read harder books and you'll do your workbook (if you're better than Roberta). Have a good time, kid, because it won't last long. Soon you'll have to go to the third grade where they really have hard work to do! Maybe I can ask Roberta's desk in third grade to write to you, too.*
> *Love,*
> *Clarence, Your Desk*

We have added to the supply of books this year with children's paperbacks. The children and I receive brochures every month from two companies that publish inexpensive, high-quality children's books. The children take their individual brochures home and bring back the completed order forms with the necessary money. I mail these and add the bonus books, one of which we get for each 10 books the children order. Then we all eagerly await the arrival of our new books. In this way, I have added about 25 new books to our classroom library.

All in all, it has turned out to be a very good year for me and, I think, for almost all my children. Most of my discipline problems have lessened as I established some routines and began to give the children some limited choices. I still have some days when I wonder why I ever wanted to be a teacher. Mike is most difficult to handle, and my promises to myself to be firm and patient with him just seem to dissolve when I am faced with one of his regular disruptions. He tells me they are moving right after school is out. Some third-grade teacher somewhere will have her hands full next year. I am sorry he is moving because I am sure Mrs. Wise would be able to calm him down. Paul is another one of my failures. He seems to be perking up and making some progress, and then he goes into a somber, detached state during which he might as well not be here. I don't know what is going to happen to him. And Daisy—she has made some progress in her work and behavior—mostly because she can't stand to have her center art time taken away, but she is still not an easy child to live with. Maybe Mrs. Wise can get through to her, too. I have such faith in that lady. I would never have made it through the year without her.

I *have* made it through the year, however, and I will be ready for next year. I told Mrs. Wright the other day that if I learned as much every year as I have this first year, I would never have to fear getting stale and bored. She said that teaching was many things, some positive and some not so positive, but that she had never found it to be boring. Red says that one thing he learned this year was that in teaching, there are so many intriguing problems to be solved! I guess that if I can continue to view my crises as "intriguing problems to be solved" I will someday be a good, capable, creative teacher.

THE STUDENT TEACHING SEMINAR

Norma L. Nouveau, veteran of one year in the classroom, had been asked by Dr. Link to talk with her student teachers at their weekly seminar. At first, Miss Nouveau protested that she was the last person who should be asked. After all, she was still learning herself, and she didn't think she had anything of significance to contribute.

Dr. Link explained that several students in the class had asked her to find a first-year teacher who would talk to them. They wanted to know what it was *really* like when one started teaching. Although teachers like Mrs. Wise could contribute a great deal to the seminar, they had been teaching too long to focus honestly on the first year of teaching. And, she added, she had been observing Miss Nouveau's progress throughout the year and was pleased with the growth that had been taking place. Miss Nouveau finally consented to address the class. "But," she cautioned, "I'm not promising that it will be any good."

"If you just tell them what you have lived through this past year," Dr. Link replied, "they will be more than satisfied."

That, she resolved, was precisely what she would do. These students would find out the truth from her before they had to live through it themselves! She requested that they meet in her room.

The afternoon of the seminar, Miss Nouveau stood at the back of her room while Dr. Link greeted the carefree students. After Dr. Link had introduced her, she began her talk by saying, "This year I have worked harder than I ever dreamed I would have to, and even so, things have gone well only at times." She then related the inaccurate judgments, errors in placement, discipline problems, and poor assignments she had made. As she spoke, she noted looks of disbelief turning to looks of pity and fear as she related anecdote after anecdote. Not wanting to discourage them, however, Miss Nouveau then began to relate the positive things that had happened to her and the consequent changes she had made in her program, especially since Christmas. When she finished, several hands went up for questions.

"If you knew you weren't doing very well in October, how come you kept right on doing things wrong? I mean, if *I* were doing something I knew was wrong, I wouldn't just keep on!"

"Well," answered Miss Nouveau with a smile, "maybe you would and maybe you wouldn't. I would have thought that same way a year ago, but it's so different when you're actually there day after day with the children and you know you're totally responsible for their instruction. There's neither the opportunity nor the knowledge to do it any other way! I was fortunate, though, to be in a school with a principal who cared, other teachers who helped me, and an elementary supervisor who showed me alternatives. Though they were all as busy as I was, they gave freely of their time and advice. If it hadn't been for them, I know I would have resigned at Christmas."

"What would have helped you, though, before you got to your first year of teaching?" another student asked.

"If only I had been given more experience in classrooms prior to my student teaching, then I could have spent student-teaching time learning more about classroom management. The better prepared you are when you enter your student teaching, the better you will be at the end of it. Also, if my reading/language arts course had been more practical, I would have been better prepared to teach the children."

Another student raised his hand to ask, "Could you just summarize for us a few of the most important things that you learned this year?"

Miss Nouveau thought for a moment before replying, "I learned so much it is hard to say, but I guess I learned that there is help out there if you ask for it, and that learning to be a really good teacher is too complex to go it alone. Another thing was locating the school storeroom. It's often a gold mine of books and materials just lying there, gathering dust. Also, I learned that I must have some time for myself. One reason I wasn't thinking well last fall, I'm sure, was that I had no time to do things that I had always done and that I enjoyed doing. I regret very much some of the things I did this year, and if I could be granted one wish, it would be that I could repeat this school year knowing at the beginning what I know now!

"I also learned that Mrs. Middleman was right in our very first parent meeting when she said, 'Easier said than done.' I had gotten the guiding principles in our meeting, looked at them, and wondered, 'How not? Of course I am going to have balanced instruction, and my groups will make it multilevel, and following the suggestions in the manual would take care of thinking and language and feeling.' But putting into practice our 12 guiding principles with a real class of children is a major challenge. I will be more confident next year—but hopefully not cavalier!"

"How are you going to start next year, since obviously you won't repeat what has been done?"

"I thought you might ask that," responded Miss Nouveau confidently. "As a matter of fact, I have given a lot of thought to that, and I think I am prepared to get next year off to a better start. I will begin the year right off teaching children how to use my centers and making sure they know their center privileges depend on their doing their work with a good effort. I will give an IRI to all the children, but I will interpret their oral reading and not just count errors. I probably won't get another reader as advanced as Larry—Mrs. Wright says Larry was the best reader in first grade she has ever seen. But if a child reads with fluency, has good comprehension, and makes only little errors that don't change the meaning, I will know that that reader has a more mature eye-voice span and not count those errors against her or him. I will form my reading groups according to the instructional levels I find, and I will make sure that the lowest group reads in two levels of books from the very beginning, so that everyone has instructional level or easier reading every week. I also will begin imitative reading and the one-on-one coaching with my most struggling readers much sooner than I did. I will use my timer, stick to my schedule, and try to incorporate everything I learned this year from the first day. I know I will have new problems to solve, but I will put into practice what I learned and we will all start out ahead."

As Miss Nouveau paused to catch her breath, Dr. Link interrupted to say that she regretted having to announce that the seminar time was up. Miss Nouveau and most of the students turned in astonishment to view the clock and confirm that indeed an entire hour had fled past. "Just like teaching," observed Miss Nouveau. "When you are thinking about what you have to say and do, it seems as if there is an enormous amount of time to fill. But when you start doing it, there is never enough time." The students chuckled. A few stayed afterward to talk privately with Miss Nouveau. Dr. Link looked on proudly.

CHILDREN'S BOOKS/MATERIALS CITED

Allison's Zinnia, by A. Lobel, Greenwillow, 1990.
Amelia Bedelia books by P. Parish, HarperCollins, various dates.
Anno's Counting Book, by M. Anno, HarperCollins, 1986.
Anno's Mysterious Multiplying Jar, by M. Anno, Philomel, 1983.
Boxcar Mysteries series, by G. Warner, Whitman, various dates.
The Empty Lot, by D. Fife, Little, Brown, 1991.
Encyclopedia Brown Sets the Pace, by D. Sobol, Scholastic, 1989.
The Great Kopak Tree, by L. Cherry, Harcourt Brace Jovanovich, 1990.
Halloween by G. Gibbons, Holiday House, 1996.
How Much Is a Million? by D. Schwartz, Scholastic, 1986.
If You Lived with the Sioux Indians, by A. McGovern, Scholastic, 1984.
The Magic School Bus at the Waterworks, by J. Cole, Scholastic, 1988.
The Magic School Bus Lost in the Solar System, by J. Cole, Scholastic, 1992.
Miss Nelson Has a Field Day, by H. Allard, Houghton Mifflin, 1988.

Miss Nelson Is Back, by H. Allard, Houghton Mifflin, 1988.
Miss Nelson Is Missing, by H. Allard, Houghton Mifflin, 1987.
Nannabah's Friend, by M. Perrine, Houghton Mifflin, 1989.
Nate the Great, by M. W. Sharmot, Dell, 1977.
The Planets: Neighbors in Space, by J. Bendick, Millbrook, 1991.
The Reasons for Seasons by G. Gibbons, Holiday House, 1995.
Spider Storch's Teacher Torture, by G. Willner-Pardo, Albert Whitman, 1997.
The Stars: Lights in the Night Sky, by J. Bendick, Millbrook, 1991.
The Sun: Our Very Own Star, by J. Bendick, Millbrook, 1991.
They Dance in the Sky, by J. Guard & R. Williamson, Houghton Mifflin, 1992.
Two Bad Ants, by C. Van Allsburg, Houghton Mifflin, 1988.
When the Woods Hum, by J. Ryder, Morrow Junior Books, 1991.

Mrs. Wise: Third Grade

THE PARENT MEETING

Vera Wise walked around the room, carefully placing materials for the parents to examine when they arrived for the meeting later that evening. She went about the task methodically, for she had been having parent meetings for most of her 31 years as a teacher, long before they became an "in" thing to do. As a matter of fact, she was the one who had suggested to Mr. Topps, some 10 years before, that these meetings become a regular part of the school routine. She had also initiated the parent conferences that everyone now held twice yearly. Moreover, she had been part of the group who had drafted the schoolwide guiding principles the faculty had worked on at a retreat several years ago and were still using.

There were those who called her an innovator and those who said it was amazing that a woman of her years could be so up-to-date! Mrs. Wise chuckled over that one. She told them all that it had nothing to do with innovation or age—she simply knew what her children needed and how *she* could best teach them.

She was always exhilarated by these meetings, as she was by the parent conferences. It was astonishing how much one could learn about a child in half-hour conferences with the parents. She made the parents feel relaxed by sitting in a chair beside them rather than in the more formal position behind the desk. She had acquired a knack for knowing what to say and how to say it that helped put parents at their ease, informed them of their child's progress, and elicited from them the maximum amount of information about the child. Tonight, however, she was to meet the parents *en masse*. She enjoyed explaining what she and their children were going to be doing, for she loved teaching. She was not totally looking forward to the day in the near future when she would be retiring.

Shortly before 7:00 P.M., the parents began to arrive. Mrs. Wise directed them to sign up for the October parent conference and to volunteer on any of several volunteer sign-up sheets she had laid out. She didn't begin the meeting until 7:05, however, for long years of experience had taught her that many parents would arrive late no matter when the meeting was to begin.

"Hello. Some of you I know quite well because I have had other children of yours. Some of you are new to me as I am to you. I know that we will become well acquainted this year. I want to urge you *all* to come visit the classroom. I have only two requirements for those classroom visits: (1) that you let me know in advance when you want to come, so that I can let you know whether or not it is convenient, and (2) that you plan to stay at least an hour, so that the children will settle down and forget that you are here so that you can really see the program. I warn you! You may be put to work. Any extra hands in my class can and probably will be used. Just ask Mr. Topps! I'm sure that is why he has been avoiding my classroom for the last couple of years."

She paused for breath and to let the laughter die down. "Here is a handout of our school's literacy guiding principles. The handout is the same as the poster I have hanging in the room over there to remind everyone who walks in here what they should be seeing. We, at this school, decided many years ago that we felt strongly enough about the place of children's literature and children's writing in the curriculum that we would make a concerted effort to incorporate them into our classrooms. For instance, you can see that guiding principles 7 and 8, 'Read aloud to students daily' and 'Schedule self-selected reading,' address children's literature specifically. Guiding principles 6 and 9, 'Have students write every day' and 'Connect reading and writing to all subject areas,' specifically address writing. I have developed my entire reading and language arts program around books for children and children's own writings. This year I am going to especially work on those cross-curricular connections. In order to make reading and writing situations as natural as possible, I have implemented a literature-based program that focuses on ensuring that students receive a balanced literacy program—guiding principle 1. Let me explain to you how it works.

"As you look around the room, you see that I am fortunate enough to have hundreds and hundreds of books that are part of our permanent classroom collection. I have been collecting these books for years. I get them from a variety of sources. My friends know never to throw out a book without checking with me first. Across the years, parents—including some of you—have given me children's books, which I add to our collection. I haunt flea markets, yard sales, thrift shops, library discard shelves, and bookstores, and I must admit that I have bought a lot of the books in this room with my own money. Don't feel too sorry for me, though, because I love books and I enjoy reading them myself and then sharing them with the children. Some people shop for clothes; I shop for books!

"In the last few years, I haven't had to buy too many books using my own money. The school system realizes that children who love reading become good readers and that immersing children in lots of wonderful books is an investment that pays off. Every year now, I am allotted a sum of money to buy books. I also apply every year for our district's teacher grants, which allow me to purchase books for the classroom. I have used almost all my funds to buy multiple copies of books, and it is these books that I use for guided-reading lessons and that the children will be discussing in their literature response groups. I also used some of my book money to buy us a brand new set of *World Book* encyclopedias and to get classroom subscriptions to several magazines for children. This year we will be getting *Cricket*, *Kids Discover*, *Sports Illustrated for Kids*, *Zillions*, *Ranger Rick*, *3–2–1 Contact*, *National Geographic World*, and *Kid City*.

"In addition to all the books and magazines that reside permanently in this room, the children and I make good and frequent use of the school library, the public library, and even, when we need some hard-to-find things, the university library. I have also bookmarked several research sites on the Internet that help us to locate information and resources as well. As you might imagine, Miss Page, the school media specialist, and I work together a lot.

"The books that you see in this room are my reading program. I know that some teachers use a reading series for part of their program, and I have used them in the past, but I have so many wonderful real books—including multiple copies of lots of the best books—that I don't see any need for the children to read anything but the real thing. Be assured, however, that I will be teaching your children the strategies and skills that are required by our curriculum guide for third grade. But even more, I want to ensure that your children become independent readers. So I work on guiding principle 10, 'Teach the decoding and spelling strategies that reading and writing require.' And I do a whole lot more.

"When you have taught 31 years, taken as many reading courses and workshops as I have, and used many different language arts series over the years, you learn what the critical reading and writing strategies are and how to help children develop these. You also know how to meet the needs of the range of students who are in the room. I aim to make as many of my lessons as multimethod or multilevel as possible in order to accommodate this range. That aim is consistent with guiding principle 2: 'Make instruction multilevel.'

"I will be doing short focused lessons with the children several times a week, and in these focused lessons I will teach them the comprehension and composition strategies they need. They will then apply these strategies to the pieces they are reading and writing. I will make sure the strategies get followed up in the literature response groups, writing workshop, and in individual conferences.

"For most of the year, expect that your child will be reading at least two books at a time. During our Readers' Workshop each morning, the children are given books to read. It is these books that I use to make sure that the children are reading a wide variety of literature, applying the reading strategies I teach them, and it is these books that they are discussing in their literature study groups. Sometimes I assign the book and sometimes I let them choose among four or five titles, but what they read during Readers' Workshop is determined by me with some input from the children.

"Equally important is our afternoon self-selected reading time. Each day, when we come back from lunch, we settle down for some self-selected reading. I make no demands on them during this time except that they are quietly reading something of their own choosing. While they read, I have individual conferences with the children about their reading. The children sign up when they want to conference with me, and if I check my records and I haven't conferenced with a particular child for two weeks, I sign that child up for a conference. On Friday afternoons, we take our after-lunch time to share what we have been reading in small groups.

"I find that reading and writing workshop time and self-selected reading allow me to focus on developing guiding principles 3, 4, and 5: 'Use language as the foundation for reading and writing,' 'Teach reading and writing as thinking,' and 'Use feelings to create avid readers and writers.' We think about and react to our own and others' writings."

Mrs. Wise glanced up at the clock and frowned. "Just like during the day here, there is never enough time to do everything as thoroughly as you would like to. We have to be in the cafeteria in 10 minutes for the schoolwide PTSA organizational meeting, so just let me explain a few other critical components of our language arts program.

"Each morning, in addition to our Readers' Workshop, we have the Writers' Workshop that I mentioned earlier. Most of you know that we do process writing here at Merritt and that your children do lots of first-draft writing and publish some pieces. This year, because most of your children have some facility with writing, we will work more on revising and editing first drafts so that their writing is more polished.

"In addition to process writing in which the children choose their own topics, as the year goes on, we will take several weeks of time during which I will teach them how to write specific things. In these focused writing lessons, I often use what they are reading as springboards to writing. Reading and writing support one another. When children write about what they are reading, they have a wealth of information and ideas to draw from. Writing also increases their comprehension and enjoyment of reading, because as they write, they must think about and decide how they feel about various aspects of their reading.

"Finally, we will spend some time each day in activities designed to move them along in their word and spelling knowledge. Like most of the other teachers, I have a word wall on which I put the words I see commonly misspelled in their writing. We add five words each week and practice spelling these when we have a few minutes between activities. As you see, the words I have put up already—*friends, because, would, people, to/too/two, they're/their/there, don't*—are words some adults still have trouble spelling and using correctly. We will also be doing lots of word sorting, which will increase their knowledge of how to spell many words.

"Most of you have already sent the three notebooks your children need. I know three is a lot, but one is a writing journal for writing ideas and their first-draft writing, one is their literature log, and the other is their word book in which they sort words and put the words they find that fit certain patterns. All three of these notebooks are critical to our program, and we will use them all year. If you have a problem getting the notebooks right now, let me know. I do have a few squirreled away.

"I also will be assessing your children early in and throughout the school year. The more I understand what they know and are able to do, the better I can teach them. I will work very hard to keep you informed of your child's progress through conferences, notes, phone calls, weekly newsletters, and report cards. I do both of these because they help me teach your children better, but as you can see, they also fulfill guiding principle 11, 'Use observation to assess learning and plan instruction,' and 12, 'Inform parents of expectations and progress.'

"We have to move to the cafeteria now, but I will answer any general questions about the classroom as we walk to the cafeteria or if you stay a few minutes after the meeting there. I will have a lot more specific information to tell you about each of your children when we have our conference in October. Remember that I consider this *our* classroom—mine and your children's and yours—and I hope that you will all schedule some time, once we get up and running in a few weeks, to come and see how hard we work and how much we love it."

MONTHLY LOGS

September

Now that this busy summer is over, climaxed by Norma Nouveau's marriage in August, I'm ready to begin my last year of teaching. I've been around a long time. I've seen fads come and go in education, and I have observed the cyclical nature of these fads—the whole-word approach, phonics, whole language, and others. I am, I suppose, reluctant to change, but the program that I have developed for my students is one that I am comfortable with and one that has proven itself to me. Years ago I read about individualizing instruction through children's literature, and this is the technique I have continued to use, though with modifications.

I always assess the children before I begin instruction, as well as doing ongoing assessment. So many teachers have indicated to me that they could not carry through with the literature-based curriculum plans that they had established. With further questioning, I often discover that either they have not assessed the children to see what they know and can do, so that they can plan intelligently, or they have simply taken the same old material and put the children through it at different rates. Both of these are contrary to the nature and spirit of a literature-based curriculum.

There are as many systems as there are teachers who use literature. The system that I have used for years with my students is one that fades to more student independence. When children first come into my room, they have often been through a reading series program that is highly structured and sequenced. One of the most difficult tasks I face, therefore, is weaning them away from an overdependence upon the teacher for instruction.

I am finding that these children have had fewer problems adapting to my program than some classes. Norma Flame did an excellent job with them toward the end of the year.

As part of my initial assessment, I administer an interest inventory. That is one of the papers they find in the folders on the first day. I walk around the room while they are working on it, so that I can identify those children who are unable to read the inventory and therefore need to have someone read it to them. I soon discovered that children like Larry, Pat, Hilda, and Roberta were quite willing to be amanuenses for children such as Butch, Chip, and Paul. They were a great help. Items such as "You are going to be living all alone on the moon for one year. You can take only a few personal things with you. What three things will you take?" and "I sometimes feel . . ." produce many clues to the needs, perceptions, and values of children. With some of this information in mind, I can help the children to find reading materials that will be both interesting and informative.

I have finished administering the Informal Reading Inventory to all the children. I always wait until we are a week into the school year before giving the IRIs, because some of my children haven't cracked a book all summer. If I test them before they get back into reading, I will get levels that are lower than their actual levels.

I have used a variety of commercially published IRIs over the years. Currently, I am using the Johns *Basic Reading Inventory* (1998). One of its advantages is that it has three passages at each level. This allows me to check oral reading and silent reading as well as listening comprehension for some children. He includes word lists that let me find the grade level at which I should have each child begin reading the passages, from preprimer level through grade 10. Mostly, though, I have students read aloud a passage and ask the comprehension questions. With a student like Paul, I wondered how much he understood even though he could barely read anything orally or silently. So I read aloud a series of passages to measure his listening comprehension. If students get borderline scores or huge discrepancies between their word identification score and their comprehension score, I have them read aloud a second—and sometimes a third—passage at that level to try to get the most reliable indicator of their reading level that I can. So I have modified the test's instructions to give me the information I need to begin teaching. I also monitor reading levels through the year.

I tested two children each day during their afternoon self-selected reading time. I began with a passage I thought might be on their level, based on their records from previous years and their performance on the word lists. I then moved up or down a grade level until I found the level at which their word identification dropped below 95 percent or their comprehension dropped below 75 percent. Their instructional level is the highest level at which they can read with at least 90 percent identification accuracy and 75 percent comprehension.

As happens every year, I have a wide range of reading levels in my classroom, with a few children still reading at first- or second-grade levels, and many reading well above third-grade level. Here are the September instructional levels for my children, according to the results of the *Basic Reading Inventory*.

Alex 4th	Jeff 3rd
Alexander 2nd	Joyce 3rd
Anthony 4th	Larry 8th +
Betty 5th	Mandy 6th
Butch 2nd	Manuel 3rd
Carl 3rd	Mitch 3rd
Chip 2nd	Mort 2nd
Daisy First Reader	Pat 6th
Danielle 6th	Paul Primer/First Reader?
Daphne 5th	Rita 6th
Hilda 7th	Roberta 6th
Horace 5th	Steve 4th

This is about the range I usually get, with a few more children at sixth and seventh grades and of course Larry, who read the highest passage I had—eighth grade—with no problem at all. I was pleased to have only six children reading below grade level, and four of them are only one year behind. I have lots of good easy books, so finding things for Alexander, Chip, Mort, and Butch to read during Readers' Workshop won't be any problem. I will have to include some extra easy books from time to time to accommodate Daisy and Paul. I am not really sure how well Paul reads. I tested him on three different days on all four primer and first-reader passages, and his performance was very erratic. His word identification is pretty good for sight words, and he did use some letter-sound knowledge and context to figure out some words in one of the passages. In another passage, however, he seemed unable to do anything with words he didn't immediately recognize. His comprehension was also erratic, and I am not sure he was telling me everything he knew in answer to the questions. I am sure he can read primer level, and he can read some first-reader material—probably depending on the topic and what kind of day he is having.

I am going to steer both Paul and Daisy to some of my very easy books for their self-selected reading and conference with them for a few minutes at least twice a week. I need to partner them up with someone for some of the Readers' Workshop selections. Finding a partner for Paul won't be hard. Daphne has already let me know that she "helps Paul," and Horace is very kind to him also. Daisy, however, is so difficult to get along with that I may have to pay someone to be her partner!

While the IRI scores give me an initial picture of how well my children read, I use oral reading analyses throughout the year to help me determine if a particular book is at the appropriate difficulty level for a particular child and what reading strategies the child is using. I do these oral reading analyses during our individual conferences during self-selected reading, and based on these regular observations, I know how each child is growing and what particular reading strategies to emphasize.

I have also gotten my first writing sample to put in each student's growth portfolio. This growth portfolio is part of what I use to determine how the children are growing and developing in their reading and writing strategies as the year goes on. I include many different samples of their process writing on their self-selected topics—both first drafts and published pieces. I do however think it is very informative to be able to look at each child's effort to write to the same task. To do this, I give them basically the same task to write about at the beginning, middle, and end of the school year. This year, I had them describe what they liked best about Merritt Elementary School. We talked a little about Merritt Elementary. Most of the children have been here since kindergarten, and they enjoyed reminiscing about lots of the fun things they had done here. I then asked them to imagine that someone new had moved into their neighborhood and to think about what they would tell that person about Merritt Elementary. Their writing task was to describe Merritt Elementary and tell as much as they could about it, emphasizing the things they liked best about school. I gave them as much time as they wanted to write a first draft. I have copied and dated this first draft and put it in their growth portfolios. Next week, I am going to put them in small groups to share their Merritt Elementary pieces and then ask them to revise the pieces in whatever way they choose to—and can. Finally, I will review the items on the Editor's Checklist they began last year with Miss Nouveau, have them edit their own pieces using this checklist, and have them write a final draft. I will put this final draft in their growth portfolios along with the copy of their first draft, and I will have a very good idea of their writing abilities, including first draft, revision, and editing. By looking at what they can do now, I will know what kind of focus lessons to teach during process writing, when to begin some more structured focused writing lessons, and what to work on with individual children during writing conferences.

In January, when they have forgotten what they wrote in September, I will once again ask them to describe Merritt Elementary, particularly the things they like best about it, and go through the same first draft, small group sharing/revision, and editing process. I will do this one more time in May. It is amazing how much growth you can see in their writing when you have them write about something they know a lot about at three different points in the year, using the same procedure to get the samples. One of the most difficult things about teaching children to write better is that, because writing is such a complex process, even when there is a lot of growth in their writing, third-graders still have a long way to go. When you look at these three writing samples along with the writing they select for their showcase portfolio, you can see and document how far they have come.

Self-selected reading is going well. This is always easy to start at Merritt, because the children expect to have part of their day devoted to "just reading." We have just gotten started with our Readers' Workshop and Writers' Workshop. Next month, we will do our first big word sort and begin hunting for words. Most of my previous classes have really enjoyed these word activities, and I think this group will too.

October

October is always one of my favorite teaching months. I have set up all the routines and done the initial assessment, and we can get down to really doing things. I also like that we have four weeks of uninterrupted teaching time. Holidays and vacations are fine, but they do interrupt the teaching flow.

Writers' Workshop is going quite well. I begin each day with a short 5- to 6-minute mini lesson in which I write something and then do a little editing on it. I have added—one thing at a time—the conventions Miss Nouveau had on their Editor's Checklist last year and will begin next month to add some new ones. Most of the children have published one piece, and my most prolific writers—Hilda, Pat, Danielle, and Steve—have already published two.

When the children are ready to publish, they sign up with me for an initial conference. I check to see that they have three good first drafts (*good*, of course, is a relative term—good for Joyce would not be good for Daphne, and three pieces that show some effort are good for Daisy or Paul). I talk with them about which one they plan to publish and how they want to publish it. Some children love to copy their first drafts into spiral-bound books and add illustrations; others like to use the word processing software along with the clip art; still others like to write it out, scroll-like, on long butcher paper. Once they have my okay to publish, they select two friends and read their draft to them. The friends know that they are to comment on what they like and make suggestions that will make the piece better. (Better is defined as clearer, more interesting, more exciting, more suspenseful!) Often, the friends make suggestions about illustrations or particular clip art that would enhance the writing.

The writer then revises the chosen piece for meaning, using the friends' suggestions if the writer thinks they are good ideas. I require that in their first-draft notebooks they write on every other line so some revision can be done on the blank lines, and I spend more time in these conferences with children at both ends of the ability continuum.

My Readers' Workshops are organized around three kinds of units—author units, genre units, and topic/theme units. This year I decided to start with an author unit. I like to start with something of high interest to the children and something quite easy to read, so that they can learn how to write in their literature logs and how to discuss in their literature response groups. I have always found that almost all the children love Beverly Cleary books. Many of her books are quite easy to read, but even better readers enjoy and empathize with Ramona, Beezus, Henry, and the rest of the gang. I began the unit by putting out all the Beverly Cleary books I could find and talking with the children about them. Many of the children had already read some of her books, and they talked about the characters—Ribsy included—as if they were old friends. I told them that we were going to spend a few weeks reading and rereading these Beverly Cleary books, and they all seemed delighted at the prospect. I showed them that I had enough copies of *Henry Huggins* so that everyone could read this one and that when we finished this, they would get to choose the next Beverly Cleary book they wanted to read.

Next, I distributed the books and told them to read only the first chapter. I told them that they could read by themselves or with a friend, and that when everyone had finished, we would make our first entries into our literature response logs. The children grabbed their books and went off to read. Many of the children partnered up, and as I had expected, Daphne grabbed Paul and took him off with her. No one grabbed Daisy, so once they all got settled, I went over and read the chapter with her, taking turns reading the pages and helping her use word identification strategies such as pictures, context, and spelling patterns. She did quite well on her pages and clearly loved the individual attention.

When I saw that some of the children had finished, I told them to take a piece of scrap paper and write down a few of the important things that had happened, so they would be ready to help us write our response log entry. When Daisy and I finished, I went to the overhead and asked the children who were through to join me, indicating to the others that they should join us when they finished. The children and I discussed the first chapter informally as other children joined the group. When almost everyone was there, I showed them how we would write in our response logs.

Using the overhead, I wrote at the top of the page the book title and then the chapter title and pages we had read. I then began a sentence about the main character by writing:

Henry Huggins is . . .

The children told me lots of things about Henry. Then, working together, we constructed a sentence about Henry, which I wrote on the transparency. Next, I wrote this beginning of a sentence:

Henry wants to . . .

Again, the children shared ideas and came up with a sentence to describe Henry's problem, which I wrote on the transparency. Finally, I wrote:

I think Henry will . . .

The children had lot of predictions about what would happen next. I listened but didn't write any of these down. When they had shared their predictions, I had them return to their desks, get out their brand-new literature response logs, and write the book and chapter title and pages to head their first page as I had. I then had them copy the *Henry Huggins is* and *Henry wants to* sentences that we had composed. Finally, I asked them to write their own ending to the *I think Henry will* sentence.

We continued these procedures through this whole first book, working together as a class to discuss the chapter read, then jointly composing a sentence or two that summed up some major points from the chapter, and finishing by having the children copy our class-composed sentences and make their own predictions for the next day.

By the time the children finished the book, they all understood how our response logs would work and were getting very good at summarizing one or two important events and making a prediction. I did have to collect the books each time they finished reading and make them pledge on their honor not to read ahead. They are so eager to have their predictions be right that they will cheat if you let them!

When we had finished reading *Henry Huggins* together, I showed them six other Beverly Cleary books of which I had six to eight copies of each. I read them a little bit of each book and then had them write down on a slip of paper their first, second, and third choice of which book they wanted to read. Several children complained that they wanted to read them all, but I reminded them that time and books were always limited and that they would have to choose. I told them that after we finished reading and discussing these books, they could choose to read the ones they hadn't read during Readers' Workshop, at home or during self-selected reading time.

Looking at their choices, I formed them into five groups, with four to six children in each group. I tried to put a mix of children in each group, and I assigned Chip, Butch, Mort, Daisy, and Paul to the easiest book they had chosen. Daphne put her three choices down but also wrote on her choice sheet, "I would like to read the same book Paul reads if you have enough. I like to help him."

What an angel she is!

The procedure we used for the second Beverly Cleary book was basically the same as the one we used for *Henry Huggins,* except that the children got together in their response groups, discussed the story, and jointly composed two or three sentences summing up what happened. Each child then returned to his or her desk and wrote what he or she liked best about the part read that day and made a "secret" prediction for the next day.

When we finished all the books, we had a Beverly Cleary party. I pretended to be Beverly—the guest of honor—and the children told me what they liked and asked me lots of questions. This unit was a big hit with the children. Many of them (including Daisy!) are currently reading all the Beverly Cleary books their group didn't read. I was just thinking that I would start next year off with this same author unit, and then I remembered I won't be starting next year off with any unit! I'll be retired! I have really mixed emotions about that, but there is so much traveling and other projects I want to do that I can't do just in the summers.

November

A new student has arrived—Tanana—and I am afraid that she will have some rather severe adjustment problems. Tanana is an Inuit child and is so accustomed to wilderness and freedom that she must be finding her new life here rather confining. I have asked two of the girls, Daphne and Betty, to be her special friends until she becomes acclimatized. Those two girls are very outgoing and friendly and will help Tanana feel at home here.

Whenever a new student moves in, I give him or her a few weeks to adjust to us, and then I do the same kind of assessment I did with all the children at the beginning of the year. I could tell right away that my interest inventory was not going to mean much to a child from a culture as different from ours as Tanana's, so rather than have her fill that out, I talked with her and wrote down some of the things she liked to do. I put out a variety of books and had her pick the three books she would most like to read or have read to her. I got a writing sample from her by asking her to describe the school she had gone to in Alaska. I gave her the IRI, and her word identification is much higher than her comprehension. I am sure that this is because comprehension is so prior-knowledge dependent, and Tanana just doesn't know a lot of the things all children growing up here would know. She could pass the comprehension criteria on the first-reader passages but not on the second-grade passages. I think, however, that her reading level will quickly get to at least third-grade level as she learns more about our culture and language.

When Tanana arrived, I decided to focus our Readers' Workshop on the topic Other Times and Places. I had several good books set in earlier years of this country as well as books set in other countries, and with Tanana's arrival, I took advantage of the chance to help children think about how people lived in other times and places. Together, we read Cynthia Rylant's *When I Was Young in the Mountains* and Karen Ackerman's *Song and Dance Man*, and then the children chose from a variety of books that take place in other times and places. I formed groups, trying once again to give everyone their first, second, or third choices and to assign my lowest readers to the easiest book they had chosen. I put Daphne, Tanana, and Paul in the same group, and Daphne read the chapters of their books with both of them. I told her she had found her calling and asked her if she was planning to be a teacher when she grew up. She just smiled happily and nodded.

I once again modeled for them how to respond in their literature response logs. I used sentence frames that lead them to compare and contrast life then and now and make decisions about what would be better or worse. I also included a sentence frame to get them to make their own personal response to what they were learning:

The most fascinating thing I learned today was . . .

To connect reading and writing, I tied in some focused writing lessons on descriptive paragraphs with this theme. I used the books we were reading to point out examples of some good descriptive paragraphs. We talked about the words authors used to let us see and feel what the faraway and long-ago places were like. I then wrote a paragraph describing the farthest-away place I have been—the coral reef in Australia. (The children were fascinated with the notion that it had taken 18 hours on the airplane to get there, and with the notion that day here was night there and vice versa. I brought in some books and other literature I had picked up in Australia, and these are very popular reading materials during self-selected reading.) I then had the children talk about the farthest place they had been and write descriptive paragraphs that would make that place come alive for those of us who hadn't been there.

Having written about what they knew firsthand, I had them work in their response groups to collaboratively write descriptive paragraphs about some of the settings for the books their groups were reading. We took a week off from our process writing to do these teacher-guided lessons on descriptive paragraphs. We are now back to process writing, and I can already see the insights they gained about descriptive writing being used in the self-selected topic writing of many of my children.

We have also gotten started into our word sorts, which I use to move them forward in their knowledge of spelling/decoding patterns. I make these word sorts multilevel by including a variety of spelling patterns used in short and long words. For the first sort, I used common spelling patterns for the vowel *u*. I gave the children a sort sheet, and I made a transparency from this sort sheet to use with my overhead.

The most fascinating thing I learned today was_____

Forming the tops of the columns were the major spelling patterns represented by *u*, along with an example word for each. The first day we used this sort sheet, I had the children fold their sheets so that they couldn't see the last two columns—*sure* and *ture*. (I covered those columns on my transparency also.) I then showed them 15 to 20 words that had the vowel *u*. As I showed them each word, they pronounced it and then wrote it in the column they thought it belonged in. When they had had a chance to write it on their sheets, I let them tell me which column to write it in on my transparency. At the end of that first lesson, our sort sheets looked like this:

OTHER	u	ue	u-e	ur	sure	ture
	us	sue	use	burn	insure	nature
menu	run	true	mule	turn		
	must	blue	mute	urban		
	snub	due	cute	turtle		
	runt		amuse			
	strum					
	bus					

On the second day, we used the same sheet again and kept the last two columns covered. We sorted another 15 to 20 words into the first five columns. Some of these words had more than one syllable, and I had to remind the children that it was the syllable that had the *u* that we were focusing on. I also had to remind them that it had to have the same spelling pattern and the same pronunciation as the model word that headed each column.

On the third day, I had them open their sheets, and I uncovered my transparency so that all columns were visible. This is what the sheets looked like at the end of the third day:

OTHER	u us	ue sue	u-e use	ur burn	sure insure	ture nature
menu	run	true	mule	turn	measure	creature
tuna	must	blue	mute	urban	assure	picture
	snub	due	cute	turtle	treasure	mixture
	runt	statue	amuse	return	pleasure	mature
	strum	value	reuse	hurt	pressure	adventure
	bus	rescue	compute			
	minus	continue				
	numbers					
	sunset					
	summer					
	submarines					

The first three days of our sorting activities are usually devoted to reading sorts—that is, we pronounce the words before asking the children to decide which column they belong in. On the fourth day, I do a blind sort. The children get a new sorting sheet just like the one they used the first three days, and I use a new transparency. I use the same words we have used on the first three days, but on the fourth day, I say the word but do not show it (thus the name "blind sort"). The students put their finger on the column to show where they think it should be written. I then show them the word, and they write it and I write it. On Friday, we do a blind writing sort. I say the word, and they have to try to write it in the correct column before I show it to them. This is the hardest one of all, but having worked with these words on the previous four days, most of the children are able to write the word in the correct column.

At the end of the fifth day, I have the children use two facing pages in their word sort notebooks and set up the columns as they were on their sheets. They then pick one or two of the words we sorted and write these in the correct columns. Their sorting notebooks are now set up for the best part of word sorting—the hunt. The children have one week to find other words that fit the patterns and write them into their own sorting notebooks. They can find words anywhere—around the room, on signs, or in books they are reading for Readers' Workshop, self-selected reading, and even science, social studies, and math. They do this hunting on their own and are all eager to have lots of words—especially big words—to contribute to our final sort.

For the final sort, I put a huge piece of butcher paper all the way across the chalkboard. I set up the columns as they were set up on the original sort sheets—using a different-colored permanent marker for each. We then go around the room, letting the children have a turn coming up and writing one word in its correct column, pronouncing that word, and for obscure words, using it in a sentence. We keep going around until we run out of words or space on our sort mural. Usually, we fill up the easy columns—*u* as in *us*, *ur* as in *turn*—but have space left on the more difficult ones. I hang the mural along the back wall, and children can continue to write in the correct columns the words they find.

We do a sort like this about every three weeks. We spend the first week together, working through the five-day cycle (reading sort, blind sort, blind writing sort), the next week hunting, and the last week experiencing the delight of finding a few more words to fit the pattern. The children responded quite enthusiastically to this sort, and I am going to do one more before the Christmas break.

December

We have done plays this month! Children love plays, and there are many good holiday plays as well as others that children enjoy acting out, so that December is the perfect month for plays. We began by choosing some plays already written as plays and later in the month wrote our own plays based on award-winning books. Each group devised a play for one of the kindergarten, first-, or second-grade classes. They became as excited about this as they were about the approaching holiday season, so that December became a little harried (more harried?).

Each group selected a book they wanted to act out. Some groups chose a picture book, so they could do the whole story. Others selected a scene or a chapter from a longer book. No matter which, they all went through the same webbing process to convert their story into a play. I modeled this using a picture book they all had loved, *Sleeping Ugly* by Jane Yolen.

I began by rereading the book aloud, webbing the characters and their traits and motivations, events, props, costuming, and setting as I went along. There was a huge web begun on the chalkboard. This was very time-consuming, and after the first several pages, a bit overwhelming to them. They could not see how I could read and look for so many things at once. I stopped that day and told them we would come back to it the next day.

Day Two: I assigned each table group to one aspect to pay attention to. Hilda's table was to list characters as I read aloud, and they were to put descriptors next to those characters that told what the characters were like. On the chalkboard, I was also listing this information as I went along. Jeff's table was to list props that would be needed to stage this as a play. Again, I listed what I noted on the chalkboard web. Other tables had other parts of the web to pay attention to. I told them not to copy what I was writing, but rather to write what they heard in order to help find things I might miss. After reading about two pages this way, I asked groups to tell me some of the things I had missed so I could add them to the big web. For example, I had not listed Princess Miserella's horse as a character, but Hilda's table thought of him as a character because he had purposely not taken Miserella home, even though he could have. That purposefulness, they argued, made him a character. I conceded to their reasoning. There were lots of props I had not listed that Jeff's table included: dishes for the shelves, little animals to stand around, and so on. So my web grew there as well. Each table had added in more things than I had, except "events"; I had identified far more than they had. I suspect this is tied to their understanding of what is an event. Some of the research articles I have read in the past seem to have struggled with that as well!

We completed the *Sleeping Ugly* web in this way, and I put them to work applying the same strategy to their own story. But this time, members of the group were to each read their story to themselves and list the aspects of their assigned element. Butch's group, who were staging *Stellaluna,* divided up the web this way: Butch was listing props; Mandy listed characters, traits, and motivations; Manuel identified events; Alexander listed scenery ideas to show the setting; and Roberta identified costuming needs. They each put their section on the group web and then reviewed it together to clarify the parts and make sure everyone understood and agreed with the listed elements.

After each web was completed (at least in a first-draft form), I called them all back together for a mini lesson on how to take those elements they had listed and turn them into a play. We reviewed the format that a play is written in, and I gave each group a template for a reference.

Another helpful holiday deed was sending volunteers from my class to Helen Launch's kindergarten room to write down the children's dictated letters to their parents. Helen decided this would make a nice gift from the children. She asked them to tell their parents about an incident they remembered and to tell them what is wonderful about their family. Even Butch and Mitch have become quite the little helpers this month. Hmm! Maybe there is something to extrinsic motivators after all.

January

Well, my expectations about this term's student teacher seem to be supported by her deeds. Amah Yung is a most eager young woman, staying late in the afternoon to complete a bulletin board or game that she is making for the children.

The children have, for the most part, become quite attached to her. She and Joyce have really bonded. They talk at great length on the playground, and I have noticed that Joyce is beginning to get really involved with her work. She doesn't need to be reminded to do it and even seeks extra things to do now. Part of the reason might be that Amah Yung discovered Joyce's interest in unusual and unexplainable happenings, and she has been bringing some of Zilpha Keatley Snyder's books for Joyce to read. She especially enjoyed *The Egypt Game* and *The Changeling*. Right now she is reading *Below the Root*, a book that I found fascinating. Joyce is really growing up!

We have had an unusually busy month. Readers' Workshop focused on folklore. I chose this genre to study partly because I have always loved fairy tales, folktales, and legends and partly because there are so many wonderful things for the children to read that cut across all the reading levels. I have versions of some of the fairy tales, as well as *Pecos Bill* and *Babe the Blue Ox*, tales that are easy enough for everyone but Paul to read independently, so I could have Chip, Daisy, Butch, and the other low readers read by themselves rather than with a partner. I am always concerned that children develop independent silent reading ability during this third-grade year, and this folktale unit provided the children with lots of easy choices.

I steered my super readers—Larry, Pat, Danielle, and others—in the direction of myths. I read *Hades and Persephone* to the whole class and talked with them about Greece and Greek mythology. The children were amazed to discover that at the time these myths were first told, most people believed that they were true. After I finished reading this tale, I showed them some of the other myth stories of which I had multiple copies, and as I had expected, my most sophisticated readers gravitated to the myths when making choices of what to read for their literature response groups.

I included many folktales from other countries in this unit. Unfortunately, I don't have many multiple copies of the folktales from other countries, so I did most of these by reading them to the whole class. For some, I read the entire book, but for many others, I just read the first chapter or story in a collection and then made these books available during self-selected reading. The ones the children liked best were *Sedna, an Eskimo Legend*, which I hunted up in honor of Tanana; *Why the Sun and the Moon Live in the Sky*, an African tale; and *Bawshou Rescues the Sun*, a Chinese tale.

Because many of the folktales and myths have clear problem-solution structures, I decided that this was a good time to teach the children to create story maps. There are many different ways of creating story maps, but all help children to follow the story by drawing their attention to the elements that all good stories share. Stories have characters, and they happen in a particular place and time that we call the setting. In most stories, the characters have some goal they want to achieve or some problem they need to resolve. The events in the story lead to some kind of solution or resolution. Sometimes, stories have implicit morals or themes that we hope children will learn from.

There are many different kinds of story maps. I like this one I adapted from Isabel Beck (Macon, Bewell, & Vogt, 1991).

Main Characters

Setting (Time and Place)

Problem or Goal

Event 1

Event 2

Event 3

Event 4

Event 5

Event 6

Solution

Story Theme or Moral

For our first story map experience, I chose *The Three Little Pigs*. The children and I retold and acted out this favorite story, and then we worked together to fill out the story map. Here is that story map filled in for *The Three Little Pigs*.

We completed three more story maps together after watching the videos of *Snow White and the Seven Dwarfs, Beauty and the Beast,* and *Aladdin*. We also read several book versions of the tales on which these movies were based and discussed how they were different and the same. The children could not believe that there were no dwarfs named Sleepy and Doc in the original *Snow White*.

Main Characters *Mother Pig, three little pigs, big bad wolf*

Setting (Time and Place) *Woods, make-believe time and place*

Problem/Goal *Pigs wanted to be independent and have their own houses.*

> **Event 1** *Mother Pig sends three little pigs out to build their own houses.*

> **Event 2** *First little pig gets some straw and builds a straw house. Big bad wolf blows the straw house down.*

> **Event 3** *Second little pig gets some sticks and builds a stick house. Big bad wolf blows the stick house down.*

> **Event 4** *Third little pig gets some bricks and builds a brick house. Big bad wolf cannot blow the brick house down.*

> **Event 5** *Big bad wolf gets scalded coming down the chimney of the brick house.*

Solution *Pigs live happily ever after in strong brick house.*

Story Theme or Moral *Hard work pays off in the end!*

Once we had done these four story maps together, the groups had no trouble completing story maps for the tales and myths they were reading. For the most part, they completed these collaboratively, and then each child wrote his or her own story map in the literature response journal.

Because the children had so enjoyed doing the plays in December, and since folktales and myths just "beg" to be performed, I ended the unit by letting each group act out one of the pieces they had read. I showed them some wonderful books I bought last summer (*Overhead Transparencies for Creative Dramatics* by Creative Teaching Press), which had on transparency important scenery from some of the myths and tales they had been reading. When projected from the back of the room, these colored transparencies transformed our room into the dark woods through which Red Riding Hood walked or a square in ancient Greece. In addition to this instant transparency scenery, the books of transparencies contain simple headband patterns that make acting out a story a snap. Because I had planned this creative reenactment response culmination to the unit, I made sure that at least two of the stories that each group had read were ones for which I had scenery and headbands. I didn't require the groups to restrict their choice of which one to act out to only those, but they all chose a piece that had these accoutrements.

The reenactments were a big success, and we had a special evening performance for parents before one of our schoolwide PTA meetings. We also sent performing troupes to the younger grades. Miss Yung was a tremendous help to me this month, and she had a great time. I hope I didn't overwhelm her, however. As I was pulling out books and videos and the transparency books, she kept saying, "Where do you get all this stuff? I have never seen anyone with so many different things and ideas. How will I ever have what I need next year?"

In her notebook, she has pages and pages full of things she needs and wants. I, on the other hand, am wondering what I am going to do with it all—31 years of accumulated stuff is a lot of stuff! I think I will box some of it up and send it off with Amah when she leaves at the end of March. I hate to part with it, but it won't be of any use to anyone in my attic—and, come to think of it, my attic is already full.

February

Another exciting month! This month I used the broad umbrella of animals as the organizing theme for our Readers' Workshop. We read both fiction and nonfiction books, including such favorites as *Charlotte's Web* and some of the *Winnie-the-Pooh* stories. We discussed how you could tell if a book was a story or informational, and I tried to get all the children to read some of each type. We made webs for the different animals different groups were reading about and included the factual information we found in informational books. We also decided that even in a clearly fictitious animal story, there were some things that were true. Spiders do spin webs and bears do like honey. When reading animal stories, the children sometimes argued about which characteristics were true of the animals, and I helped them look up the animal in question in various reference books to resolve the disputes. We discovered some wonderful authors of animal informational books. The children were entranced with Dorothy Hinshaw Patent's books—especially *Buffalo* and *Gray Wolf, Red Wolf.* They also enjoyed the books of Carol Carrick, who writes fiction with realistic depictions of animals as well as informational books, including Mitch's favorite, *Sand Tiger Shark.*

Once we got lots of animal webs made, I used these to teach some focused writing lessons on writing reports. The children and I had read several books on whales and jointly constructed the web. I then showed them how we could take this information and write a report on whales. I modeled for them how to write an introductory paragraph about whales, then to use the information from the different spokes of the web to write descriptive paragraphs, and finally how to write a concluding paragraph. The children and I jointly constructed each paragraph— they gave me suggestions and then I put the sentences together in a cohesive way.

It took us several days to turn our whale web into this report. Steve, who is our resident nature expert and quite an artist, drew the whale illustrations.

Once we had done our whale reports together, the groups picked one of the animals they had been reading about and webbing and wrote reports based on their webs. They are getting quite good at writing collaboratively, probably because we do a lot of it as a class. They pick someone "who writes real nice" to do the actual writing, but they all add their ideas. I have them use the Editor's Checklist to proofread their reports, and they are getting much better at finding and fixing those things we have been working on all year.

Realizing that "time is marching on," I decided that I needed to move them toward more independence in their writing. After the groups collaboratively wrote their reports on an animal, we constructed as a class several webs about animals commonly kept as pets—dogs, cats, gerbils. They told me all about George in first grade and wanted to go get him and bring him for a visit. Steve informed them that George had been dead for over a year, and many were devastated when they realized that their first-grade pet was no longer with us. Steve volunteered to ask Mrs. Wright if we could borrow Samantha—but they didn't want "just any old gerbil."

I had each child choose one of the animals we had discussed, then asked them to write a report, using the web and the format we had used as a whole class and in their response groups. After writing their report, they shared in small groups, got suggestions for revision, then picked a friend to help them edit, and finally brought their paragraph to me or Miss Yung—joint editors-in-chief. They are now typing their individual reports on the computers, and we are compiling a class book on animals. Many of them have chosen their animal reports as one of the pieces to go in their showcase portfolios, and I have noticed lots more animal reports being written now that we are back to self-selected topic process writing for a few weeks.

Miss Yung has been invaluable to me this month. We have done a lot of team teaching, and our styles mesh wonderfully. She is, however, much more organized than I am and has come up with a very clever way of keeping anecdotal records on the children. I have a folder for each child with divisions for the major areas in which I write comments on a regular basis. I always note in this folder what the children bring to read to me from their self-selected reading, as well as some observations on what strategies they are using well and which strategies I need to help them develop. I also make some notes immediately after each writing conference. In addition, I sit down each afternoon for a few minutes and sift through my folders, remembering what I observed the children doing as they read and wrote throughout the day, and make some notes based on these remembrances.

Miss Yung, observing me do this each afternoon, would always ask how I could remember all this. I told her that it is hard to remember when you are just starting teaching, because you have so many things to think about at one time, but that with experience, she would find that she too could sift through the folders at the end of the day and remember specific observations she had made about different children as the day progressed. Not willing to wait for experience, Miss Yung has come up with a simple system. She walks around all day with a clipboard on which she has attached one sheet of file-folder labels. As she observes children, she puts the child's initials and the date on one of the labels and then writes down what she wants to note in the folder. At the end of the day, she peels all the labels off the sheet and puts them on the right child's folder. She also notices which children she hasn't made any observations about in several days and puts their initials on a label on the sheet she will use the next day. (Some quiet children like Rita and Manuel just don't get noticed unless you decide to notice them!)

Between writing observations down immediately after each reading and writing conference, and the labels that are always there to record observations at any time of the day, you don't have to try to remember what you saw the different children doing. In fact, I realize as I watch her with her clipboard and labels that I am probably not as good at remembering as I think I am. She will be doing almost all the teaching next month, but when I get back into it in April and May, I think I will get myself a clipboard and sheet of labels! I told both Amah and Dr. Link, her supervisor, that I intended to do this, and Amah expressed delight and amazement that she had been able to teach me something. Dr. Link said that the best teachers were also lifelong learners, and they both tried to talk me out of retirement! "It's too late," I said, "I've got travel plans made and it's time to make way for the Amah Yungs of the world."

March

Amah Yung has become invaluable to me and the students, and I told Dr. Link that I was not going to let her go! She laughed at me, of course, and said that if I felt that strongly, perhaps I would be willing to recommend her for my position, which would become vacant with my retirement this June. I assured her that I would certainly do that, for Amah has been the best student teacher I have ever had. She is so creative, willing, and sympathetic to the students! Yet she doesn't let that sympathy interfere with providing them the best possible instruction: She feels quite sad about Chip's home situation, but it is one that we can do nothing about, since his family is too proud to accept welfare. But we can't let that interfere with doing what we can for him: providing him with the best possible education.

Amah has become a real expert at managing her time. With both of us working, team-teaching style, we can accomplish even more, so I was reluctant to give her the experience that she needed in handling the entire day by herself. But I did allow her three weeks, of course, so that she had a small taste of what it would be like to be totally responsible for a class.

During those three weeks—her last three weeks with us—she had the children making "shape books." Chip made a "hand book" in the shape of a large hand. The illustrations were photos made with an inexpensive Polaroid camera, as well as others cut out from magazines. All were pictures of hands doing various things. The illustrations were labeled with descriptions of the hands' actions. One picture had a man's hands playing a piano, and the sentence said, "Hands can make music." Another showed a lady cuddling a baby and was titled "Hands can love you, too." Horace made a "foot book" using the same technique. Several other children found shape books to be an entertaining exercise.

Another project of hers was the long-awaited poetry unit. I knew that these children had had quite a lot of exposure to poetry. They had had much poetry read to them, and they had, in turn, created many poems of their own. I knew that they were ripe for the kinds of activities that Amah had in mind for them.

She began the poetry unit by reading to the children from Mary O'Neill's classic and beautiful Hailstones and Halibut Bones, a collection of poems about colors. After reading a couple of her favorites and one of mine ("What is Purple?"), she discussed with them that Mary O'Neill is saying that colors are not only things but also feelings, moods, smells, and sounds. Then she took a stack of colored construction paper from her table and asked the children to form groups of five or six and told them that each group would receive one color sheet. They were then to list all the things that the color could be, feel like, smell like, sound like, or make them feel like within the five minutes that the timer would be set for. They began to discuss furiously and to list all of these qualities. When the timer rang, there were groans of "Oh no! Not yet! Let us put down some more." She asked each group to choose someone who could read the completed list to the rest of the class. One that I thought was particularly good was this one by Rita, Jeff, Manuel, Mort, Pat, and Steve. Their color was white:

> puffy clouds
> lacy snowflakes
> glaring light
> refrigerator door
> frosty window pane
> anger
> fear
> apple inside
> crunchy ice cube
> fluffy whipped cream
> winter morning breath
> mashed potatoes

She told the children that poetry creates images, and that those images do not need to be done with rhymes. She said that she was sure that the children could create a poem from what they had listed. She said, "Let me see if *I* can make one." This is it:

> *Lacy snowflakes*
> *Against my window pane*
> *Fluffy whipped cream*
> *Puffy clouds above.*

The children were enthralled, as was I, with this creation. Immediately, each group set to work to create a poem. Amah had explained to me that she wanted the children to have many experiences in writing group poems before they attempted to write individual ones. She told me that she had come to love poetry only within the last few years, that she had dreaded and hated it before. She was sure that that was because of the way in which her teachers had dealt with it—not as something to be loved, treasured, and enjoyed, but rather as something to be analyzed, dissected, and criticized. She had vowed that she would do her best to help her students learn to enjoy poetry at an early age. A format that she used with them involved the "diamante" form that Iris Tiedt had developed. It is as follows:

noun

adjective, adjective

participle, participle, participle

noun, noun, noun, noun

participle, participle, participle

adjective, adjective

noun

The first and last words are to be opposites, and images build on the first noun through the two nouns in the middle. The transition is made here to building images for the last noun. The poem below is one written by the class.

Father

Strong, kind

Working, resting, loving

Bed, baby, boy, Mommie

Working, working, working,

Tired, busy

Mother

She also had the children complete the following phrases, and with the unifying factor of "The year" repeated at the end of the poem, she found that even the less capable children could produce a poem they were pleased with.

The year . . .
The fall . . .
The winter . . .
The spring . . .
The summer . . .
The year . . .

I knew that the poetry unit had been successful when I noticed that the previously untouched poetry books in the class library became the most demanded ones, and when poetry began to appear in their writing notebooks. The children recited poetry to one another on the playground. If only they keep this enthusiasm!

April

My, how the time is passing now. With April over, only one more full month of school remains. I always begin to panic at this time of the year, wondering if I will accomplish all that needs to be done. Oh well, done or not, the year *will* end! I've started to go through my file cabinets so that I won't be here all summer, trying to move out of this room. One accumulates a lot in 31 years.

While cleaning, I came upon the file folder for literature-based curriculum compiled the year that I first began to become discontented with what I had been doing and was searching for something more satisfying for myself and the children. I had read a lot of articles in my professional journals, attended workshops, and taken courses at the university. I tried, then, to put all of the information together in a way that I could deal with it. I thought that I was ready after we returned from our spring break (in March of that year). There was still enough time to work out some of the problems and to give it a fair try, realizing that if it didn't work, I wouldn't have wasted an entire year of the children's time.

For the rest of that year, I used trade books for most of my reading instruction and began doing Readers' Workshops. The children responded well, but I had very few books of which I had multiple copies and no whole-class sets of books. I used what I had here, plus what I could check out from the school, public, and university libraries, and we got through the year, but I couldn't offer children very much choice, and just gathering up the books took a huge chunk of my time.

The second year, I used reading series and trade books, alternating which we would read in. I had purchased some multiple copies of trade books, and the school purchased some more that could be checked out from the library. Gradually, I got to the point where I am today. My reading program is totally literature based, and I give the children complete freedom in what they read for self-selected reading and a lot of choice in what they select to read and discuss in their literature response groups. I have some selections that we all read and a lot of pieces that I read to the whole class. I make sure to include lots of variety in topics, authors, and genres so that my children all get a fairly balanced reading diet.

Our topic this month was sports! In talking with the children and looking at their interest inventories, I realized that sports is one topic almost all my children are interested in. Many of them play sports—baseball, soccer, tennis—and with the university so close, lots of my children go to basketball and football games. There is also a lot of excitement and interest this year in the upcoming Olympics. I included stories in which children play sports, including *Thank You, Jackie Robinson* by Barbara Cohen, *Never Say Quit* by Bill Wallace, and *Scoop Snoops* by Constance Hiser. I also included biographies of sports heroes. They read about some of the old pros but seemed to enjoy most the *Sports Shots Books*, which chronicle the lives and careers of modern heroes, Michael Jordan, Florence Griffith Joyner, Wayne Gretzky, Michelle Kwan, and Joe Montana. Of course, we used reference books such as *Amazing but True Sports Stories* and *Inside Pro Football*. Both this year's and the back issues of *Sports Illustrated for Kids* were great references.

I also used the sports theme for several guided writing lessons. The students remembered writing their animal reports and compiling them into a class book.

This month, they all became sports reporters. We watched together a video of a championship basketball game and then worked collaboratively to write up the game for *Sports Illustrated for Kids*. I told the class that reporters were always given a limited amount of space, and so we had to limit our article but make it exciting at the same time. When we had finished our class-composed article, the children chose another sport for which I had a game or match on video—baseball, football, tennis, soccer, swimming, or gymnastics—and worked in groups to write an article describing that.

We completed two fairly sophisticated word sorts this month. For the first one, we worked with some common endings and suffixes and emphasized the spelling changes that occur when these endings are added. I gave the students their sort sheets, and on the first day, I had them fold their papers so that we were sorting only words that had no ending or words that ended in *en, er,* or *est.* We had previously sorted words with endings that needed no spelling changes. All the words I gave them for this sort required that they make some change in the root word before adding the ending. On the next two days, I included more *en, er,* and *est* words and others that ended in *ment, less,* or *ness.* Following our usual procedures, I gave them a clean sort sheet on Thursday and did a blind reading sort, followed by the hardest task of all on Friday—a blind writing sort in which they had to decide where to write the word and write it before I showed them the word. The following week, they hunted words that fit these patterns and wrote them in their word sort notebooks. These words are harder to find than the ones sorted by vowel patterns that we did earlier in the year, and they had a hard time filling up the butcher paper columns during our culminating sort. Roberta and Horace teamed up together and figured out that if you started with words ending in *y,* you could get a lot of words to add. Their list included many *nasty, nastier, nastiest, nastiness/silly, sillier, silliest, silliness* combinations. Hilda complained that this wasn't fair, because they surely had not found all those words in their reading. Roberta picked up the dictionary and claimed that she had been reading it!

No Ending	en(e)	er(y-i)	est(y-i)	ment	less	ness(y-i)
sun	*sweeten*	*sunnier*	*meanest*	*agreement*	*winless*	*greediness*

The other sort we did was also a challenge. We sorted for words that ended in *el, le,* and *al,* along with words that ended in *able* and *ible.* The children were frustrated by the fact that you couldn't tell by hearing these words which way the end would be spelled. I pointed out that with some words, you can't be sure which way it will be spelled; you just have to write it and see if it looks right and sometimes use the dictionary to check.

Other	el	le	al	able	able	ible
	label	*turtle*	*general*	*table*	*notable*	*edible*

The children have begun compiling their showcase portfolios. We are having our first show for parents in mid May, and the children all want to put their best foot forward. I have limited them to five pieces each—and they must include at least one piece in which they have written in response to something they read. For each piece they select, they are writing a brief description on an index card, indicating why they chose this piece and what they were trying to do with it. Some of my most prolific writers are having a terrible time deciding which five to include, while Daisy, Mort, and Chip are complaining, "You mean we have to find five things we are proud of and want everyone to read? That's too many!" I am taking them on a field trip to the university next month, and one of the things we will go to is an artist's showing. I hope that will help them understand what our showing is all about.

May

I always have approach-avoidance conflicts at the end of the school year, but this month has been especially emotional. It is strange, but I can picture in my mind and name almost all the children in the first class I taught 31 years ago (yegads, I am getting old—they are in their mid-forties!), and I am sure I will always remember this class. These last few weeks, as they have been assembling their showcase portfolios and I have been selecting samples from their growth portfolios to put in their cumulative portfolios, I kept thinking that they were the best class I ever had. I wouldn't have believed it at the beginning of the year, but I will even have fond memories of Mort and Daisy!

It was apparent from looking at their beginning-of-the-year, midyear, and end-of-the-year writing samples in which they described Merritt Elementary and told about what they liked best that they have all shown tremendous growth in both their first-draft writing ability and their ability to revise and edit a piece of writing. The growth was most striking for the students who came in furthest behind. Paul can write coherent pieces now. While these pieces are short and not terribly interesting, they do say something and hold together, and he is able to improve them a little when he edits and revises. Daisy, Butch, Chip, Joyce, and Jeff have all shown marked increases in their writing ability. Tanana is writing more and is willing to write, but her language is still quite immature, and often her sentences don't sound quite right.

I did not give end-of-the-year IRIs to all the children, because I could tell from my observations of them during Readers' Workshop and from my oral reading analyses taken during self-selected reading conferences that they were growing in both their ability to read and respond and in the breadth of their reading interests. I did give IRIs to my below grade-level children, however, because I wanted to see how far they had come.

Paul, who entered reading at either primer or first-reader level, can read most material at second-grade level if he is having an "alert" day. Daisy is also at second-grade level, but she just missed the third-grade instructional-level criteria by a few words, so she is moving along. Butch, who was reading at second-grade level, now reads at third-grade level. Of course, that still puts him one year behind when he goes to fourth grade next year, but he did make a full year's growth. Chip, Alexander, and Mort, who read at second-grade level at the beginning of the year, tested fourth-grade level. I am so proud of them! Chip didn't surprise me, because he is a real worker and he really got into books this year. Mort did surprise me. His daily work and attitude didn't show much improvement. If he applied himself, he could probably be a very good student. Tanana's instructional level tested third grade, and again her word identification was much better than her comprehension. She has shown amazing growth, however, and I know that with Ms. Maverick's integrated knowledge-building curriculum in fourth grade, she will continue to grow in her knowledge of the world; consequently, her comprehension will improve.

I am delighted with the growth shown by my very best students. Larry, Hilda, Danielle, Pat, Mandy, and Roberta have become quite sophisticated readers and writers. They have all broadened greatly what they like to read about and the different types of writing they can do. They are confident in their abilities and—except for Roberta, who is still too bossy—they are very helpful to the other children in literature response groups and in revising/editing conferences. Ever since I started to organize the classroom around literature and writing and include many multilevel activities, I have noticed remarkable growth for the children on the two ends of the continuum. I am not sure that the way I teach makes much of a difference for the Mitches and Carls in the world, but I know that it makes a difference for the children who come to me reading and writing substantially below or above where you would expect third-graders to be.

We finished up the year with "Your Choice" Readers' Workshops. I put out all the multiple copies of books that we hadn't used yet and let children choose from them all, then formed literature response groups based on their choices. They decided what they would write in the literature response logs and completed these individually before going to their discussion groups. Because I modeled for them so many different ways of responding, the children had no trouble thinking of what they wanted to say. As I circulated among the groups, I saw children with their logs open and heard them reading some statements such as:

> I think the funniest part was when the dog got into the game.
> I didn't think she should have told her mother what had happened when her friends had sworn her to secrecy.
> I know what is probably going to happen next. They are going to lose the game and the coach will quit.

Hearing my readers make statements like this on their own convinces me that they have learned how you think about and respond to what you are reading. Because they are so in the habit of thinking this way, I bet they will continue to do this even if no one makes them write their responses down. Literature response logs are not so much for me to know what they are thinking as they are to help them clarify for themselves what they are thinking.

THE THIRD-GRADE MEETING

Mrs. Wise smiled as Sue Port departed. Some teachers felt considerable fear of that small but dynamic Ms. Port whenever she entered their classrooms. Not Mrs. Wise! She remembered when Ms. Port had been *her* student teacher some 15 years ago. It was on Mrs. Wise's recommendation that the school system hired Sue and later promoted her to the position of curriculum supervisor. Now Mrs. Wise was smiling, for she had just been asked if she would present the program for the final meeting of the third-grade teachers. "My valedictory," she thought. "Oh, well. I suppose they had to ask me now, since I won't be here next year. I was hoping, though, that I could get away without even attending, let alone being the program!" After 31 years of these meetings, she was *ready* to retire; she had often said that the meetings were things she would never miss about school.

But now to plan what to do! She began by going through some of the materials that she had selected for this final meeting, dragging out samples of books that she had used during this past year. She had asked to have the meeting in her own room, so that she would not have to transport all of her paraphernalia across town to the room in the administration building where these meetings were usually held. Here she would show the other teachers the learning centers that occupy the children's time, as well as the card catalogue system that the children had devised. She sat down to plan the meeting for the following week.

One week later, Mrs. Wise was completely organized and ready for the meeting. She greeted the teachers who entered her room and then began the meeting by expressing her pleasure at seeing all her old friends and acknowledging her sincere delight at the interest they had shown in her program. She told them that she was eager to share with them the kind of program that she had been using for many years. Some of those present had visited her classroom in the past, and she invited them to make any comments that they felt were pertinent.

"Knowing me, you can expect to see a lot of books this afternoon." As she said this, she reached down and opened two large boxes, which were indeed full of books. As she talked about her classroom, she pulled out books to illustrate what she had read to the children, which books the whole class had read, and the kind of books she had let them choose from to read and discuss in their literature response groups. She showed them Jeff's literature response log (Jeff had been in the hospital the last week of school, so Mrs. Wise was using a lot of his things to demonstrate what the children did; she would drop everything off at his house after the meeting). She showed how she structured their responses early in the year, but how they were able to independently write their own personal responses by the end of the year.

She also had Jeff's writing notebook, his word sort notebook, and the five pieces he had selected for his showcase portfolio. She showed these also as she explained how she did both process writing and guided writing lessons to move all the students forward in their writing ability.

On transparency, she had some of the webs the groups had made, from which they wrote their animal reports, along with the transparencies she used for the word sorts they did. She also had brought along the class book they made on animals and the butcher paper sheet on which they had accumulated their words from their last word sort.

As Mrs. Wise was showing them all these things and describing what they did, she could see some agitated faces. She stopped talking once she had shown them all the main things and said, "This was what I wanted to show you. What else would you like to know?"

A lot of hands went up, and Mrs. Wise called on a young teacher she had not seen before. This teacher said, "Mrs. Wise, I am awed by what you have shown us, but I wouldn't have any idea how to do this. Where do you get all the books, and how do you decide what they should read and write, and how do you know who is doing what?" Mrs. Wise could see that a lot of the more experienced teachers were thinking this too, and they all looked relieved that it was one of the beginning teachers who had asked the question. *She* wasn't supposed to know everything!

Mrs. Wise smiled and told them how she had begun gradually. Only after several years of transition had she accumulated the knowledge, organization, and books to allow her to do an "All Real Books" program. She talked about buying books with her own money in the old days but bragged about Mr. Topps and Merritt Elementary's decision to put more of their funds into classroom libraries and to let the teachers decide what they needed.

She also talked about her assessment system and showed them the IRI and interest inventory she gave at the beginning of each year, along with the repeated Merritt Elementary School writing prompt. She showed them the folder she kept on each child, in which she kept her oral reading analyses and observations after each reading and writing conference. She showed them her clipboard with file folder labels and told them how she used these to record her observations and then moved them to the appropriate folders. She could tell that everyone was impressed by this simple solution to the difficult-to-manage anecdotal record system, and then she told them that it was Amah Yung, her student teacher, who had thought of this. (At the mention of Amah, the young teacher whose question had instigated this explanation looked first amazed and then delighted. After the meeting, she explained to Mrs. Wise that Amah was her sorority sister, that she had no idea she had been Mrs. Wise's student teacher, and that she was going to call her this summer and "pick her brain.")

Mrs. Wise went on to tell them about the three kinds of portfolios she used: growth portfolios that contained samples she had chosen and in which she kept her anecdotal records, showcase portfolios that the children put together to demonstrate their literacy prowess, and cumulative portfolios that contained the samples each teacher selected to move with the child from year to year.

The teachers had other questions, mainly about what she did "with the low kids" and "how she challenged the high ones." This gave Mrs. Wise a chance to explain why she believed her approach to literacy was most beneficial to the low and high achievers. "For an average child like Jeff," she mentioned, pointing to his samples that had been passed around for the teachers to look at, "I'm not sure my literature-focus classroom really matters, but I can tell you that for students like

Daisy and Chip on one end and Larry and Hilda on the other, the multilevel instruction, the cooperative learning, and the amount of choice I give them makes a world of difference."

A hand went up and Agatha Nostic said, "Now, Vera, are you telling us this Jeff was just one of your average children?"

"As average as they come," responded Mrs. Wise. "He tested third-grade level on the beginning-of-the-year IRI, and I have his initial writing sample here, which is actually a little below average in many ways for the beginning of third grade. If I were going to pick one of my kids to have his appendix out so that I could show off his things here at this meeting, it surely wouldn't have been Jeff!"

Mrs. Wise glanced up at the clock and then summed up what she did and how it fit her philosophy of teaching. "I have probably been teaching third grade longer than anyone in this room—even you, Agatha—and I have tried about every fad that came along and jumped on a lot of the bandwagons and taught a lot of 'new and improved' reading series. After all these years, I am sure of just a few things. Children are all different, and they have different interests, attitudes, home experiences, and reading and writing abilities. Some children need more structure and instruction. Some children really thrive in situations where they can work with partners and small groups. All children profit from being immersed in a wide variety of wonderful books and being given a lot of time and support to write. The program I have developed has structure and instruction. We do things to build word knowledge—primarily our word wall and word sorting. I teach them reading and writing strategies through the focus lessons I do at the beginning of Readers' and Writers' Workshops. In addition to teaching, however, I give them time to do the activities I want them to value, and I let them make lots of choices of what they will read and write."

Mrs. Wise paused to notice the nods of agreement around the room. She had had the feeling when she began that some of these teachers were not very sympathetic to what she was doing, but now there was a noticeable change. Several of the teachers wanted to know how to begin her program.

She began to gather up her materials, preparatory to leaving the meeting, when Sue Port, with a grin on her face, told her to sit down, for the best part of the meeting was yet to come. Through the door, borne by two of her oldest friends, came a cake of mammoth proportions. The inscription read "Good-bye, Vera. We'll miss you." She was stunned and unable to speak for a moment, but one of her friends thought she heard her mutter under her breath, "I'd rather have a martini."

REFERENCES

Johns, J. L. (1993). *Basic reading inventory*, 5th ed. Dubuque, IA: Kendall/Hunt.

Macon, J. M., Bewell, D., & Vogt, M. (1991). *Responses to literature*. Newark, DE: International Reading Association.

Tiedt, I. (1970). Exploring poetry patterns. *Elementary English*, *47*, 1083–1084.

Children's Books/Materials Cited

Amazing but True Sports Stories, by Phyllis Hollander & Zander Hollander, Scholastic, 1986.
Babe the Blue Ox.
Bawshou Rescues the Sun.
Below the Root, by Z. K. Snyder, Atheneum, 1975.
Buffalo: The American Bison Today, by D. H. Patent, Ticknor & Fields, 1986.
The Changeling, by Z. K. Snyder, Atheneum, 1970.
Charlotte's Web, by E. B. White, HarperCollins, 1974.
A Convention of Delegates, by D. J. Hautly, Atheneum, 1987.
Cricket magazine.
The Egypt Game, by Z. K. Snyder, Atheneum, 1967.
Gray Wolf, Red Wolf, by D. H. Patent, Houghton Mifflin, 1990.
Hades and Persephone.
Hailstones and Halibut Bones, by M. O'Neill, Doubleday, 1961.
Henry Huggins and other books, by B. Cleary, Avon, various dates.
Inside Pro Football, Scholastic, 1992.
Kid City magazine.
Kids Discover magazine.
National Geographic World magazine.
Never Say Quit, by Bill Wallace, Scholastic, 1992.
Overhead Transparencies for Creative Dramatics, by Creative Teaching Press, 1987.
Pecos Bill.
Penny Power magazine.
Ranger Rick magazine.
Sand Tiger Shark, by C. Carrick, Houghton Mifflin, 1991.
Scoop Snoops, by C. Hiser, Scholastic, 1986.
Sedna, an Eskimo Myth, by B. Brodsky, McDermott, 1975.
Sleeping Ugly, by J. Yolen, Coward, McCann & Geoghegan, 1981.
Snow White.
Song and Dance Man, by K. Ackerman, Knopf, 1992.
Sports Illustrated for Kids magazine.
Sports Shots Books, Scholastic, 1990.
Stellaluna.
Thank You, Jackie Robinson, by B. Cohen, Scholastic, 1989.
The Three Little Pigs.
3–2–1 Contact magazine.
When I Was Young in the Mountains, by C. Rylant, Dutton Children's Books, 1982.
Why the Sun and the Moon Live in the Sky, by E. Dayrell, Houghton Mifflin, 1990.
Winnie-the-Pooh stories by A. A. Milne, Dell, 1987.
World Book Encyclopedia.
Zillions magazine.

Ms. Maverick:
Fourth Grade

THE PARENT MEETING

Yetta Maverick greeted most of the parents by name as they entered the door of her fourth-grade classroom. Six years before, she had known no one and had missed the easy familiarity she had established with the residents of the small mountain community where she had taught during her first three years as a teacher.

"Welcome," she began. "As most of you know from our annual book fairs, I am Ms. Maverick. I am pleased to see so many parents here tonight. In many schools, there is a tremendous turnout of parents for the kindergarten and first-grade meetings, but attendance decreases as the grade level of the children increases. You are to be commended for your continuing interest in the education of your children.

"I want you to know that I think fourth-graders are the very best age children to teach. Nine-year-olds are just so eager to learn—about everything—and they have the basic reading and writing skills that allow me to spend more of my time on reading and writing to learn, rather than on learning to read and write. It's a good thing that your children have already come such a long way in their literacy journey because, as you may know, fourth grade is also the grade in which statewide tests are given in writing, science, and social studies. Some fourth-grade teachers resent this subject-area testing, but it actually plays right into what I like to teach. I love to learn about real things—history, geography, real people, how machines work, the planets, and geology have always fascinated me. When I was in fourth grade, I was going to be an oceanographer, and I read all the science-oriented books I could get my hands on. So expect to see your children coming home excited about, talking about, and collecting information about whatever our current science or social studies unit is."

As she spoke, Ms. Maverick handed out the following schedule:

	Monday	Tuesday	Wednesday	Thursday	Friday
8:30–9:00	Group Meeting and Planning for the Day / Teacher Read-Aloud				
9:00–9:25	Self-Selected Reading and Individual Conferences				
9:25–10:20	Reading Workshop	Reading Workshop	Reading Workshop	Science or SS Unit	Science or SS Unit
10:20–10:40	Break/Recess				
10:40–11:40	Math	Math	Math	Science or SS Unit	Science or SS Unit
11:40–12:10	P.E.	Music	Art	P.E.	P.E.
12:10–12:45	Lunch	Lunch	Lunch	Lunch	Lunch
12:45–1:45	Writing Workshop	Writing Workshop	Writing Workshop	Science or SS Unit	Science or SS Unit
1:45–2:15	Words/Spelling	Words/Spelling	Words/Spelling	Science or SS Unit	Science or SS Unit
2:15–2:45/3:00	Centers/Projects/Individual and Small Group Conferences				

"I want you to look at our schedule now," she continued, "because it is a bit different from that used by other teachers your children may have had. It has taken me many years of teaching fourth grade to come up with some structure that allows me to give all the essential components adequate time, and this is what works best for me. We start our morning with a planning meeting in which we talk about what we will be doing during the various times. I lead the children in a discussion of 'what we will accomplish today.' Too many children come to fourth grade just doing what they are told but without a clear sense of how what we're doing helps them become better learners or how they are adding to their understanding of how the world works. I want your children to approach the rest of the day in a purposeful way in which they see the various tasks as 'things that get them someplace'—not just 'things she told us to do.' So we will not just talk about what we are going to do when, but how and why and how doing this will help us be smarter and better learners.

"The second thing that will happen each day is that I will read to them. It amazes me to read statistics that say most intermediate teachers don't read to their children daily because they don't have time! I don't have enough time either, but reading to children is one of the major ways of motivating children to read, increasing their language and concepts, and helping them learn how you think as you read. Most of you know that thinking, feeling, and language are the underpinnings of reading and writing, and at Merritt, we take seriously the 12 guiding principles we all agreed to several years ago. Reading to children each day is one of the most important vehicles we have for building language, developing thinking, and encouraging a love of books. I try to read a great variety of books, but I must admit I prefer informational books—books that tell about real people, places, and happenings. I also tie some of my read-aloud books into our science and social studies units, thus getting a few more minutes of content time in. So, when you ask your children what I am reading to them, don't be surprised if they tell you things like 'a book about whales' or 'a biography of Rosa Parks.'

"Next, the children have their self-selected reading time. I schedule 25 minutes for this every day. This is a little long for some of your children this early in the year, so I have started with 15 minutes and will increase gradually. At fourth-grade age, children can all read, but some are still not in the habit of sustaining their reading for long enough to really get into the book they are reading. Getting them to the point where they can sit and quietly read for 25 minutes is my goal, and I am sure we can do this at some point in the year. While your children read, I hold individual conferences with them. I conference with a fifth of your children each day. We only have three to four minutes for the conference, but you can accomplish quite a lot in that time, and when you multiply that times 36 weeks, that is a substantial amount of individual time during which I can touch base with every child every week, assessing reading strategies and encouraging individual reading interests.

"The other things that happen every day are our morning break or recess time, specials (which fourth grade has scheduled for 11:40 to 12:10), lunch, and our end-of-the day center or projects time." At this point, Mort's mother raised her hand, and Ms. Maverick acknowledged her.

"That's what I've been wondering about. I know that there is a lot to cover in fourth grade, and while I don't object to the children playing, I don't think they need 30 plus minutes every day to play in the fourth grade."

Ms. Maverick bristled just a bit but tried to smile as she explained, "Center and project time are not play time in this class. The activities the children do during this time are all connected to what we are learning and the skills we are working on. Sometimes the children are working in assigned centers, and sometimes they are making choices. Often, this is when they work on individual and group projects that come out of our science and social studies units. They do research and writing and work on drama and media projects to consolidate and then share what they have been learning. I got the idea of the end-of-day center time from Mrs. Wright, and I use that time to work with small groups and individuals while children pursue their own learning goals.

"Many of you know these 12 guiding principles, which the Merritt faculty came up with five years ago." Ms. Maverick pointed to a poster on her wall, on which the following statement was displayed.

> *At Merritt Elementary, we believe that all children can learn to read and write. We hold high expectations of every child. To make these expectations a reality, we all agree to have our instruction reflect 12 guiding principles:*

1. Provide a balanced literacy program.
2. Make instruction multilevel.
3. Use language as the foundation for reading and writing.
4. Teach reading and writing as thinking.
5. Use feelings to create avid readers and writers.
6. Connect reading and writing to all subject areas.
7. Read aloud to students daily.
8. Schedule daily self selected reading.
9. Have students write every day.
10. Teach the decoding and spelling strategies reading and writing require.
11. Use observation to assess learning and plan instruction.
12. Inform parents of expectations and progress.

"My center time helps me to achieve the first one and the second one. To me a balanced program means lots of things—a balance of types of materials the children read and write, a balance of whole-class, small-group, and individual arrangements, a balance between teacher decisions and children choices. Having the afternoon center time and the individual and group time it provides helps us to have a more balanced literacy program. It also helps me make it more multi-level. Your children are all fourth-graders, but their reading and writing levels span about six years. I make my instruction multilevel in a variety of ways, including having children choose material on their reading level during Self-Selected Reading and having them do writing at some point every day. They can only write on their own level, you know. The afternoon center/project time is another time when I can individualize what different children work on and help each child move along, regardless of where he or she begins."

Ms. Maverick glanced at the clock and saw that the meeting time was almost gone. "Trust me on this one for a month or so," she said. "Ask your children each day what they accomplished during the center/project time, and then see if you think they are just playing."

Quickly, Ms. Maverick explained the rest of the schedule and how the schedule helped her carry out the guiding principles. "All teachers have to follow state guidelines in terms of the amount of time given to each subject area. My schedule conforms to those guidelines, but I don't give the subjects equal time every day. Rather, I spend longer blocks of time on some days to equal the right number of minutes across the week. As you can see, our Monday, Tuesday, Wednesday schedule is different from Thursday and Friday. On Monday, Tuesday, and Wednesday, we have almost an hour of reading workshop, an hour for math, an hour for writing workshop, and 30 minutes to work on words and spelling. On Thursday and Friday, all that time is given to our science or social studies unit. This allows long periods of uninterrupted time to really get into the topics, and yet we still have separate times to make sure the fourth-grade reading, writing, and math curriculum requirements are being met.

The other thing that may not be so obvious is that we do read and write on our unit days. In fact, I teach many comprehension lessons and focused writing lessons on these days that help children learn the specific strategies required for informational text. Also, don't think science and social studies get forgotten on Monday, Tuesday, and Wednesday. Some of what we read during Reading Workshop and write during Writing Workshop is related to our units. Many of the big words we study and learn how to spell during our words time are connected to our units. In fact, I take very seriously principle number 6, which reminds us that we are committed to connecting reading and writing to all subject areas."

Ms. Maverick could hear parents from other rooms moving noisily through the hall on their way to the cafeteria for refreshments and the schoolwide meeting. She finished up by telling her group that she would be getting her first newsletter out to them soon and that she would be asking them to come in for individual conferences in about a month.

"Meanwhile, if you have any concerns about your child or how we 'do fourth grade,' our classroom door is always open, and I welcome your ideas and, yes, even your concerns!"

MONTHLY LOGS

September

What an unusual class of children this is! I thought that over the 10 years I have taught I had seen every possible combination of children, but this class disproves that theory. Of course, I expect to find great differences among children by the time they get to fourth grade, but I have never before seen the range represented by the span between Paul, who reads almost nothing, and Larry, who qualitatively reads almost as well as I do and quantitatively reads more than I do. Then there are the personality differences. Roberta cannot do the right thing no matter how hard she tries, and Betty, her twin sister, can't do anything wrong. Joyce and Hilda are both very capable, intelligent, and extremely independent.

I am pleased, however, with the adjustments most of the children have made to my program. I always enjoy getting Mrs. Wise's children because they have had so much experience working together in groups. It is still a shock to me to see Amah Young teaching in her room next door.

I am especially pleased with Daisy. According to her records, she just never got anything done. She is working now, although I think she is doing it for me rather than for herself. Each time she does anything, she comes to me for approval. I pat her on the head, because I want her to establish the habit of sitting down and accomplishing something, but I am trying to help her develop some internal feedback. Yesterday she brought me a picture she had painted. I said, "Yes, it is lovely. Didn't it feel good to do it?" I have a feeling this is going to be a year-long process, however; I have seldom seen a child with so little intrinsic motivation and self-confidence. For the moment, I am thankful that she is working for whatever reason. Paul is the weakest reader in the class. I will work individually with him during the afternoon time.

Mort is a pill! If I hear that child sigh and say, "Well, it doesn't matter. I don't care," one more time, I may lose my composure and shake him! I know, however, that I would be in trouble and it wouldn't do any good. Yesterday I said to him, "Mort, what do you like to do when you go home after school?"

He replied, "Oh, mostly I just sit around and get bored. Sometimes I watch television." As far as I can tell, he has no friends, no interests, and no aspirations. I guess I should think of him as "a real challenge."

I always begin the school year by doing some assessment of how well my children read and write and how they feel about reading and writing. I began by looking at the portfolios sent to me by Mrs. Wise. It is always enlightening to look at the three writing samples she has them do on the same topic. It encourages me when I see how Paul, Daisy, Jeff, Butch, and Tanana developed in their writing with Mrs. Wise's excellent instruction. I figure if they grew that much last year, they will certainly continue to develop with all the writing I plan for them this year. Even the writing of the best writers, Larry, Pat, and Hilda, showed remarkable growth across third grade, just proving once again that even bright, able, motivated, industrious children profit from good instruction. As I was looking through these writing samples in their portfolios, I was reminded once again of Mrs. Wright's contention that Writing is the most multilevel block.

I got a beginning-of-the-year writing sample from the children, using the same procedures Mrs. Wise uses but on the topic of "My Favorite and Least Favorite Things." I looked at these and compared them to their May third-grade sample. The writing of most children remained fairly stable across the summer, although the most struggling writers showed some regression, and Mort wrote almost nothing. It appears he has no real favorites—or "unfavorites."

Mrs. Wise also indicated their reading levels at the end of third grade. All but Paul, Daisy, Tanana, and Butch were reading at or above fourth-grade level on the Informal Reading Inventory, with Daisy, Tanana, and Butch reading just one year below level and Paul reading two years below. This was consistent with the standardized test results from last year, which showed that all the children except these four—and Mort, who probably didn't bother to read the test—read above the 50th percentile, with Larry, Pat, Hilda, and Roberta knocking the top off the test! I had Paul, Daisy, Tanana, Butch, and Mort read to me the first two pages in the first selection of our adopted reader and took an oral reading record as they read. Then I closed the book and asked them to retell the beginning of the story. Mort read it fine and clearly understood it, although it was like pulling teeth to get him to tell me. Butch had trouble with 11 out of the approximately 200 words, and his retelling was spotty. Tanana read very slowly but only missed four words. She had trouble retelling the story, but when I probed, she knew more than she could express. Daisy read "like a house on fire" missing 15 words and never stopping to look back. Not surprisingly, she wasn't able to tell me very much of what she had read. I had her go back, however, and forced her to read one sentence at a time, and she then did correct several of her errors and was able to tell me more. I concluded that Butch, Tanana, and Daisy, though a little under the criteria for instructional-level reading, could profit from reading in fairly easy fourth-grade-level material (the first selection is a little easier than the later ones) if they were given a lot of support from me or a partner. Who will be willing to be Daisy's partner is another question! Paul, on the other hand, is not able to approach reading at fourth-grade level. I stopped him at the end of the first page, and I read the second page to him. I don't know how well he comprehended, because he doesn't talk to me very much. I will have to have him with me or find him a very supportive partner whenever we are in Reading Workshop, and I am reading with him alone in books on his level each afternoon for 10 minutes during our Center/Project time.

My attempts to assess their reading and writing interests were quite successful. I told them that we were going to read some—but not all—the selections in our adopted reader. I also told them that we were not going to read them in the order they were in the book but were going to skip around. "I need your help," I said, "to decide which ones we will read and which ones to start with." I then gave everyone a sheet on which I had listed all the major selections in the book. We spent three days during Reading Workshop previewing and talking about the selections. We identified the author, and I asked the children if they had ever read any books by that author. They got quite excited when they recognized selections by Judy Blume, Eloise Greenfield, and Chris Von Allsburg. We identified each type of selection. Most of the children seem to prefer stories, mysteries being particularly popular. They were less enthusiastic about the informational selections, including biographies. We looked at the pictures of each major selection and predicted what it would be about. We read the shorter selections—poetry and brief magazine-type articles as we got to them. Finally, after previewing all the selections, I asked the students to rank each on a 0–3 scale, with 0 meaning, "I don't want to read it" and 3 meaning, "I really want to read it soon." We tallied up the scores and *Tales of a Fourth Grade Nothing* by Judy Blume, *Jumanji* by Chris Van Allsburg, and all three mysteries contained in the book got the most points. All the selections got some votes, with the social studies informational pieces and biographies bringing up the rear.

Because their reading interest was so high, we began our reading workshop with *Tales of a Fourth Grade Nothing* one week and *Jumanji* the next week. For the third and fourth weeks, I gathered up copies of two other Blume and three other Van Allsburg books and used the procedure I learned from Mrs. Wise of reading to students the first few pages of each book and then having them indicate their first, second, and third choice for what they wanted to read. They were quite excited about this and a bit amazed I knew how to do it! "I bet she stole the blook club idea from Mrs. Wise," Roberta remarked. Looking at their choices, I formed five groups, putting the children who needed help in the easiest book if that was one of their choices and the more advanced readers in the harder book if they had chosen it. I was amazed when I read Daphne's choice response. It read,

> Dear Ms. Maverick,
>   I would like to read all the books so it doesn't matter but if I could I would like to be with Paul. I have been helping him read since first grade and even though he is still not too good, he is much better than he was. If you put me in his group, I will help him and he will be able to read it.
>   Sincerely,
>   Daphne Sweet
>   P. S. Mrs. Wise always let me be in the same group as Paul.

You learn something every day when you give children choices and ask for their opinions. I have been wondering how to handle Paul during Reading Workshop, and all of a sudden, here comes Daphne, ready, willing, and able!

I learned a lot about my children's attitudes toward reading and particular reading interests through having them survey different types of texts and make choices about what they like. I am also learning through our Self-Selected Reading conferences. I have divided the children into fifths according to the days of the week, an idea I learned from Mrs. Wright, as Roberta pointed out to everyone. (I think Roberta is beginning to wonder if I have any teaching ideas of my own, but she will soon find out I do!) Each day, once they are all settled in their spots with plenty of things to read within arm's reach (we have a No Wandering rule during Self-Selected Reading time), the five children who are designated that day of the week come for a brief conference. We have the routines pretty well established now. The children come in alphabetical order (we will reverse that halfway through the year), and each child gets three to four minutes. To prepare for our weekly conference, they have learned to:

1. Choose a book you like and can read.
2. Pick two pages from the book to read aloud to me.
3. Be ready to tell me what you like about this book and why you chose these two pages.
4. If you have not finished the book, tell me what you expect will happen or what you might learn.

5. If you have finished the book, tell me what kind of book you are thinking about sharing with me next week.

I have role-played this with the children and put these on a "Getting Ready for Your Own Special Conference" poster. During the conference, I make anecdotal records for each child of the book they bring, how well they read and understand it, why they chose that book, and their plans for next week. We have only had two weeks of conferences, but most children are getting the idea and seem to like the fact that they are the ones in charge of their conference.

Their feelings toward writing are on the whole quite positive. We talked about writing and what they had written in one of our first morning planning meetings. I invited them to bring any published pieces they could find at home, and I was amazed at how many they brought. Most of them had all three published books from first grade and some pieces published in various ways from second and third grades. They are clearly used to writing on their own topics, and they seem eager to pick a piece to publish, which we will get up and running next month. Just as with reading, they seem more comfortable writing personal narrative about themselves and stories than with informational writing. I am letting them choose what they want to write and publish now, but as the year goes on, we will do some focused writing activities in which they will learn to write descriptive and informational pieces.

While we have not actually begun the social studies unit on our state yet, we have done some readiness activities in preparation for this unit. One of the concepts that is very difficult for children to grasp is the notion of time and sequence. Last year I had my class construct a time line showing the important events in our state and their corresponding dates. Although the children learned from this activity, it was very difficult for them to conceptualize the differences in time. Last year's class never understood that the spaces between the depicted events were proportional to the actual time elapsed between these events.

In order to provide readiness for the state time line and to help the children apply time passage and sequence to their own lives, I had the children make a time line depicting the important events in their lives. I began by having the children put their chairs in a circle and asking them to call up the important things that had happened in their lives. The children were all eager to respond, and everyone had something to share, since the subject was one they all knew lots about. Rita recalled her first trip to the library, when the librarian told her she was too young to have a library card. Tanana remembered moving here from Alaska and how scared she was when she first came to Mrs. Wise's classroom. Larry recalled the first Hardy Boys book he had read. When all the children had contributed something to the discussion, I suggested that we might create some "life lines" to show all the important events that had already taken place in their lives. I showed them how we could use string and little slips of paper with words and illustrations to depict our individual histories.

The children were most enthusiastic, so we began right then. I gave each of the children a long sheet of paper and asked them to put their birth date in the top left corner and the current date in the bottom left corner. Although many of the children knew the month and day on which they were born, only Larry, Pat, and Hilda knew the year of their birth. I then asked the others how they thought they could figure out the year in which they were born. After some discussion, they worked out the mechanics of subtracting how old they were from the current date and filled in the year on the chart they were making. In the meantime, I modeled by making my chart on the board. Next to my birth date, I wrote "Ms. Maverick was born" and next to the current date, I wrote "Ms. Maverick is helping her class to make their own life lines." The children then followed my example and put appropriate entries next to their own names.

They then listed the important events in their lives. I told them not to worry too much at this point about the date or the order but just try to get down about 8–10 events. Most children had no trouble at all listing a dozen events. Paul, however, needed a great deal of help with this, and I fear his life line represents my thinking more than his. When the children had finished listing the events, I asked them how they thought we could find out the approximate date of each event. Several suggested their parents kept lists of everything, and that if they could take the charts home that night, they could fill in many of the dates. The others suggested they could fill in by knowing in what order things happened in relation to the events with known dates.

The next day they returned with dates and many more events filled in on their charts. We then cut the charts and organized the events into the proper order. Next began the construction of the actual life lines. Since all of the children in the class were either 8 or 9 years old, we decided to cut the strings either 9 or 10 feet long. In that way, each foot could represent a year. Any events that happened in the same year would be placed close to one another. If there were a year or two in which no events occurred, that would be represented by the unfilled space for that year. We also agreed that because we were going to hang these around the room for others to read, we should try to spell the words correctly and to use readable handwriting. Each child then measured and cut his or her string and marked it off in one-foot lengths. They also cut and measured strips of colored paper to three-by-six-inch dimensions. While the children were doing this, I acted as editor, helping children correct the spelling and punctuation on their charted events so that they could copy them correctly on their life line slips.

Somehow, it all got done! The children illustrated the events and taped the slips to the strings. Those who finished first helped the others. The life lines now hang below the windows and the chalkboards, and whenever the children have a spare moment, they can be seen reading their own or someone else's life history. This activity, which started out as readiness for our state's time line, had value in and of itself. The children helped one another and learned more about one another. They learned that we share many common experiences and that other experiences are unique to each individual. They do seem to have a better sense of time sequence and proportion, and they have certainly practiced their math, reading, and writing skills. I will do this again next year!

The other readiness activity this month was constructing a map of the school. We will do a lot of work with maps when we begin the actual study of our state next month, and for many children this is their first exposure to maps. I wanted them to connect maps to their own life space before asking them to generalize to the less tangible world outside. After a discussion about maps and what would be involved in constructing a map of our school, we walked around the whole building to observe what we would include in our map. The children suggested, and I listed on the board, all the things we might want to include in a map of our school. I then grouped the children in pairs, and each pair took responsibility for going to a particular classroom or area of the building, measuring that area, and constructing that part of the map. When all the children reassembled with their measurements, we measured the total length and width of the building and then decided what proportion of that length and width the various rooms comprised. For a while, it looked as if we had a lot less total space in what we had measured than what there actually was in the building. Larry was the one who realized we had forgotten to consider the space taken up by the hallways. After measuring these, we were able to decide on a scale. Each pair of children cut from colored paper the model for the room or area they had measured and labeled it appropriately. We then pasted the individual rooms on a piece of appropriately sized poster board and, six days after we started, had our map of the school. Well, actually, we had it for only a day or two before it was commandeered! Mr. Topps noticed it when he came in to visit and remarked that we had done a first-rate job and that this map was just the thing he needed to hang outside the office so that visitors could find their way around. He asked if he could borrow it for a while. The children all autographed it, and it now hangs outside the office.

October

As long as I can remember, October has been my favorite month. When I was a child I loved October because my birthday came in October. In college, October was football games and rallies. Now that I am a teacher, October is the month in which my new class "gels"; the children have learned the routines and we start to accomplish things. I love accomplishing things—checking them off my list—and this desire to accomplish things is beginning to show in most of my children.

All the students, even Mort and Butch, seem to really look forward to my morning read-alouds. This month, I read *Fourth Grade Is a Jinx* by Colleen O'shaughnessy McKenna, and *Anastasia on Her Own* by Lois Lowry. I also read relevant parts about our state from Wilma Ross's *Fabulous Facts About the 50 States* and two books just about our state.

We are now having a full 20 minutes of Self-Selected Reading time each day. The children come on their scheduled day, and most have done their preparation for the conference. I remember when I first taught and tried to have conferences, I tried to prepare for each conference. It was impossible to read all the books my fourth-graders were reading and to figure out what to ask them. Finally, one day, I realized that I was doing all the thinking, planning, and organizing that the children should be doing, and I began devising ways to make the conference truly their conference. My five rules for getting a conference ready are taken seriously by almost all my children, and I now look forward to my short but purposeful conference with each of them every week. I follow their lead, encourage their reading tastes, observe their reading strategies, and find out more about them as people. The only thing that worries me is, what other routines could I establish that would both make my job easier and give students more ownership and control over their own learning? I'm sure there are things I am still not doing that would help me move students toward more personal responsibility and accountability. I think I will talk with Kenny about this over the weekend. He teaches at the middle school and is constantly trying to move students along in these areas.

Both reading and writing workshops are going well. We read the three mysteries from our anthology together, and then children chose from five mysteries of which I had multiple copies. I really worked on the strategies of following sequence and drawing conclusions during this mystery unit. Each day, after reading one section, we would list the major things that had happened in the correct order, make predictions for what would happen next, and list the clues that led us to these predictions. I appointed everyone detectives, and everyone seemed to enjoy taking on this new role. Larry and Hilda especially enjoyed our mystery unit and are reading Sherlock Holmes books during Self-Selected Reading—mysteries which are much too difficult for typical fourth-graders, but not for Larry and Hilda.

We have begun our revising/editing publishing process during our writing workshop. My rule is that they can sign up to publish when they have three good first drafts. Each day, as we begin writing workshop, I gather the children who think they are ready to publish. The number varies each day, but the procedure is the same. They bring me their writing notebook, show me the three first drafts, and indicate the one they have chosen to publish. I look quickly to make sure they do have three "good" first drafts. Some children really want to publish everything, so they write one good first draft and then dash off two others to try to fool me. I inform them that I have been teaching fourth grade since before they were born and I know a "dashed off" piece when I see one. I tell them that I understand they want to publish quickly, but rules are rules, and they must write three good pieces and then pick one. I then send them back to their desks and tell them I look forward to seeing them again soon, when they have three good first drafts. Of course, what is "good" for Hilda differs from what is "good" for Tanana, but you can still tell when a reasonable effort has been made—and when it hasn't.

Once any "slackards" have been dispatched back to their desks, I work with the children on revising their pieces. I explain to the children that what authors write is sent out for review, and the reviewers tell what they like, ask questions about things they don't understand, and make suggestions. I use the mnemonic TAG to help the children remember what helpful reviewers do. In fact, I have a poster on which I have written:

> *To be a helpful reviewer, listen carefully and then:*
> *Tell what you liked.*
> *Ask questions about what you didn't understand.*
> *Give suggestions for making the published book terrific.*

As each child reads the piece aloud, we all (I and the other soon to be published authors) listen carefully, and then I tell something I liked and invite the others to do the same.

> "I liked how you make it funny by telling how your mom tricked you."
> "I liked the part where you realized this was a surprise party for you."
> "I liked how you ended it."

Next, I ask a question and invite other children to ask questions if they have anything they were unclear about or something else they would like to know:

> "How did your mother kept this a surprise if all the stuff was set up in the dining room?
> "How many kids came to the party?"
> "What did you get for presents?"

I serve as recorder for this, writing down our questions and any answers the author provides. Next, I try to give a helpful suggestion and ask if anyone else has suggestions:

> "Perhaps you need to do more at the beginning with the setting, describe the dining room set for the party and then describe you "grounded" to clean the garage."
> "Why don't you name the kids as they are quietly sneaking in the back door."
> You could use better words to show how mad you were about being grounded—like "furious" or "really bummed out."

Again, I record the suggestions and hand this record to the author. We are now ready for the next author to share, to listen well, and think of what we could say when it is our turn to tell the author what we liked, ask questions, and give suggestions.

After the children who are ready to publish have their revising suggestions, they return to their desks to make any revisions needed. I always have them write on every other line in their notebooks, so they have space to add things, cross things out, and put carets (∧) where they are going to insert longer chunks. I have shown them how to write any new parts on a separate sheet of paper ready to insert in the correct place.

Next, I turn my attention to the children whose piece is ready for me to play editor-in-chief. After revising their piece, each child picks a friend to help him or her edit for the things on the current checklist. We have been adding these gradually, and I have been modeling the process by choosing someone to "be my editing friend" and help me edit the piece I write every day in my minilesson at the beginning of writing workshop. Currently our editing checklist looks like this:

1. Do all the sentences make sense?
2. Do all the sentences start with caps and end with punc?
3. Do all people and place names have caps?

4. Do all the sentences stay on the topic?

5. Does the piece have a beginning, middle, and end?

6. Are words I need to check the spelling of underlined?

Once the child, with the help of a friend, has done some self-editing for the things on the checklist, I give the piece a final edit. Then the child goes over to one of the computers and uses our publishing program to type and format the piece. Adding the illustrations is the final step. Some children draw by hand, but many use the computer drawing tools, and they all love finding appropriate clip art.

Currently, the children are in all different stages of writing, revising, editing, and publishing. Larry, Butch, Roberta, Hilda, and Tanana have finished their first published piece and are now back writing three good first drafts. I keep up with where they all are by having them put their cards in the appropriate slot of my writing steps chart.

Working on 3 good first drafts	Ready for revising conf.	Revising	Editing with a friend	Ready for editor-in-chief conf.	Publishing
Larry	Betty	Anthony	Mort	Alexander	Pat
Butch	Alex	Carl	Paul	Mandy	Mitch
Roberta	Daisy	Steve	Rita	Jeff	Manuel
Hilda	Joyce			Danielle	Horace
Tanana	Chip				Daphne

We are now off and running on our state unit. Each unit actually has three overlapping phases. At the beginning, I provide the children with a great deal of input from many different sources. During most of this first phase, we work together as a whole class, building some interest and motivation for the unit, becoming familiar with new and specialized vocabulary terms, and discovering enough information so that we can begin to raise some questions to which we can seek answers. During the second phase of the unit, while we continue many whole-class activities, the children are also doing extensive reading, listening, and viewing, either individually or in small groups. Finally, they engage in several culminating activities that help them to organize and synthesize the information gained during the unit.

Throughout the unit, we do a variety of activities designed to foster concept development and to increase the store of words for which they have rich meanings. As much as possible, I try to provide direct experience for concept and meaning vocabulary development. We take field trips to the source of real places, objects, people, and events, and the children and I are always on the lookout for things to bring into the classroom that will make new words and unfamiliar concepts real to us. Of course, we cannot go to see everything or bring it into the classroom, so I rely on pictures, videos, web sites, and other media to build concepts and help develop their language foundation. When I introduce new vocabulary to the children, I always try to put these words in topical word sets. During our state unit, I will begin topical word sets for maps, state government, and places to visit. I display these words in the room, along with appropriate pictures, and the children learn to read and spell them as well as develop rich meanings for them.

My kickoff motivator for this unit was a large white outline map of our state, which I had drawn by projecting the image of an overhead transparency map onto the bulletin board at the rear of the room. After tracing the projected image, I cut along the outline and stapled the giant white map to the red-backed bulletin board. I did this all late one night (with Kenny's help) so that the children's attention would be drawn immediately to the giant blank white map against the bright red background. They noticed it immediately and were intrigued by its size and blankness. Several correctly guessed that it was an outline map of our state. I had the children move their chairs closer to the board and began to lead them in a discussion of our state. Little by little, in response to their comments and questions, I wrote the name of a particular landmark in its proper location. I let the children help me decide where these landmarks should go by consulting several maps that I spread out on the floor as we talked. At the end of this initial motivating session, we had (1) located our town, the state capital, several other cities, lakes, and rivers, (2) talked about what went on at the capital and began to use words such as *governor, lieutenant governor, legislators, laws,* and *taxes,* (3) used directional words such as *north, south, east,* and *west* and noted these directions above, below, and on the appropriate sides of our map, and (4) begun to discuss various places that the children had lived, visited, or had some other connection with.

I told them that as we studied our state, we would use again and again many of the words we had used in our talk. They would need to be able to read the words in order to find out more about our state, and they would need to be able to spell them in order to be able to write about it. Mitch, Jeff, and Daisy didn't look too happy at the thought of additional work, so I smiled reassuringly as I picked up a black marker and several half sheets of different colored construction paper and let them help me remember the "special" words we had used that morning. I then let them watch me print these words on the colored slips of paper. As I was doing so, I remarked about the relative length and distinct features of the words, pronounced the words carefully, and had the children pronounce each word after me. I then had Mitch climb on a chair and tape the words to the wall above the bulletin board. I noted that we had 11 words to start with, and that we would add more as we continued to study about our state. I then prepared the children for our following morning's activities by showing them a little color-headed pin and a triangular shaped slip of paper. On the triangular slip, I printed the following in tiny letters:

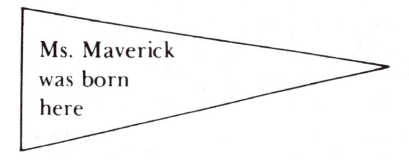

Then I pinned this slip to our map high in the northwestern corner.

Next to the pinned flag, I wrote the name of the community in which I was born. The children were fascinated and all wanted to make little flags. I assured them that that was tomorrow's activity, and that in the meantime, they should look at the maps and try to figure out places they had been to or knew of, so that we could put flags on the map for them. I also suggested that they talk with their parents and perhaps even look at a map with them to determine such family history information as their parents' birthplaces, where aunts and uncles lived, and the names and locations of places they had visited. For the rest of the day, there was always someone at the back of the room, looking at our giant map and investigating the smaller ones that I had placed on a table under the bulletin board.

The next day the children came bursting into the room loaded with maps and family histories they had brought from home. We immediately gathered in the back of the room, and the children began to spread out their maps, sharing the information they had with one another and trying to locate the places they wanted to flag on our giant map. While still giant, our map was no longer blank. It was covered with place names and flags, all of which the children had some personal affiliation with. We even have a flag marking the city to which their former classmate Mike had moved. Mrs. Flame would be happy to see that. She still worries about how Mike is doing. We also added the names of several neighboring towns and a few lakes and rivers to our state vocabulary.

The interest and excitement generated by the giant map motivator has grown throughout this month, as has the number of words in our state vocabulary. We now have 32 words up there, and as I use these words again and again in different contexts, I try to remember to point to the words and remind the children of the other contexts in which we used them. We take 10 minutes during our afternoon words/spelling time to practice these words. Each child takes out a sheet of paper and numbers it from 1 to 10. I then call out 10 of the words on the wall. As I call each word, the children are allowed and, indeed, encouraged to look up at the wall and find the word and then write it on their papers. The trick to this technique is that they are not to actually copy the words; they must look up and then down at their papers and then up again, taking a mental image of the word and then reproducing this mental image. When all 10 words have been called out, the children check their own papers by chanting the spelling of each word. Most days, all the children get 9 or 10 right, and because they are so successful at it, they love to do it. The other day during recess it rained, and when they were trying to decide on an indoor game, Horace suggested that we do the spelling words again! I couldn't believe it, but that's what they "played," with Horace being the teacher and calling out the words. From now on, once the children are very familiar with the words, as they are now, I shall let the children take turns "being teacher" and calling out the words. Strange—I always think I am allowing the children as much participation as possible and then discover something else that I am doing that the children could do with benefit.

I have done several comprehension lessons this month during our Thursday/Friday unit time. Through these lessons, I help them increase their knowledge about our state and work on increasing their vocabularies and improving their comprehension skills at the same time. For some lessons, I select part of a newspaper or magazine article or a short selection from a book and type it on my computer in large print. I then run the typed sheet through the copying machine to make a transparency. Using my overhead projector for comprehension lessons has several advantages: If the passage I select is unusually difficult to read, I can change a few of the words or omit sections to make it more readable. I don't waste a lot of paper making 25 copies of the same thing, and I can focus the attention of the children where I want it. I do, however, always show the children the source of the original article so that they know that what they are reading is "something real."

I begin my preparation for the lesson by identifying any words or concepts I think will present difficulty for many of my children. I make a distinction between unknown words and unfamiliar concepts. In the first directed reading lesson, for example, the subject was "things to do in our state." I had taken this article from the magazine section of the Sunday newspaper. Two concepts that I thought would not be familiar to most of my children were *rapids* and *currents*. In both cases, most of my children would probably be able to identify the words but would not have a meaning for those words appropriate to the particular contexts in which they were being used. The word *current* they might associate with the term *current events*, and for *rapids*, while they might have the concept of speed, they would probably not readily associate this concept with fast-moving water.

In addition to the two relatively unfamiliar concepts, *current* and *rapids*, I also identified several words for which most of my children would have listening-meaning concepts but would not be able to identify in print. These unknown words for the "things to do in our state" selection included *reflection* and *parachute*. In both cases, I was quite sure that the children would have a concept for these words once they were able to identify them but doubted that the "big word decoding skills" of most of my children would allow them to figure out the pronunciation of these familiar concepts but unknown words.

Having identified several unfamiliar concepts and unknown words, I then decided what to do about them. Sometimes, I build meanings for unfamiliar concepts or tell them the pronunciation of unknown words before they read the story. More often, however, I alert the children to the existence of these unfamiliar concepts or unknown words and challenge them to see if they can figure out what a word is or what the concept means as they read the selection. This encourages the children to use the context to figure out the meaning or pronunciation of words. This is what I did with *current, rapids, reflection*, and *parachute*. I wrote these four words on the board and asked a volunteer to pronounce *current* and *rapids*. Betty gladly pronounced them. I then asked them if anyone could give me a meaning for *current* or *rapids*. Manuel suggested that current has something to do with electricity and Steve said that it means "like in current events." For *rapids*, Roberta said that "without the *s* it means fast." I told them that the definitions they had given were right, but that, as I hoped they knew, words have many different meanings and that the words *current* and *rapids* in the selection we were about to read had meanings different from the ones they knew. I then told them that, as they were reading the selection, I wanted them to see if they could figure out what these different meanings might be. I hinted to them that the other words and sentences near the words *current* and *rapids* would give them the clues they needed to solve the mystery.

To add another element of mystery, I pointed to *reflection* and *parachute* and told the children *not* to pronounce the words. I told them that these two words were different from *current* and *rapids* in that they knew what these second two words meant but might not recognize them in print. I suggested that as with *current* and *rapids*, the words close to *reflection* and *parachute* would allow them to solve the mystery. Once the children had read the selection, they explained what they thought *current* and *rapids* meant in this context, identified the other words that had let them figure that out, and compared these meanings for the words with the meanings they already knew. Many of the children had also figured out the unknown words, *reflection* and *parachute*, and explained which other words had led them to solve the mystery.

Having identified and decided what to do about unknown words or unfamiliar concepts, I then decided for what purpose I was going to have the children read the selection. In a comprehension strategy lesson, my goal is always that the children are better at reading for a specific purpose after reading the selection than they were prior to reading the selection. Sometimes I work on improving their literal comprehension. I may decide that after reading the selection, we will put the events of the selection in order, or that we will read in order to answer the fact questions: Who? What? When? Where? How? For other selections, I may decide that we will work on being able to state main ideas in our own words.

I teach many lessons designed to sharpen the children's inferential comprehension ability. In these lessons, I show them only a portion of the text and ask them to predict what will happen next. I write these predictions on the board and let the children vote to decide which one they consider most likely to occur. I then display enough of the text so that they can check their predictions. Finally, I ask the children who made the correct prediction to read me the words in the passage that allowed them to make the correct prediction. In this way, the children who are not very good at inferring see that inferences are based on something that is directly stated in the text.

The first year I taught, I referred to inferential comprehension as "reading between the lines." One day, I watched one boy squinting at his book and then peering over the shoulder of the boy in front of him who could "read between the lines." It suddenly occurred to me that, from a child's vantage point, it was conceivable that he believed there was something between the lines that he couldn't see or that was only between the lines of other people's books. Since then I have stopped using that particular phrase. I have begun to ask those who can make inferences to point out the words in the text on which they based their inferences. This allows the children who can't make inferences to begin to observe the way the process works in the minds of those who can.

For the "things to do in our state" lesson, I decided to focus the children's attention on the main ideas of each paragraph. I displayed only the portion of the text that mentioned a particular place and asked the children to read so that when they finished they could tell me in a sentence what the main attraction was at each place. First, I let the children read silently. When most appeared to have finished, I let a volunteer read the section aloud. In this way, Paul and others whose reading skills are still limited could get the content of the selection and participate in the comprehension activity.

After each section was read silently and then orally, I asked a child to tell me in one sentence what the main thing was that people went there to see. I then made a list on the board that gave each place name and the sentence describing its main attraction. When we had completed reading about the eight places, I read over the list I had made on the board and pointed out to the children that, in addition to stating the main attraction, these sentences were also the main ideas of each paragraph. Main ideas, like main attractions, are the most important ideas (attractions), the ideas (attractions) most people would like to remember after reading (visiting) a paragraph (place). While we will continue to work on identifying and stating main ideas all year, this lesson was a good one to begin with because it helped to make the concept of main idea a little more concrete.

As a follow-up to this comprehension lesson, I put the children in eight cooperative groups. Each group was to make a flag for one of the eight places we had read about, write the place name and the main attraction on the flag, locate the place using the ever-growing supply of maps we now have in the room, and pin the flag to our giant map, which was no longer blank.

We have taken our first field trip this month, to visit the local newspaper. I bring daily copies of both the local and capital newspapers to school each morning, and since we began the unit on our state, the children have become quite interested in them. Before we took the field trip, I had the children put their chairs in a circle, and we began to talk about the local newspaper and to formulate some questions to ask Ms. Daley, the editor. I listed these questions on a large sheet of chart paper and, on our return, we checked the chart to see how many of our questions had been answered.

We then got out a local map and looked at the various routes we could take to get from our school to the newspaper office. We tried to decide which route would be the shortest and which would be the quickest. Because there was much disagreement about the best route, I asked the children how we might plan an experiment to find out. After much discussion, the following plan was arrived at. Each of the five cars (Mrs. Penn, Mrs. Smith, Mrs. Hope, and Daphne's grandfather had volunteered to drive) would take a different route. One person in each car would be responsible for writing down the beginning and ending mileage. Another person would time the trips. The other riders in the car would keep track of the number of lights, stop signs, intersections, and so on. It was agreed, of course, that each driver would drive carefully and obey all speed limits.

Finally, Friday arrived! The cars set out at the same time. Mrs. Smith arrived first, but Mrs. Penn had taken the shortest route. I arrived last, and my passengers were not too pleased about that, especially Butch!

The receptionist took us on a tour around the buildings and then took us to Ms. Daley's office. The children behaved very well and, because they had discussed and planned before coming, asked some very good questions. I was just beginning to relax and pat myself on the back for preparing them so well when the inevitable happened. A reporter came into Ms. Daley's office with some copy. She introduced him to the children and asked them if they had any questions. Hilda asked him a question about a story she had read recently in the paper, and as he was answering her question, he turned to Ms. Daley and said, "Why don't you take them down into the morgue and show them some of the dead ones?" Roberta's head twitched with excitement; Betty screamed! The reporter quickly explained that the newspaper morgue had "dead" newspapers, not dead bodies, while Mrs. Smith and I consoled Betty. A striking example of the multiple meanings of common words!

We went into the morgue and spent a long time there. Ms. Daley showed us the newspapers that recorded such historic events as the end of the Civil War, the Lincoln and Kennedy assassinations, and the state's celebration of its 100th birthday. She pointed out the difference between history books that are written long after the actual events have occurred and newspaper accounts that are written immediately. She also pointed out how newspapers are one very important source of historical data. The children were particularly impressed when she showed them a copy of a biography of a famous general and explained that the writer of that book had spent many days in this very morgue doing research about our town where this general had grown up.

Upon our return from the newspaper, we looked at our collected data, computed the mileages and times, decided that the shortest route in distance was not the quickest route, and discussed reasons why this was so. We also looked to see which of our questions had been answered and decided that six had been answered quite thoroughly, three partially, and two not at all. Finally, I did a focused writing lesson in which, after I had modeled, each child composed a short letter to Ms. Daley thanking her for her time and telling her what he or she had found most interesting about the visit. Here is Roberta's letter:

Dear Ms. Daley,

Thank you for letting us come down to visit your newspaper. There was lots to see and I can only apologize for Betty's screaming in your office. She is always doing things like that and I can't understand why. The dead newspapers were interesting but I would have liked to have seen some dead bodies since I never have. Being a newspaper lady I bet you have seen hundreds of them.

Sincerely
Roberta Smith

November

During Reading Workshop this month, we read a science fiction selection from our anthology, and then they chose from a variety of science fiction books of which I had multiple copies. I read to them the classic science fiction title *A Wrinkle in Time* by Madeline L'Engle. Clearly, this unit has increased their interest in science fiction. Looking over my conference sheets from last week, I see that over half the children brought a science fiction book. I am quite pleased with the balance I have established between teacher-decided reading and student choice reading. By making sure to include a wide variety of genres, authors, and topics in what I read aloud to them and what we read during Reading Workshop, I make sure they are familiar with and know how to read all different kinds of books. Letting them choose their books for our daily Self-Selected Reading time helps them develop their own particular reading interests—but those interests broaden when they have experienced everything available. Hopefully, I will even turn some of them on to social studies informational books and biography once I have read more of those to them and we have read some during Reading Workshop. I have put those off until later in the year, because they are more motivated when I begin with what they already like. But we will get to them in the new year.

I have been doing some "What Looks Right" (Cunningham & Hall, 1998) lessons during our afternoon Words/Spelling time. Looking at their spelling in their first-draft writing, I was pleased to note that almost all my children spell by pattern, rather than "one letter, one sound," the way most younger children do. In English, however, there are often two common spelling patterns for the same rhyme. That there are two patterns is not a problem when you are reading. If you are reading and you come to the unknown words *plight* and *trite*, you can easily figure out their pronunciation by accessing the pronunciation associated with other *ight* or *ite* words you can read and spell. It is a problem, however, when you are trying to spell. If you were writing and trying to spell *trite* or *plight*, they could as easily be spelled *t-r-i-g-h-t* and *p-l-i-t-e*. The only way to know which is the correct spelling is to write it one way and see if it "looks right" or check your probable spelling in a dictionary. What Looks Right lessons help students learn how to use these two important self-monitoring spelling strategies.

For the first lesson, I chose the *ite-ight* pattern. I headed two columns on the board with two words my students could all spell, but with the different patterns, *bite* and *fight*. I had students draw two columns on their paper and set them up just like mine.

    bite   *fight*

Next, I had students say these words and notice that they rhyme but that they don't have the same spelling pattern. I explain to students that in English, using a rhyming word to read another word will work almost all the time, but that spelling is more complicated because some rhymes have two common spellings. "Good spellers use rhyming patterns but also have a visual checking strategy. After writing a little-used word, they look at it to see if it looks right. If it doesn't look right, good spellers try to think of another rhyming word with a different spelling pattern and write that one to see if it looks right. Finally, if you need to be sure of the spelling, you look it up in a dictionary by looking for it the way you think it is spelled." I explained that the activity we were going to do is called "What Looks Right" and would help them learn to check their own spelling the way good spellers do.

"I am going to say some words that rhyme with *bite* and *fight* and write them using both spelling patterns," I told them. "Your job is to decide which one looks right to you and write only that one. As soon as you have written it the way you think it is spelled, I want you to find it in the dictionary to prove your spelling is correct. The first word I will write is *kite*. If *kite* is spelled like *bite*, it will be *k-i-t-e*, if it is spelled like *right*, it will be *k-i-g-h-t*." As I was saying this, I was writing these two possible spellings in the appropriate columns. Most of the students recognized the correct spelling immediately and wrote *kite* under *bite*. They then found *kite* in the dictionary and proved it and I crossed out *kight*.

I did a few more examples with words that most of them were familiar with—*tight*, *white*, and *quite*. The students clearly enjoyed getting these right and then finding the words that proved it. I let students sitting near each other look up the words together if they had chosen the same spelling. Next, I wrote a few words that were less familiar to them—*spite*, *fright*, and *flight*. Many of the students were less sure about these, and I pointed out that if they hadn't seen these words several times and noticed their spelling, they would just have to guess at one and see if they could find it in the dictionary. If they couldn't find it the way they had guessed, they looked for the other pattern and found it and changed the spelling on their papers. When words time was up for that day, my chart looked like this:

bite	*fight*
kite	~~kight~~
~~tite~~	tight
white	~~whight~~
quite	~~quight~~
~~flite~~	flight
spite	~~spight~~
~~frite~~	fright

Because words time was up for that day and I wanted to continue the lesson tomorrow, I had the children initial their papers ("Busy people don't have time to write out full names on working papers") and clipped their papers to the chart.

The following day, after we had spent a few minutes practicing the spelling of our unit spelling words, I quickly handed out the papers, calling them by initials. RJS—Roberta June Smith—grabbed hers. BAS went to Betty Ann Smith. Some children put only two initials—Mort claims not to have a middle name and Butch "ain't telling"; but whether two or three, they all get a kick out of my calling out their initials.

We resumed the lesson as I wrote *site* and *sight* on the chart. Most of the children recognized *sight* and quickly wrote it. A few weren't sure and chose *site*. Imagine their surprise when they found both of them in the dictionary! We read the two definitions and sentence examples and then made up a few of our own:

> The newspaper office was the site of our first field trip.
> The blind man lost his sight in the war.
> Your room is a sight!

I had the children add whichever one they hadn't chosen to their sheets, and I left both *site* and *sight* on the chart. Horace remarked that this was a neat one because, "You couldn't go wrong!" I smiled as I wrote *might* and *mite* on the chart. Again, most children recognized *might* but a few picked *mite*. Once again, we found them both! Many children had not heard of the tiny animal mite—but Daphne pointed out that it must be like those nasty dust mites that her grandmother is allergic to. Again, we read both definitions and sentence examples and discussed the picture of the mite. "See how helpful the dictionary is," I sermonized. "If you write a word and it doesn't look right, you can check to see if it is there, and if not, you can find the other pattern. If can also tell you which homonym you need for what you are writing."

Then I told them, "I am going to write a word that I doubt any of you have seen, so you will probably all have to guess. The word is *blight*." Under *bite*, I wrote *blite*; and under *fight*, I wrote *blight*. "When you find the one that is the correct spelling, we will read the dictionary definition, but a blight is a bad thing, often destroying crops. A blight destroyed all the potatoes in Ireland many years ago and forced many Irish people to come to America for food. Quickly, make a guess and then see if you can find your guess."

Larry, Hilda, Pat, and Roberta, who almost always know the correct answer, were clearly stumped on this one and didn't want to guess. I chided them, however, to "trust their luck," pick one, and see if they could find it. "You can change it if you pick the wrong one," I assured them. Eventually, the correct spelling got found, we read the definition, and everyone got *blight* written under *fight*. I did the same with the unfamiliar words *trite* and *plight*. Roberta wanted to write the ones she wasn't sure about in both columns. "Only if you think you will find it both ways like *sight, site* and *might, mite*," I warned. Once more, our time was up. I collected the papers and clipped them to the chart. "We need these one more day," I announced.

The following day, after once again calling them by initials, I told them that using the dictionary to see which pattern is the correct spelling also works for two- and three-syllable words. What if you were writing and you needed to spell *invite*. Would it be like *bite, invite* or like *fight, invight*? As I was saying this, I was writing it both ways on my chart. The children quickly made a choice—most recognized *invite*—and went hunting in the dictionary to "prove" it. I noticed that the speed with which they could find a word in the dictionary had increased greatly in just these three days. I then wrote seven more words using both spelling patterns, working from most familiar to least familiar: *headlight, eyesight, uptight, bullfight, excite, ignite, dynamite*. The children all enjoyed working with these more sophisticated words, and it increased the range of the lesson so that there were things about spelling for even Larry, Hilda, and Pat to learn—truly a multilevel activity. At the end of the third day, my chart looked like this:

bite	*fight*
kite	~~kight~~
~~tite~~	tight
white	~~whight~~
quite	~~quight~~
~~flite~~	flight
spite	~~spight~~
~~frite~~	fright
site	sight
mite	might
~~blite~~	blight
trite	~~tright~~
~~plite~~	plight
invite	~~invight~~
~~headlite~~	headlight
~~bullfite~~	bullfight
~~uptite~~	uptight
~~eyesite~~	eyesight
excite	~~excight~~
ignite	~~ignight~~
dynamite	~~dynamight~~

I had the students read and spell the words with me and then helped them to summarize what good spellers do and don't do.

> "Good spellers don't spell words one letter at a time. They use the spelling patterns they know from other words. If a word you write does not look right, you should try another pattern for that sound. The dictionary will help you check your probable spelling and let you know which homonym has the meaning you want."

I did one more What Looks Right lesson with them this month, using the *ane/ain* patterns. Because the children understood the procedures and have gotten much speedier at finding words in the dictionary, this lesson only took two days. I plan to do a few of these each month because I can see how it is making them more strategic and independent in their spelling. Here is the Jane/rain chart:

Jane	rain
~~trane~~	train
sane	~~sain~~
~~brane~~	brain
lane	~~lain~~
~~chane~~	chain
~~stane~~	stain
~~gane~~	gain
cane	cain
plane	plain
mane	main
crane	~~crain~~
~~Spane~~	Spain
~~sprane~~	sprain
~~complane~~	complain
~~explane~~	explain
hurricane	~~hurricain~~
~~entertane~~	entertain
~~contane~~	contain
~~remane~~	remain
octane	~~octain~~
cellophane	~~cellophain~~

Our field trip this month was to the county seat. This was an all-day field trip, and we packed a picnic lunch. Thank goodness it didn't rain! We prepared for this one as we had for the newspaper office, by having discussions and coming up with a list of questions we wanted answered. This time, Hilda wrote down the list to make sure that we came back with at least a partial answer to all our questions.

In the morning, we visited the county courthouse. When we got to the county clerk's office, a young couple was waiting to get a marriage license. All the boys plus Pat and Roberta thought that was hysterical. The children were most fascinated by the sheriff. They wanted to know what happened when a person got arrested and what a sheriff and his deputies did. The sheriff showed them the county map, which was very detailed, and helped them to locate our school and some of their homes.

When we went into the court, the judge was hearing a traffic case. He revoked the license of a person arrested for driving recklessly and speeding. This impressed the children greatly. When we got to the tax assessor's office, Hilda was busily checking her list to see what we might have forgotten to ask. When her question was finally asked, it came out as "We want to know how you decide how much taxes everyone should pay, and my Dad says you must be a friend of our next door neighbor's because his house is twice as big as ours and he pays less taxes."

That afternoon we toured the county historical museum. The children were especially intrigued by the original state flag and the lists of names of all those who had died in the major wars we have fought. The restored log cabin behind the museum added much realism to our study of how people used to live in our state, and the children were fascinated by the Indian artifacts.

Upon our return to the classroom, we made a list of all the people we had visited or seen in the courthouse and what their functions were. We also referred to our question chart and, with Hilda's help, did indeed have at least a partial answer to all the questions we had raised. I then helped the children form five groups. Each group composed a letter thanking one of the people who helped us on our visit.

The field trips we take each month require a lot of effort and planning, but I know that they are worth it. The children learn so much–not just on the day of the trip but in the preceding days, as we prepare for the trip. I don't ever plan one for December, however. It is hard enough to get accomplished all we need to do and all the inevitable holiday things in that shortened month.

December

As I was sitting down to write this month's journal, I noticed my final words from last month's journal. Famous last words! We did indeed take a field trip this month—quite unexpectedly. Normally, we don't go to the state capital. It is almost a two-hour trip, and the legislature is usually not in session during the fall when we are studying our state. Early in the month, however, the legislature was called into special session in order to consider a new water pollution bill. Everyone in the state has been debating this issue for some time now, but it took a tragedy to get the legislators moving. Four weeks ago, five people died in a small downstate industrial town. The cause of death was determined to be the high level of industrial chemical wastes in the water, way above the standard already set but never enforced. The antipollution forces were able to rally support around this emotional issue, and the governor called the legislature into special session to consider a more stringent water pollution bill with provisions for enforcement and severe penalties for lack of compliance.

The children came back to school on the Monday after the five people had died, and they were all upset. Many of them brought the various newspaper stories and related the discussions they had had about this issue at home. The children, unlike the adult population, were almost unanimous in their insistence that the water pollution standards be much stricter. Not being burdened with financial responsibilities, they could see the need for clean water much more clearly than they could understand the financial strain the new controls would put on industry and, if industry is to be believed, the entire state population.

Of course, we put our chairs in a circle immediately and discussed the problem. I tried to raise questions and interject information that would allow them to consider the issue in its broadest terms. Many of the children were unclear about words like *chemicals* and *bacteria*, and I began to make mental notes on which words we might want to explore more fully and add to our wall vocabulary. I decided that the subject was such an important one and the children were so naturally motivated that a unit on ecology and pollution would be first on our agenda after we finished our current unit.

It was Mrs. Penn who suggested that we take the children to the state capital. She came in after school that very afternoon and told me that she would be going over to meet with a citizen's action group later in the week and that she would be glad to make all the arrangements at the capital and to be one of our drivers. She added that she had seen Mrs. Smith that morning and had mentioned the possibility to her and that Mrs. Smith had agreed it would be a great experience for the children to see the legislature in session and that she, too, would be willing to drive. I told Mrs. Penn that I would talk it over with the children but that I was all for it.

The children, of course, were most excited. In addition to the general excitement of going on a trip that long and being "at the capital" was the excitement generated by the knowledge that Ms. Maverick had never taken any of her other classes to the state capital. They were not just doing the same trips all the other fourth grades did; they were doing something very special and very grown-up. As I watched their delight in this specialness, I vowed to try to think of something special for each class of children I taught.

The preparations for the trip took most of the month, and many of the activities that I had planned for this middle part of the unit went by the boards. The transportation problem was solved by Mrs. Penn, who commandeered Mandy's father and Larry's mother. She also arranged for our tour through the capitol and our visit to the gallery while the legislators were debating. In addition, she got our local representative, Buddy Stans, to agree to come up to the gallery when the session broke for lunch and talk with us and answer our questions. Our list of questions for Mr. Stans took three sheets of chart paper.

Lunch was a problem. We were going to leave at 7:00 A.M. so that we could get there, park, go on a 10 A.M. tour through the capitol building, and be in the gallery from 11 A.M. to noon. A picnic lunch was a little risky at this time of year, and I thought it would be good for all the children to have the experience of eating in a real restaurant. They had all eaten at fast-food drive-ins, but many of them had not been to a restaurant, ordered from a menu, or paid their own bill plus tax and tip. The problem with taking them to a restaurant, of course, was that many of them could not come up with the money, and that many families who would come up with the money really couldn't afford it.

As I was thinking about the lunch problem, I was also gathering up the week's supply of newspapers to take to the recycling drop point. I then remembered that some organizations had collected money for various causes by having paper and aluminum drives. It occurred to me that if our class could collect paper and aluminum for recycling as well as deposit bottles for return to the grocery stores, we might make enough money for everyone to have lunch. We might also become more personally "pollution conscious."

In two weeks, we collected hundreds of pounds of paper and aluminum and returned $56.85 worth of bottles to the grocery stores. Several parents made voluntary donations to our lunch fund, and we ended up with another $80. The children thought this was a fortune until we divided by 25 and realized that each person's share of the fortune was only $5.47.

Mrs. Penn had found an inexpensive restaurant close to the capitol that was accessible to people in wheelchairs like Danielle and had arranged for the 29 of us to eat there. She had also gotten several sample menus, and from these each child figured out the various combinations of food he or she could buy with $4.56 (which is what each child actually had to spend after paying the 5 percent sales tax and 15 percent tip).

In order to prepare them for their visit to the capitol and the legislature, I showed a video entitled *Your State Government*, which is put out by the state chamber of commerce and the state department of education. Just as when I am going to have the class read something I do a reading comprehension lesson with them, I do a viewing comprehension lesson with a video. After previewing the video, I determine which unfamiliar concepts I want to teach and whether I will help them to build these concepts before, during, or after the video. Often the video provides visual experience for words that I cannot provide direct experience for. I stop the video at the appropriate point and discuss the picture that makes real the unfamiliar word or concept.

I then determine my purposes for having them view the video and decide how much I will show at a time. Unless it is strictly for entertainment, I never show a video all the way through. Rather, I set the purpose for viewing a particular segment, stop the video and discuss the fulfillment of that purpose, set another purpose, and begin the video again. If the video is one that the children seem to especially enjoy, I will often show it again the following day in its entirety. I then try to think of an appropriate follow-up activity to the video. My purpose in this follow-up activity is to help the children organize, generalize, evaluate, and apply the new information gained from the video.

Mr. Perkins came this month before we went to the capital. He brought his routing slips and maps and talked to the children about all the reading he has to do in his job as a truck driver. The children were quite impressed. He also showed us the best route to take to the capital and told us some interesting things to watch for on the way.

The actual trip was exhausting but very exciting. We left promptly at 7:30 A.M. The parents provided some apples and crackers for each car so that the children could have a little snack when we first got there. The woman who escorted us on our tour through the capitol was very sweet and very smart, so Betty and Daphne have decided to be tour guides when they grow up. While we were in the gallery, one of the "anti-the-more-stringent-bill" legislators was talking, and the children were quite upset. I think they began to get some notion, however, that there are always two legitimate, defensible points of view. Mr. Stans was great! He spent almost 30 minutes talking with us. He commended the children on their paper/aluminum/bottle collection and told them that another way they could make a difference was by getting in the habit of writing to their legislator and letting him or her know their opinions on current issues.

Lunch was fun! The children were well prepared, and most knew exactly what they wanted. The only person who overspent was Daisy. I didn't realize it at the time, but Mandy's father had to bail her out with 34 cents. I told him he should have left her to wash dishes!

We did do a few other things this month besides holiday things and our big trip. Our Reading Workshop focused on folktales, tall tales, and legends. As usual, we read some selections from our anthology and then had a book-choice week. We also did some focused writing lessons in which we wrote some tall tales. We made a class book of these and bound them together and produced copies for all the children to give to relatives for holiday gifts.

We had a whole-school party on the day before school let out for the holidays. Mr. Sweep, the custodian, was retiring after being here since the day the school opened 27 years ago. While we were all sad to see him leave, that sadness, for me, was lightened by the knowledge that Mr. Moppet, Chip's father, needed the job so badly. He has been out of work for months, and he and his family are too proud to accept "charity." I have, however, been seeing to it that Chip has some breakfast when he gets here in the morning, and now that his father is the school custodian, I know they will be all right.

January

This month we finished our state unit. No small feat, I can assure you! For culminating activities on this unit, I decided to have small groups work on several different activities: a time line, a mural, a historical drama, a newsletter for parents telling about all our trips and what we had learned, and a book about our state. I described the projects to the entire class, letting them know what they would be doing on each. I then had the children write down their first and second choices for the project on which they wanted to work.

Paul, Manuel, Chip, Anthony, and Carl worked on constructing a time line for our state. The completion of this project was, indeed, much facilitated by the experience of making the life lines that they had done in September. They began by listing important events in our state's history and verifying the dates on which they occurred. Miss Page, our librarian, helped them to find some of the references they needed for this part of the project. They then decided to use a 20-foot piece of string and to let each foot represent 10 years. While Paul was not much help on the researching end, he worked diligently to copy the dates and events onto the markers that would go along the line.

Rita, Mandy, Danielle, Larry, and Horace made a lovely bound book entitled *Facts You Should Know About Our State.* They took much of the information we had gained from our discussions, reading, videos, and field trips and wrote several topical pieces. They also included maps, pictures of the state flower and bird, and representations of the several flags our state has had. They typed these on the computer and made a title page and a table of contents. They then bound it with a lovely cloth cover, as they had learned to do from Mrs. Wise, and took it to the library to show to Miss Page. You can imagine their delight when she told them it looked good enough to be a library book. The children asked if it could really *be* a library book, so Miss Page pasted a pocket in the back, typed up a card, gave it an appropriate number, made a card for the card file, and shelved it with the other books about our state. Needless to say, it doesn't stay on that shelf long. Every child in our room wants to check it out to read, and now they are all asking to make books to put in the library.

Betty, Mitch, Butch, Hilda, and Alexander did the newsletter for the parents. They wrote about many of the activities we had done, but most of the page space went to our field trips. Hilda appointed herself editor, and I was amazed at how tactfully she coerced all the others into doing a "professional" job. Butch and Alexander, both of whom are whizzes on the computer, did most of the computer work, including using the scanner in the computer lab to put in some of the photos we had taken on our trips. The parents were quite impressed with the newsletter, and I took the opportunity to point out to Butch's father and Alexander's mother during our conferences that there are great job possibilities for technologically savvy people.

Mort, Tanana, Daisy, Steve, and Daphne did the mural that covers the side of the room. This mural depicts the changes in the way people lived, traveled, and dressed in our state over the past 200 years. Again, Miss Page's help was invaluable in steering this group to reference works that contained many pictures. She also arranged for this group to view several videos that helped them be accurate in their representations.

The drama group, Roberta, Alex, Pat, Jeff, and Joyce, presented several short skits representing significant events in our state's history. The funniest one was their skit of the legislators debating the new water pollution bill. Pat was the "anti" senator, and Roberta, Alex, Jeff , and Joyce sat and booed and hissed as she spoke.

Most of the work on these culminating projects occurred during our afternoon Center/Project time. This is when children can work together in groups on some days and work individually on other days, depending on what needs to be done. I have centers on the periphery of the room, and children can always be found in these areas. In addition to the computer center, the writing center, the library center, the listening center, the math center, and the art center, which are always options, I have a center related to our science topic. Next month, there will be a variety of science experiments related to pollution. Most of the time, the children are working on activities of their own choosing, but sometimes I assign them specific things to do. This is also the time when projects begun during our morning unit time are carried out and when further research is done. Miss Page has an open door policy in the library, and most afternoons, some of my children are in the library researching some part of our unit topic.

I spend most of my time during the Center/Project time working with small groups or individuals. If a child has been absent for several days, I work with that child to get caught up. If a child has had serious behavior problems that day, she or he spends some of the center time with me trying to figure out why the problems occurred and what we can do about them. Both Mort and Daisy have spent quite a bit of their center time "debriefing" their day with me and planning how tomorrow could be better. Mort doesn't seem to mind missing some of his center time, but Daisy gets quite angry because she loves the art center. Her behavior recently has been more considerate, and I think she has decided that she would rather spend time painting late in the day than having a "heart-to-heart" with me.

I spend 10 minutes every afternoon reading and writing with Paul. Although not a good reader for fourth grade, he can read and write better than I initially thought. When he is having a good day, he can independently read material at second-grade level. I have been letting him choose what he wants us to read together. He has a special notebook, and each day after we read, he writes (with my help) a couple of sentences about the book we have read. He is now able to compose and correctly write simple sentences, and I am going to expand the writing to include more complex sentences and paragraphs. Recently, he has gotten into the *Curious George* books and is reading every one I can find. He also enjoys rereading them during Self-Selected Reading time and listening to the tapes in the listening center during the afternoon. He and Daphne are fast friends, and sometimes during Center/Project time, I see him in the reading center, reading *Curious George* books with her. I also see her reading to him other books he chooses. Paul is one of those children you never stop worrying about. He is sad and withdrawn much of the time but has times when he appears involved and happier. I am just grateful that he is here at Merritt where just about every teacher accepts the fact that, even with the best instruction, not all children will be at grade level and that all children—especially less able ones—need TLC.

Although these culminating activities occupied much of our time and energies this month, we did accomplish some other things. I took a second writing sample by having them write once again on the topic of their favorite and least favorite things. Once they had finished, I returned to them their beginning-of-the-year sample. They compared the two and listed what they could do better now. Most children were amazed at how much better they were writing—longer sentences, more descriptive words, better spelling and punctuation. Some couldn't believe they had really done their best on the earlier sample. I assured them that they had done their best but that they were indeed becoming better writers. "Why do you think we have been doing all this writing, revising, editing, and publishing?" I asked. "It's not just to keep you busy. It's to help you become sophisticated writers." Mort looked skeptical! I also looked at the samples and was also amazed. I noted some things we all needed to work on and then put both samples away until it was time to do the final sample in June.

We have had lots of fun devising math word problems for each other to solve. The ground rules were that (1) each word problem had to involve our state in some way, and (2) the person who made up the problem had to be able to solve it. The children worked out the problems at odd times during the day, and then, just before lunch, five children would come and write their problems on the board. The rest of us would then work at solving the problems. The children learned that writing clearly stated mathematical word problems that contain all the information needed to solve them is a difficult task.

February

We finally got to our Ecology/Pollution unit. It has been a lot of fun, and I found many ways to help the children become involved in the community. We discussed interviewing techniques and constructed a little questionnaire to find out what people are doing about energy conservation and pollution. The children interviewed neighbors, relatives, and business owners, and we prepared a report, which we distributed to all the people interviewed. Newspapers, magazines, and television broadcasts provided much of the input for this unit, because this information needs to be the most current available.

During one of our initial sessions, the children and I decided on some categories under the general heading of ecology and began a bulletin board for each of these subtopics. The children brought newspaper and magazine articles and pictures, shared them with the class, and put them on the appropriate board. I made videotapes of the nightly national and local newscasts and played back for the children those parts that applied to our study. I also arranged for many members of the community who are involved in specific ecological concerns to come in and talk with us about their particular involvement. As a culmination to this unit, the children and I drafted a list of recommendations for conserving energy and preventing pollution, which we sent to Ms. Daley. The letter was published with all the children's names under it. The children were pleased, but their parents were ecstatic! Copies of that paper with its 15 suggestions for conserving energy and preventing pollution have gone to doting aunts and grandparents all around the country.

The children are very careful not to waste anything anymore and are quick to point out wasteful habits in others. Sometimes these others are not so pleased to have their faults aired in public. One day in the cafeteria, Mrs. Flame took her tray up to deposit it. She hadn't even touched her roll or her cake. Butch informed her that if she didn't want to eat something, she shouldn't take it in the first place!

I read many appealing informational books to the children in connection with our pollution unit. Two books put out by The Earthworks Group, *Kid Heroes of the Environment* and *50 Simple Things Kids Can Do to Save the Earth,* are both chock-full of tips and projects that real kids really can do. We have gotten many excellent ideas from these two sources. *Greening the City Streets: The Story of Community Gardens* by Barbara Huff was another practical resource. We also enjoyed many of Dorothy Hinshaw Patent's photo essays, including *Where the Bald Eagles Gather, The Way of the Grizzly,* and *Where the Wild Horses Roam.* I also read them a marvelous fiction book with an ecological theme, *Trouble at Marsh Harbor* by Susan Sharpe, which the children all enjoyed and which many of them chose to read to themselves later.

I organized our reading workshop this month around the ecology theme. Our anthology has a whole section on it, and we spent three weeks reading the selections contained there. The children were amazed, and very pleased to learn, how the plant and animal populations in Yellowstone have come back after the terrible fires there during the summer of 1988. They were fascinated by the information they learned in the short magazine article on "Smoke Jumpers." Butch, Mitch, and Roberta have all decided that is what they will be when they grow up! They were intrigued by the notion of a rain forest and suggested we make a field trip to the Amazon. We couldn't do that, but we did find some good videos, which helped us to imagine what it would be like.

When we are all reading the same thing in our anthology, I use a variety of formats, depending on what seems appropriate. We read most of the short magazine and poetry pieces together as a class. For the longer pieces, we usually preview them together. In addition to using this preview to help my children access and build prior knowledge, I introduce new vocabulary and relate it to the selection. I also lead them to notice all the special features of the text—especially in informational pieces. We read all the headings and talk about how they give you a clue about what to expect there. We also read all captions that go with pictures, and give special attention to interpreting every map, graph or chart. When there are respellings of words in parentheses after difficult-to-pronounce words, we take a minute to figure out the pronunciation of each word and talk about how helpful this "on the spot" respelling key is and how it works.

I always set a purpose for their reading. With an informational selection, we often begin a graphic organizer such as a web, chart, or timeline based on our preview. Students know that they are to read the selection so that they can help us complete the graphic organizer. We seldom do the actual reading of the longer selections together, however. I remember from my own elementary school days, sitting there while everyone took a turn reading a paragraph and wondering if it would ever end! In addition to being boring and not instilling positive feelings about reading, round-robin reading is not very efficient. I know that teachers tell the other children to "follow along," but I doubt that many actually do. In order to read well, children have to read a lot—not just their one paragraph from a 10-page selection.

I use a variety of formats to get the selections read. Sometimes, I assign the children to reading partners. Sometimes, especially when we are reading a play or rereading a story to plan how to act it out, I put the children together in small acting groups. Often, for the first reading of a selection, I give the children the choice of how they want to read it. I did this with the piece about Yellowstone. We had previewed the text and begun a web. I then told the children that I would give them 25 minutes to read the whole piece and plan what they would add to our web. I gave them each a small index card and told them that when they finished reading, they should pick one spoke of our web and write down whatever facts they thought should go there. I also told them that we all read at different rates, so some of them would probably finish before the time was up and have lots of time to write down facts, and others might not have quite long enough to finish, but that when the timer went off, we would begin completing our web. I then told them that they were grown-up fourth-graders and were becoming more responsible every day, and that I was going to let them choose how they would read the selection.

"You can read it by yourself, if you like, but if you make this choice you will not get any help from your partner or me, so you must decide if you can read it on your own and have some facts to help us complete the web. Another option is to read it with a friend. The only rule here is that both of you must want to read it together, and you must read quietly so that you don't disturb the individual readers or the ones reading with me. Reading with me is the third option. I will be in my reading chair, and anyone who likes can come over here and we will read the selection together."

The children all seemed pleased that they were getting to make this choice. Some children immediately found their "best friends" and began reading. Pat and Hilda went off together. Roberta went to read with Steve. Larry and Horace went off together. Butch and Mitch partnered up. Daphne took Paul to a quiet corner and began reading and explaining it to him.

Tanana, Jeff, Chip, Betty, Manuel, and Alexander chose to read with me. I read parts of some pages to them and asked them to finish the page to themselves. I then let volunteers read aloud sentences containing facts they thought they should add to the web. As I was reading with this group, I monitored the partners and the ones reading individually. I had to give Butch and Mitch a warning, because they were fooling around. After I threatened them with having to join my group, they settled down to read. Daisy was drawing instead of reading, and Mort was staring out the window, so after one warning, they were moved into my group.

At the end of 25 minutes, we reconvened and began completing our web, which we finished the next day. As we were completing the web, I had them read parts aloud to clarify misunderstandings or confusing parts. Once the web was done, I chose one subtopic and modeled how you could turn that information into a summary. The students each chose a subtopic—any but the one I had written about—and wrote a summary of that subtopic.

The children have all been keeping learning logs this month as we have studied about pollution. Each day as we are finishing our unit time, I give them 10 to 15 minutes to write down what they have learned and their reactions to it. This is an emotional issue for my children, who have very strong feelings about "their earth" and what is being done to it, and their journal entries are filled with concerns, fears, and anger. I am trying to let them express these emotions but also to steer them toward thinking about solutions and what they individually, we as a school community, and our governmental bodies can do about it.

We have done many activities this month in celebration of Black History Month. I read them several excellent biographies of famous African Americans, including *Jesse Jackson* by Patricia McKissack, *Frederick Douglass Fights for Freedom* by Margaret Davidson, *Freedom Train: The Story of Harriet Tubman* by Dorothy Sterling, and *I Have a Dream: The Story of Martin Luther King* by Margaret Davidson. I also read them some fiction that had strong African American main characters, including *A Girl Called Boy* by Belinda Hurmence and *Phoebe the Spy* by Judith Berry Griffin. We talked a lot about biographies, and my children once again amazed me by informing me that autobiographies were when you wrote about yourself! When they saw how surprised I was that they knew this, they explained about the "When I Was Your Age" tales that Mrs. Wright used to write and that they convinced Miss Nouveau to write. I was amazed at how interested the children were in biographies and autobiographies, so we have launched a research/publishing project. All the children have chosen some currently living famous person, and we are going to publish a book of biographies. Their chosen people run the gamut from sports heroes to rock stars to politicians to actors and actresses. They are researching their chosen people now, using resources including *TV Guide* and *Sports Illustrated.* We have posted a list in the room of who is researching whom, and almost every day children bring in things for each other that they have found in newspapers, magazines, and other sources. This project is an exciting one, and my children have already asked Miss Page about having it be "a real book in the library."

March

Having primed their interest with my read-alouds last month and in conjunction with our biography writing project, we have read biographies this month during Reading Workshop. Once again, we divided the time up between reading in our anthology, which contains two biographies, and then choice groups in which they indicated their first, second, and third choices from five biographies of which I have multiple copies. Given that they were all simultaneously researching people to write their biographies, they were very interested in how authors knew what they knew. One of the biographies in our anthology was quite factual, but the other one, while about a real person, was called a "fictionalized" biography. It had lots of quotes in it attributed to the person as a child, and the children all wanted to know how the writer knew she said that. I tried to explain that biographers do not make up events, but they sometimes make up words to make the person they are writing about "come alive." They have to be sure that the words are consistent with the personality, but these are not the exact words.

Opinion is divided among my children about whether or not they should make up quotes in their biographies. I am leaving that decision up to them, but we have been noticing how you punctuate quotes and have added a quote example to our editing checklist, which now has 10 items on it:

FOURTH-GRADE EDITING CHECKLIST

1. Do all the sentences make sense?
2. Do all the sentences start with caps and end with punc?
3. Do all people and place names have caps?
4. Do all the sentences stay on the topic?
5. Does the piece have a beginning, middle, and end?
6. Are words I need to check the spelling of underlined?
7. Are *were* (we, you, and they) and *was* (I, he, and she) used correctly?
8. Do words in a series have commas?
9. Do the words I used paint a vivid picture?
10. Do quotes have correct punc—Ms. Maverick says, "Check your quotes."

This month, I have added a "book board" to our reading center. I selected 50 titles from our classroom library that are at a variety of reading levels and that are generally popular with my fourth-graders. I then wrote these titles on sheets of white paper and covered the bulletin board with them. I then cut small red, blue, and yellow rectangles and put them into pockets I made along the bottom of the bulletin board. Now that all was ready, I gathered my children together and announced a new contest. In this contest, books, not people, were going to be the winners. Together, we read the titles of the 50 books. Among these were books some of my children had already read, and they commented briefly on them. I then explained that whenever they read one of these 50 books, they were to decide what color best describes the book. If it was "super, a book everyone should read," they would put their name on a red rectangle and attach this rectangle to the appropriate white sheet. If the book was "awful, boring, a waste of time," they would put their name on a yellow rectangle and attach this rectangle. If the book was "OK, enjoyable or informative, but nothing super special," that book would get a blue rectangle with their name on it. "From time to time," I explained, "we will have discussions during which you can tell us why you think a certain book rated a red or a yellow."

The board has been there only four weeks and already there are many red, yellow, and blue autographed rectangles attached to several of the books. The children love to see their names and ratings attached to the books. When they see a book with several red rectangles, they all try to get it and read it. One book has three yellow rectangles. Now everyone is reading it to see if it is "really that bad." Pat has rounded up extra copies of several books from the public library, and Danielle's dad bought her several paperback titles at the bookstore.

The book board is a new idea I tried this year and so far I am delighted with the results. The children are motivated to read and attach their ratings to the books. I have seen classrooms in which the number of books read by each child was kept up with and in some cases rewarded with T-shirts or other items. While I think it does encourage some children to read, I also have noticed that some children start reading only very short books or very easy books. The goal seems to become the number of books read, rather than the enjoyment and appreciation of the books. Because the book board keeps up with how many children have read and how they rated each book, rather than how many books each child has read, children are motivated to read many books but not to just accumulate titles. We have had two book discussions so far. Both were lively interchanges in which some children tried to convince others that the book was really a "red" or really a "yellow." I was reminded of the deadly dull oral book reports I had my students do during my first year of teaching. How could I have done that! For some time now, I have been curious about why children seem to understand what they listen to so much better than what they read, even when they can read almost all the words. I discussed this with Kenny, who is taking a graduate reading course, and he suggested I try some listening-reading transfer lessons (Cunningham, 1975). To do a listening-reading transfer lesson, the teacher uses two selections (or two sections of one long selection). One of these selections is read to the children and the other is used for them to read.

I decided to do my listening-reading transfer lesson using one of the biographies from our anthology and to emphasize sequence as the comprehension strategy, since determining the correct order of events is important to understanding biographies. I divided the biography into two parts and planned two parallel lessons.

I began my lesson as I always do, by having the children preview the text with me, talking about all the pictures, graphs, maps, and charts, and reading all the headings and picture captions. I told the students there would be some important words which I wanted to discuss afterwards, so that we could figure out as much meaning as possible from the context. I wrote the words *segregation, constitution,* and *amendments* on the board and had the children pronounce them with me. "As I am reading, you will hear these words, and after we read, I want us to talk about what they mean and why they are important to Thurgood Marshall's biography." I then taped to the chalkboard five sentence strips on which I had written the major events from the part I was going to read, but not in the correct sequence. I read these events to the children and set the purpose for listening. "Listen as I read so you can help me put these events, which are now jumbled, into the order in which they actually occurred." After listening to the first part of the biography, the children helped me rearrange the strips to put the events in their proper order and explained how they knew which should go first, second, and so on. We then discussed the words *constitution, segregation,* and *amendments,* what they meant, and why they were important in his life. I reread the portions of the text that used these words, and we concluded that even though we had heard the words before, we didn't really know much about them and we learned a lot about them from our reading.

Next, I told the children that they were going to finish reading the biography and do the exact same kind of thinking while they read that they had done while listening to me read. I wrote the words *civil rights*, *unequal*, and *Supreme Court* on the board and told the children that we would talk about the meanings of these after they read. I then gave a sheet on which I had written the major events of the second part of the biography and told them that their job after reading was to cut these jumbled events apart and get them in the correct order.

"I want you to do exactly the kind of thinking as you read that you did when you listened to me. Think about the words on the board and how what you read will help you bring meaning to those words. Think about the order in which things happen, and after you have read, get these important events in the right order." As usual, I gave children the choice of reading and completing the sequencing activity by themselves, with a friend, or in a group with me. I then told them that they had 30 minutes before we would reconvene and check our ordering together.

The children quickly chose a friend or curled up by themselves or joined me. Daphne was absent, so Paul, who almost always reads with Daphne, joined my group. Daisy went off by herself, and I warned her that I expected to see her reading and that she had better make a good effort at getting the events in order.

Our classroom had a busy working buzz for 30 minutes as the children (individually, with a friend, or with me) read the selection and cut and reordered the events. When we gathered together again, we agreed on the correct order. It was a bit tricky, because the biography mentioned some things later in the text that had actually happened earlier, but different children who had gotten the correct order read the parts aloud and explained how you knew what had happened before what. We then returned to the words *civil rights*, *unequal*, and *Supreme Court*, talking about what they meant and reading aloud parts from the text that helped us figure out this meaning. Finally, I "debriefed" with the children, helping them to think about what we had done. We talked about the commonalities between listening and reading.

"When you are listening and reading, you have the same words and ideas. In reading, you have to figure out the words while you are thinking about what it means. Reading is harder because you have to do two things at the same time. But you should always try to do the same kind of thinking. If you read and you realize you have been too busy figuring out the words to know what you are reading, you should go back and reread and 'listen to yourself' read so that you can think the same way you do when you're listening. When you read and listen, you can add lots more meaning to words you just knew a little about."

April

This month, we began our final science unit on Adaptation and Change. We studied animals and plants as part of this unit. I decided to focus my Reading Workshop on animals and to contrast fiction and nonfiction. We all read *Misty of Chincoteague* by Marguerite Henry and *Old Yeller*. We talked about how these two books were fiction but that you could still learn a lot about animal behavior from stories. We made a list of "true facts" about horses and dogs that we had learned from these books and checked in some reference sources.

The children then made their first, second, and third choices from four Gail Gibbons books—*Spiders, Wolves, Sea Turtles,* and *Cats.* We constructed webs to organize the information gained from these books and then used the webs to write reports on these animals. Currently, the children have all chosen another animal and are doing research on that animal using the web to record what they find. We will publish an animals book next month.

I have begun to do some book-sharing groups every other week at the beginning of Center/Project time on Thursday. Kenny has been taking a course on Classroom Organization and Management that has spent a lot of time looking at the research on motivation and engagement. Most of what they have learned I realize I have already incorporated into my day. I read aloud to the children every morning and at other times throughout the day. I choose my books to read aloud from all different genres, authors, and topics because I firmly believe that a child who does not like to read is just a child who has not yet found the right book. Of course, I provide time, books, and encouragement for Self-Selected Reading. In my conferences, I "ooh and aah" about their book choices—no matter what they are—and I try to build their self confidence by pointing out their good strategies and the clever thinking they do about books.

The piece that I was missing—if the research on engagement and motivation is correct—was interaction among children about what they are reading. They talk with me about their books, but there was no place in the schedule for them to systematically and regularly talk to one another. I decided to use the first 15 minutes of Center/Project time on alternate Thursdays to get the children together to talk about their books. Each Thursday, I form five sharing groups by pulling their names randomly. Each member of the group then has a few minutes to share what she or he is reading and why she or he likes it, and to answer questions from group members about the book.

Our social studies unit this month has been on Alaska. We always study other cultures after we finish our state unit, and I have been concerned about helping Tanana adapt to our culture. It occurred to me last month that one way to help her feel more comfortable would be for us to learn more about her and her home. Tanana was a great resource during this unit and helped us empathize with native Alaskans who see their traditional ways threatened by the advance of civilization.

We have gathered and used many books about Alaska, and as a member of the American Automobile Association, I was able to get many maps and brochures from them. I read the class two informational books, *In Two Worlds: A Yup'ik Eskimo Family* by Aylette Jenness and Alice Rivers and *The Igloo* by Charlotte and David Yue. I have also read them some contemporary fiction with Aleutians as main characters, including *Julie of the Wolves* by Jean Craighead George.

The children and I are on an imaginary journey, and we have a time machine that allows us to move back and forth in time as we move through the vast and diverse state of Alaska. The children are all keeping logs of our trip, and each day they record the date, place, temperature, and so forth, and their thoughts and feelings about all that we are seeing. At first I was afraid that the children might consider the time machine and log idea kind of "hokey," but they have wonderful imaginations and delight in using them and are clearly into our Alaska adventure.

After talking with Mrs. Wright, I decided to try a "List, Group, and Label" lesson as a kickoff to our unit. I asked the children to tell me all the words they thought of when they heard the word *Alaska,* and I listed them on the board. When the children had exhausted their Alaska vocabulary, I read the entire list to them and asked them to listen as I was reading for any that seemed to go together in some way. Mrs. Wright had suggested that the next step was to let individual children list the things they thought went together, tell why they put them together, and give a label to that group. I did this, but in order to get greater participation, I let each child write on a slip of paper the items he or she wanted to put together. Individuals then read their lists and responded to my questions on why they had put those words together and what they would call that group. When each child who desired to had read his or her group to us, had explained the reason for grouping, and had labeled the group, I suggested that each one of them make another group that was different from any they had already made. We then repeated the explaining and labeling process with these second groups.

This has been a very effective technique to kick off a unit. I learned what kind of prior knowledge and preconceptions the children had about Alaska, and they began thinking about Alaska and using the specialized vocabulary: *caribou, Aleuts, pipeline.* I also think it helps their classification skills and thus their thinking skills. I plan to begin many units with a "List, Group, and Label" lesson.

We are constantly discussing things in this class, but I have done some more structured discussions as part of this Alaska unit. I have formed discussion groups which stay together for the entire unit. I have tried to divide my children so that each group has some leaders and some quiet ones, and I have spread out my "rowdies." The groups I formed were:

Daisy	Paul	Butch	Mitch	Mort
Alex	*Betty	Carl	Chip	Daphne
*Rita	Hilda	*Joyce	Pat	*Horace
Larry	Alexander	Roberta	Tanana	Mandy
Manuel	Anthony	Steve	*Danielle	Jeff

In order to keep the discussion focused, I give them concrete tasks to do that will require discussion and that also will result in their drawing some conclusions. Once they were in their groups, I gave them a card with their names on it and explained that the person whose name had a star next to it would be the recorder for that group for the day and would do all the writing for the group. (I picked the recorders according to their fluency with spelling and writing.)

For the first discussion, I gave each group index cards and a felt marker and told them they had five minutes to list the resources of Alaska. They were asked to write only one resource on each index card, because they would use the cards later. Since they had seen a video a few days before on Alaska's resources, and many had read about Alaska's resources in various source books, they had no difficulty thinking of resources. When the timer rang to signal the end of the five minutes, each group had a stack of cards and was still talking!

Next, I gave them two large sheets of construction paper and some tape. On the top of one sheet of construction paper, I had the recorders write, "Resources that will be used up" and on the other, "Resources that will last forever." I explained the concept of renewable and nonrenewable resources to them, and gave them a few examples from our local resources. I then gave them 10 minutes to tape each of their index cards to one of the construction paper sheets. The discussion that ensued was lively and on task. When the 10 minutes were up, we displayed the charts from each group and compared the results. When two groups had put the same resource in two different categories, the groups explained their reasoning, and if we could come to any resolution, the resource was changed to the appropriate chart. In several cases, we decided we would have to do some research to resolve a controversy, and several children volunteered to see what they could find out during our afternoon Center/Project time.

I have always believed that language was the foundation for reading and writing and that thinking was at the essence of all reading and writing. As I watched all my students talking and listening during our discussions and our List, Group, and Label lesson, it was obvious that they were using and building their language and thinking processes. I am going to have to do more of this earlier in the year next year.

May

Well, once again the year is ending, and although we did a lot, we didn't get it all done. I wonder if I will ever have a year in which I accomplish everything! I ran into Vera Wise in the library last weekend and was telling her about my year and our trip to the capital, and my book sharing groups, and how I was using much more discussion, but I also lamented that there were things I planned that didn't get done. She replied, "As long as you are a great teacher, you never will do all you planned. You have to start out with goals and plans," she chided, "but then you have to look at your children and be open to opportunities. 'The teachable moment' is more than just a phrase we all learned in our education courses, you know." I felt somewhat better after talking with her—I always do—but I still would like to have one year that goes according to plan!

This last month has been frantic. Our class did the annual book fair, and although I put all the children to work and have learned some shortcuts to all the paperwork, it still took a lot of time. We did historical fiction and plays for our Reading Workshop. After reading the play in our anthology together, the children chose from five plays which they read in small groups. Each group acted out their play for the other four groups and for Mrs. Flame's second-graders.

We assembled the portfolios that will be going to Mr. Dunn. There are some things which everyone had in the portfolio and other things that the children got to choose. Of course, we did the final "Favorite and Unfavorite Things" writing sample. This time, when I asked the children to do it, they knew that I had their beginning-of-year and January samples and wanted to see these before they wrote. "No fair," I responded. "I want you to write your best, and then you can assess how much growth you have made since January." They all—including Mort and Daisy—put their best effort into this final sample, and the results showed it. I and they were equally impressed with their growth. These three samples along with their self-evaluation of their writing growth and my evaluation are all going to Mr. Dunn. I hope he will be as impressed as I am.

The other things that are in every portfolio are each child's written summary of an informational piece we read, a story map related to some of the historical fiction, and an audiotape made during one of our final Self-Selected Reading conferences. On this tape, each child is reading two pages from a chosen book and then carrying on a discussion with me about it. They also talk on the tape about what they like to read, some of the best books they have read this year, and how their reading interests have broadened. Several children mentioned the book board and book-sharing groups as providing the impetus for them to read certain books which they heard their friends talking about. More proof I need to include these next year—probably earlier in the year.

In addition, the children chose one piece of published writing, one example of a response from their reading log, and one other "something" to represent them. "Think carefully about what you want to send forward to Mr. Dunn," I instructed. "It should be something you are proud of and have worked hard on, and something that lets him begin to know what kind of person you are—what really matters to you." Daisy, of course, chose a painting she had done. She has become quite an artist. Steve took a photo of his prize-winning science fair project. Paul, with some help from Daphne, wrote a Curious George book and wanted that sent to Mr. Dunn. Mitch constructed a map showing lots of truck routes he wanted to drive when he got his "big rig." Roberta, who has persevered in her desire to be a "smoke jumper," researched some of the major fires of this century and wrote and illustrated a report on this. Picking or creating one "thing" that represented them was clearly an intriguing task for the children. They took it quite seriously, and I realized that they have moved along toward my goal of taking responsibility for and pride in what they are learning and accomplishing.

Once the portfolios were assembled, the children made a table of contents and wrote an explanation of each piece and what that piece demonstrated about them and their reading and writing growth and interests. I shared each of these with the parents in our final parent-teacher conference. During my conference with Mort's mother, we talked about his apathy and lack of enthusiasm. We both agreed that while he still had a ways to go, he was better about doing what he needed to and even got a little bit excited about some of the things we did—particularly when he had chosen to do them. "I have been meaning to tell you all year, Ms. Maverick, that I was very wrong in thinking that the Center/Project time was a waste of time for fourth-graders. Usually the only thing I could get any feedback about from Mort was related to what he was doing during that time." I had forgotten that she was the one that voiced that concern way back in the fall parent meeting, but I was glad to hear she had changed her mind.

I am taking all the portfolios with me when I go to talk to Kenny's graduate class next month. I don't know how he roped me into this, but somehow he got me to agree to come talk to his class about my "strange but effective" schedule and about how I try to engage and motivate my students. He has promised to take me to our favorite restaurant for a spectacular meal afterwards. I don't particularly want to do this, but he has been a big help to me this year, and as Norma Flame keeps reminding me, "A good man is hard to find."

KENNY'S GRADUATE CLASS

After the break, Kenny went to the front of the class to introduce Yetta Maverick. "You have been hearing about Yetta's great ideas all semester from me," he began, "but now you are going to hear them 'from the horse's mouth'—no offense, Yetta." Kenny went on to tell a little more about Yetta Maverick, and then Yetta got up and began to talk. She was a little nervous at the beginning, "much easier to talk in front of children," she reminded herself. But once she got into talking about her class and her schedule, she forgot to be nervous.

"Getting it all done in the intermediate grades is a major challenge," she began. "I have tried all kinds of schedules, and the one I am going to show you now is one I have used for the past two years and works better than anything else." Yetta put her schedule transparency on the overhead and quickly explained how she spent large blocks of time on Thursday and Friday with her science and social studies units and had separate times for reading, writing, words, and math on the other days. She showed them examples of the kinds of things they had read during Reading Workshop and explained how she used both the adopted reader and multiple copies of books. She also talked with them about her Writing Workshop and how some weeks students were writing on self-selected topics and other weeks were devoted to focused writing lessons in which everyone worked on learning to write a particular form. She then showed them some examples of things her students had read and written connected to science and social studies units and explained how integrating reading and writing with the content areas helped the children learn more content, gave them real purposes for reading and writing, and allowed her to accomplish more by "killing two birds with one stone."

Besides her schedule, the other main topic Kenny had asked her to talk about was motivation and engagement, a topic which loomed large in the minds of almost all teachers. She began by telling them how she and Kenny had discussed the components that seemed to play a major role in engagement: success, self-confidence, interest, choice, and interaction. "As I looked across my day," she explained, "I determined that I was providing for the first four but not for interaction. I added some biweekly book-sharing sessions on Thursday afternoons during our Center/Project time to provide all my students with regular opportunities to share their reading and their opinions with their friends."

Success is related to what you ask children to do and making sure that they can succeed at it. It also matters that they see their success as related to their efforts. I spend a lot of time with my children helping them see what they are accomplishing, not just what they are doing."

She could tell by the looks on some of their faces that they didn't get the distinction. "For example," she said, "during Reading Workshop, I include a wide variety of genres, authors, and topics. I want students to learn how you read different kinds of texts, and I want them to know about the whole universe of literature which is available to them. When we finish working with a particular kind of text, I ask the children to tell me what they have learned about mysteries and how to read them, or biographies and how you read them. I don't want my students to just think, 'We read mysteries,' but rather, 'We learned a lot about how mysteries are written and how to read them.' In writing, we worked a lot with summary writing—not an easy task for most fourth-graders. I wanted my students to see that we weren't just writing summaries; we were learning to summarize. Children are more motivated and engaged when they see that they are growing and accomplishing things they couldn't do before. I provide as much success as I can, but I try to tie that success to the things they are accomplishing and to let them see the link between their effort and the accomplishment. When they don't do something correctly, I try to help them find another way to go about it so that they can succeed. I want them to think, 'I don't know how to go about this,' rather than 'I can't do this.'

"Success and understanding what you did to be successful is what I think leads directly to self-confidence. Self-confidence is not just thinking that you can do anything, but knowing that you can learn to do the things you haven't learned yet to do. Interest and choice are also critical. All of us are more motivated when the topic is one we are interested in and when we have some choice in what we do." She then explained how she tried to balance the things children must do if she was going to accomplish the curriculum goals against the need to allow children choices to pursue their own interests. She pointed to Self-Selected Reading time and her afternoon Center/Project time as two points in every day when student interest and choice played paramount roles in what they did. "But these are not the only times children make choices; there are also lots of opportunities to give students what I call 'limited choice.'"

As she said this, she pointed to copies of the five plays she had brought with her. "After everyone read the play in our anthology—to learn how plays are written and the special ways we have to read plays—they made a first, second, and third choice of which play they would like to read and put on for the rest of us. I formed the play-acting groups based on their choices, but also considering the reading ability of my students," she explained. "This play is written at a late second-grade level and is a lot easier than all the others. This one is much harder than the others. If the children who were struggling picked the easier play as any of their choices, I put them in that group. Likewise, if my advanced readers chose this hard one, I slotted them to that group. I then divided the other children to include some grade-level readers in the easier play group."

At this point, Ms. Maverick looked up at the clock and realized that although she could go "on and on," she needed to stop to let them ask questions. There were lots of questions.

A young teacher asked, "Don't the low readers resent being put in the easy book every time?" Ms. Maverick quickly explained that the groups changed every time a new type of book was being read, and that the low children were not always in the easier book group. "If they didn't choose the easy book as any of their choices, I slot them into one of the other groups and let the group support their reading," she explained. "I also don't think the children realized that one of the books was easier and one harder," she mused. "They were all reading plays, and they all had gotten one of their choices, and the composition of the group changed each time we did choice groups."

"What about when you read in the anthology," an older man asked. "Did you group them by ability then, or did the whole class read it together?"

"Neither," answered Ms. Maverick. She then explained about how the before and after reading activities were done as a whole class but the actual reading of the selection was done in a variety of ways, including some children in partners and some with her. She told them about Daphne's wish to be Paul's partner and how she sometimes let the children choose whether they wanted to read a selection by themselves, with a friend, or to join her in a group to read it.

"But what about children who choose to read it with a friend and then just fool around and don't get it read?" a teacher interjected.

"I give them one warning and then they join my group," Ms. Maverick responded, in the same no-nonsense tone her children had learned to pay attention to in her classroom.

The questions went on until the instructor finally had to call a halt to it. Ms. Maverick quickly showed them all the portfolios she had lugged to the meeting and invited them to look through these if they had a few minutes. Many teachers lingered to ask more questions and look at the children's work. Finally, they all left and a beaming Kenny took an exhausted but relieved Yetta off for a truly scrumptious late dinner.

REFERENCES

Cunningham, P. M. (1975). Transferring comprehension from listening to reading. *The Reading Teacher, 29,* 169–172.

Cunningham, P. M., & Hall, D. P. (1998). *Month-by Month Phonics for Upper Grades.* Greensboro, NC: Carson-Dellosa.

Children's Books/Materials Cited

Anastasia on Her Own, by L. Lowry, Yearling, 1986.

Cats, by G. Gibbons, Holiday House, 1998.

Curious George books, by M. Rey & A. Shalleck, Houghton Mifflin, various dates.

Fabulous Facts About the 50 States, by W. Ross, Scholastic, 1989.

50 Simple Things Kids Can Do to Save the Earth, by The Earthworks Group, Scholastic, 1974.

Fourth Grade Is a Jinx, by C. O. McKenna, Scholastic, 1989.

Frederick Douglass Fights for Freedom, by M. Davidson, Scholastic, 1989.

Freedom Train: The Story of Harriet Tubman, by D. Sterling, Scholastic, 1987.

A Girl Called Boy, by B. Hurmence, Houghton Mifflin, 1990.

Greening the City Streets: The Story of Community Gardens, by B. Huff, Clarion, 1992.

The Igloo, by C. & D. Yue, Houghton Mifflin, 1992.

I Have a Dream: The Story of Martin Luther King, by M. Davidson, Scholastic, 1986.

In Two Worlds: A Yup'ik Eskimo Family, by A. Jenness & A. Rivers, Scholastic, 1992.
Jesse Jackson, by P. McKissack, Scholastic, 1992.
Julie of the Wolves, by J. C. George, HarperCollins, 1974.
Jumanji, by C. Von Allsburg, Houghton Mifflin, 1995.
Kid Heroes of the Environment, by The Earthworks Group, Earthworks, 1991.
Misty of Chincoteague, by M. Henry, Houghton Mifflin, 1990.
Old Yeller, by F. Gibson, HarperCollins, 1989.
Phoebe the Spy, by J. B. Griffin, Scholastic, 1989.
Sea Turtles, by G. Gibbons, Holiday House, 1998.
Spiders, by G. Gibbons, Holiday House, 1993.
Sports Illustrated magazine.
Tales of a Fourth Grade Nothing, by J. Blume, Dell, 1976.
Trouble at Marsh Harbor, by S. Sharpe, Puffin Books, 1991.
TV Guide magazine.
The Way of the Grizzly, by D. H. Patent, Houghton Mifflin, 1987.
Where the Bald Eagles Gather, by D. H. Patent, Houghton Mifflin, 1990.
Where the Wild Horses Roam, by D. H. Patent, Clarion, 1990.
Wolves by G. Gibbons, Holiday House, 1995.
A Wrinkle in Time by M. L'Engle.

Mr. Dunn: Fifth Grade

THE PARENT MEETING

Ed Dunn sat at his desk, waiting for the parents to arrive. Six years before at this time he had been nervously rehearsing an almost-memorized speech, but this night he was much more confident. His first year of teaching had begun as a challenge, and he soon found himself floundering. He traced many of his problems to his mistaken assumption that everyone in the class would read and write proficiently and somewhat similarly.

Happily, with help and guidance from Mr. Topps and other teachers, he began to meet the challenge. He adjusted his instruction so that all students experienced some measure of success. Working diligently and keeping the students' best interests foremost in his mind, he fashioned a good program. By the end of the year, he believed that he had learned as much as the students.

This year, especially, he felt ready to teach. On his own, through professional development opportunities in his district, and through courses at the university, he had learned many ways to provide materials and instruction that take into account the many reading levels inevitably found in fifth grade. He had discovered that reading instruction actually can be provided while students read materials in content areas such as social studies, science, and health. He discovered that students needed help coping with the ideas encountered in texts more than just pronouncing words. Now he was to welcome the parents of this year's class and tell them about the program he planned for their children.

After everyone arrived and was seated, he began: "Good evening and welcome to your child's fifth-grade classroom. I am Ed Dunn, and I hope to get to know each of you as I teach your children this year.

"During this meeting, I will emphasize what I will be doing to improve your children's reading and writing, since that is the backbone of our studies. Even in math, fifth-graders need to read well to follow written directions and solve word problems. In middle school, high school, academics beyond high school, in their workplaces and personal lives, your children will need advanced levels of literacy.

"Ms. Maverick and I have talked at some length about the type of reading program your children had with her last year. I am very impressed with her reading-to-learn approach. To some degree, my approach to reading instruction can be seen as an extension of hers. However, I follow the traditional divisions among the content areas. By this I mean that we have periods of every day set aside specifically for language arts, math, social studies, health, and science. This basically is the way your children will spend their school days in middle school, high school, and if they go on, in college. I am introducing them to this format this year.

"One important goal that I have this year is to guide your children to the important facts and ideas in their subject-matter reading materials. For example, we will study a unit on matter and energy in science, and there are many concepts in this unit that your children probably have never encountered before. It's my job to help this class learn about things such as conductors, insulators, convection currents, waves, energy chains, collision systems, and many other concepts that probably are unfamiliar. The reading materials that Miss Launch and Mrs. Wright used in the primary grades generally contained information about familiar things such as families, sports, and pets that your children had directly experienced inside or outside of class. But the emphasis now is on reading materials that contain new, unfamiliar information.

"Not only do the youngsters need help understanding these new and unfamiliar ideas, but they are expected to remember the ideas, too. If you'll think back, after Miss Launch and Mrs. Wright had finished with a reading passage, they didn't check weeks later to see if your children could recall the contents of the passage. But now in fifth grade, the emphasis is both on understanding and remembering unfamiliar information.

"I want to carefully lead your children through their materials so they know what information is important. I have a pretty good idea of what I think should be learned, I am responsible for conveying it, and I want to make sure that all of it is highlighted. Because of this, I tend to be the one to tell the class what to read or listen for—be able to describe the water cycle, for instance—and I then ask questions or assign projects that call for extra thinking about the specified content. Often I will lecture or show a video that calls attention to the information."

Mr. Dunn paused for a second to see if the group was still with him. They seemed to be, so he pressed on to what he thought would be new to them. "Unfortunately, there is a problem with me guiding students to what they should understand and remember. The problem with this approach is that if I always choose the materials, always set the purposes for reading, and always follow up those purposes, then my students come to depend on me for guidance. They learn a good deal of information, but they easily become dependent learners. My second, equally important goal involves helping your children become independent.

"Children need the skills and the self-sufficiency to learn on their own. Feelings energize reading and writing, and children need to believe in themselves, having confidence that they can go off alone or with others and learn important ideas and accomplish important tasks. More and more they need to monitor their own progress and do what needs to be done without me directing their every move. At home you probably expect your children more than ever to clean their rooms and perform other chores without you constantly telling them what to do. In my class, I promote such independence by providing a structure that gradually releases students to self-guidance.

"Along with gradually releasing, or fading, my directions about what to do and when to do it, I also will encourage independence by continuing emphases on independent reading and writing strategies. Let me give you an example of what I mean by independent learning." Mr. Dunn displayed the following short paragraph that he had written on an overhead transparency:

> *A man named Eric Thorvaldsson came to the island in 982 A.D. Eric had been exiled from Iceland for three years for killing another man. When he returned to Iceland, he wanted settlers to be eager to go to this land, so he made it sound attractive by calling it Greenland.*

He turned to the parents. "What are some of the things independent learners would do with this information?"

After some silence, Mrs. Penn raised her hand. "We could try to get a basic understanding of the passage, but I know there's more to it than that."

Mr. Moppet spoke out. "When I was in school, I simply memorized all of the information. I usually got A's and B's on the tests because I could produce practically anything the teacher wanted. Of course, I promptly forgot most everything I had memorized as soon as the test was over too." The parents obviously could relate to Mr. Moppet's confession. Mr. Dunn noted many of them smiling and nodding their heads in agreement.

"That's exactly what I hope to keep your children away from in my class," Mr. Dunn said. "The passage I've displayed on the overhead for you contains quite a bit of information. Students could memorize facts such as the date Eric first came to Greenland, Eric's last name, and the length of his exile. However, this year we will have extensive lessons on helping students independently determine what is important, and I will provide opportunities for the class to do this on their own. Thinking is the essence of reading and writing, so we will work on thinking strategies such as determining whether or not more information is needed to satisfy a task and locating new information. These strategies are what today's fifth-graders need to be independent students, and they are ones that can be carried outside of class as your children become lifelong learners.

"I must confess that I am of two minds when it comes to helping students learn from what they read. I know I should not continually direct the class's attention to what is important, but I worry that they will miss essential information if I don't tell them exactly what to look for. In other words, I want to direct your children's reading, but I also want to let them learn how to acquire information by themselves. Children need a balanced literacy program, and I believe I can strike the correct balance, although I must admit that sometimes it is hard to find."

Mr. Dunn walked to a table with a computer on it at the side of the room. As the parents turned in their chairs to face him, he removed the dust cover from the machine. "Finally, I want to tell you about the writing-with-computers program that we will use in this class.

"Fortunately, we have had a computer lab at Merritt Elementary since your children began coming here, and all classrooms have had at least a single computer in them. I'm sure, at this point, your children know more about computers than many of you do!" Several parents nodded, chuckling and smiling.

"While we are fortunate to have a lab with enough computers in it so the largest class in our school can all be in there at the same time, Mr. Topps and I believe it would be even better if we could have enough computers in each classroom, so they could be an integral part of the entire instructional day. Because of the expense, that just has not been feasible. This year, however, I have exciting news for you. Last winter, I submitted a grant proposal that has been funded. This year, in this classroom, we are going to have seven computers just like the one here that I have brought from home." He placed his hand on top of the monitor. The parents were obviously impressed and pleased.

"The Angus Restaurant, my classroom's business partner again this year, has agreed to purchase seven computer tables with lockable wheels for us. With them, we will be able to rearrange the computers around the room, depending on how we are using them at any particular time. As you can see if you look down at the floor, Mr. Topps has had three floor outlets installed around the room so that we can plug the computers in there as well as in the wall outlets.

"I am spending all of my PTSA money from last year and this to buy two inkjet printers with special devices so that three or four computers can share the same printer. These printers will be set up in the room by the middle of October. Reading and writing are learned in a variety of ways and in various settings, and these computers and printers provide new tools for communication."

At this point, a woman raised her hand and began speaking. "Mr. Dunn, I'm Daphne's grandmother. Mr. Fields and I bought a personal computer last year to help us manage our farm. Daphne has really enjoyed several programs that we bought for her at the computer store. What software will you have for these new computers?"

"Excellent question, Mrs. Fields," said Mr. Dunn. "With money from the grant, I have obtained a site license for our class to use a single piece of software with the new computers. This software combines word processing with numerous other desktop publishing features. We had to pay three times what the program usually costs, but we are permitted to make seven copies of the program, one for each computer. We are also allowed to make copies to replace any we lose if a hard disk crashes. In addition, the grant has enabled us to purchase access to the Internet and World Wide Web. We have also purchased a number of simulations and multimedia presentations for social studies, science, health, mathematics, and literature, as well as reading, writing, and other aspects of the language arts. As you can see, this is going to be an exciting year for your children."

Mr. Dunn was relieved. He thought he had done a fairly good job summarizing the reading and writing program that he had spent so much time envisioning and producing. Given the short amount of time he had, he believed the parents would best understand and be most interested in the what he had just presented. He waited for a response.

Mrs. Penn broke the silence for everyone. "Mr. Dunn, we are all thankful that our children are here in Merritt Elementary, and we know that what you have planned for our children will continue to help them grow as they have in the past. Basically, I think I know what you mean about teaching reading along with content-area subjects, balancing guided comprehension with independent comprehension, and I'm pleased to see the computers in class. Our children clearly need to become better at understanding unfamiliar ideas, and they need to learn how to use this technology so they can succeed in the future. It looks like another great year is coming up."

"I'd like to second that," spoke up a woman at the back. "We left here when Mike was about to start third grade. We are very glad to be back. Mike is a handful, but at least here we know everyone will work with him. Miss Nouveau worked wonders with him, and I know you, Mr. Dunn, will be able to help him behave and learn."

Few questions seemed necessary after that, and the meeting came quickly to an end. Mr. Dunn again was thankful for being part of a school that promoted such positive interactions with parents, and he left even more determined to do right with the children entrusted to him.

MONTHLY LOGS

September

What a month this has been! Establishing a productive classroom environment always takes time because the children simply don't know what "this year's teacher's" expectations are. I've found that as long as I clarify my expectations, treat individuals fairly and with respect, and provide reasonably stimulating lessons that allow the children to progress, then the class runs successfully.

My schedule below shows how I divided the day. We study five main subject areas: reading/literature, writing/language arts, math, science, and social studies. Special classes include physical education, art, and music, which others teach, allowing me about 45 minutes of unstructured time. I embed some regular activities such as reading aloud to the class, self-selected writing, and spelling into the subjects. Opportunity time at the end of the day is devoted to homeroom activities involving personal growth topics such as time management and stress reduction, to finishing assignments and projects begun during the day, to receiving extra help with confusing subject matter, to self-selected reading or writing, and to recapping the day.

Time	Activity
8:30 – 8:40	Plan the day
8:40 – 9:40	Reading/Literature
9:40 – 10:35	Writing/Language arts
10:35– 11:25	Math
11:25 – 12:00	Lunch/Recess
12:00 – 12:20	Self-selected reading
12:20 – 1:00	Science
1:00 – 1:45	Specials
1:45 – 2:30	Social studies
2:30 – 3:15	Opportunity time/Close the day

I use the class textbooks occasionally, but I always bring into the classroom other printed materials, audio visuals, technology, concrete objects, and guest speakers. I refer to all these nontextbook things as *collateral sources*. This means that all are equally important. In fact, the main contribution of the textbooks is as reference sources for the topics we cover in class.

When I passed out the textbooks in each of the areas, I got quite a variety of responses from the children. Danielle immediately began poring over the pages of each book. Reading seems to provide her an outlet. Hilda pulled out her eraser and began cleaning up her books before placing them carefully in her desk. Conversely, when I distributed the social studies texts, Mike and Butch pulled out their pencils and began drawing mustaches, crossed eyes, and big ears on George Washington and Abraham Lincoln, who grace the covers of our books. Although I could remember doing similar things when I was their age, I still informed them in no uncertain terms that such action was unacceptable. They grumbled, but they erased their artwork.

Our mornings are devoted to reading/literature, writing/language arts, and math. I carry over skills from these areas to others throughout the day. For example, if we're studying capitalization in language arts, then we notice what is capitalized in the books we read and the writing we do in reading/literature, math, social studies, and science.

At present, the time set aside for reading/literature begins with me reading aloud to the class. I started teacher read-alouds the very first day of school. Each week over the summer, I tried to read one or two children's books that were new to me. This is really no chore since these books are always fast reads, and I really like children's literature, anyway. I usually find them better written and less cynical than most mass-market literature intended for more mature audiences. Last summer I made an effort to read books set in the cultures of other nations. It seems especially important for fifth-graders to understand how their counterparts around the world live, think, and feel. We live in a multicultural world. Unfortunately, social studies often seems too abstract and collective in its view. Students have trouble identifying with individuals from other countries and cultures unless they can somehow walk around in their shoes for a while. A good novel has the power to provide this kind of vicarious experience. Furthermore, there are individual, cultural, and language differences among the children we teach, and providing multiple types of culturally relevant materials seems to enfranchise students who might be on the margins.

The first three weeks of school, I read a chapter of *Journey to Jo'burg* by Beverley Naidoo to the class every day. That book was a good one to start with because it is not very long and has 15 short chapters. I wanted to be able to maintain students' interest during the read-aloud and leave them wanting more when it ended. I thought we could build up to longer books with longer chapters. The story of *Journey to Jo'burg* is set in South Africa in the time of apartheid and provides a frighteningly vivid portrait of life for blacks under that system. The children were riveted throughout. Some of them also became quite disturbed that no one had told them about apartheid before. I assured them that they had heard about it but had not really realized what it meant. I promised them if they watched the news or looked through the newspaper for a week or two, they would find out more about current race relations in South Africa. Before finishing the book, several of them shared in class what they had heard or read about South Africa in the news media. The last week in the month, I began reading *Year of the Panda* by Miriam Schlein. It is set in rural China.

After reading aloud, which seems to help students focus on academics, I turn to guiding the class through the fifth-grade literature anthology. For instance, before reading a passage I present a few vocabulary terms that I think students will need to make sense of the text, talk about experiences class members had similar to the passage, and prescribe a number of pages to read silently before talking more about it.

My language arts and math programs are based on presenting a common topic to the class and then pursuing that topic at levels that are appropriate for the children. I present whole-class lessons on each topic. The children then work on their own or in small groups with materials and exercises that are appropriate for their levels.

Even though all my students were regularly involved in writing last year in Ms. Maverick's room and in the lower grades before that, I still find it a good idea to begin the year in writing/language arts with several weeks of self-selected writing. Regardless of how much writing children have done previously, it seems that most of them are uncertain and anxious about how their new teacher will treat their thoughts that have been recorded in writing. Even the most advanced students I have are well aware that I could readily find things wrong with their writing if I held them accountable to all the conventions one finds in a traditional fifth-grade language curriculum.

Knowing how important feeling is to literacy learning, every September I work to establish a high level of trust. As usual, I begin by having students write about topics of their own choosing, followed by a time of sharing in which volunteers read aloud what they have just written. The only limitation is that what they write cannot be written to offend me, other students, or their parents. Students can respond to what others have shared, but only to make positive comments or ask questions in order to gain additional information. I keep my own comments brief and positive. By the end of September every year, I find that students are willing to write for me and each other because we have established this atmosphere of trust. Additionally, the self-selected writing we do early in the year seems to promote self confidence, with individuals realizing that their efforts are what determine their success. During the year, I regularly have students select what they want to write about as well as how they want to express themselves, but I include focused writing assignments, also.

Self-selected reading occurs each day after lunch. Like our read-aloud period, self-selected reading is a valuable teaching-learning practice that has the extra benefit of settling active youngsters and gently focusing them on academics. It also helps balance my instruction by linking specific group-presented strategies with individuals' personal attempts at making sense of what they read. During self-selected reading, the class reads silently on their own for a certain time period, and I confer with students either individually or in small groups. I frequently have an individual tell me about what they are reading and how they are doing with it. For instance, I might have someone read a small portion of the book, then tell me how it fits with what they have read to date. To elicit essential thinking processes, I ask questions such as the following:

- What have you read or personally experienced that is similar to what has happened in the book?
- What images is the book especially good at evoking?
- What is the main thing the author is saying to you?
- What have you wondered about as you read this?
- Would you like to read something else by this author?

The students generally take good advantage of self-selected reading time; I'm sure this is the result of what these children have done in their earlier grades here at Merritt Elementary. In the future, I intend to form well-defined book clubs, groups of students who have chosen the same book to read and discuss. My conversations with the book club members as a group then might cut down on the time I now spend conferencing with individuals.

In science and social studies, I plan units of instruction that develop understanding of the subject and that improve literacy abilities at the same time. Here I balance attention to content-area facts and ideas with attention to strategies and processes. In effect, I use subject-matter materials just as if they were written for formal reading instruction. If a key word is defined clearly by the context, then I have the class figure out what the word means from the context. If a passage we are reading is organized clearly, then I have the class portray that organization through graphic organizers. Additionally, students work in groups or on their own, inquiring into aspects of the topic we are studying. Most of these small-group and individual activities are with materials written at various levels of difficulty, so children often explore the same topic and complete the same task (e.g., Determine the main causes of disease; Provide evidence that animals adapt to their environment) while reading different materials.

One of the most important teaching actions I performed this month involved classroom diagnosis. Knowing that there always are differences among children, I wanted to learn about some specific differences exhibited by this class. Mort and Paul put forth very little effort in completing the social studies and science activities I assigned, so I suspected that those two had difficulty reading and writing and that difficulty caused them to appear lazy and uncaring. But I wasn't sure. That's why I spent part of the second week of school conducting a group diagnosis with our content-area reading materials. I wanted information about who required accommodations and adaptations to the assignments.

The group diagnosis that I use relies quite a bit on common sense. I simply have students complete an assignment that is roughly typical of the type of assignment that I might make during the year. The difference is that I look at the students' performance as a measure of how well they can deal with the materials, not as a measure of the grade they should receive. This is an inventory of the proficiencies students bring to my classroom; it is not a test for purposes of accountability and grading.

To construct a group reading inventory, I took a basic textbook that we have for one of our six subjects (I selected social studies this time) and identified an appropriate selection from the second 50 pages. The selection had a beginning, middle, and end; that is, it stood by itself. For the section, I wrote questions that were the same type that would normally occur during a regular class. In fact, my questions covered the topics that would receive emphasis if I were actually teaching them. One of the other fifth-grade teachers might ask different questions that emphasize different aspects of the passage, but that is to be expected.

After the class completed this group inventory, I took it home for assessment and evaluation. This year I evaluated the papers holistically, because all of my questions called for short-answer, essay-type responses rather than responses that called for circling letters or underlining words. To do the holistic evaluation,

I first read all the papers rather quickly one time in order to gain an overall perspective. Then I went through the papers again and sorted them into four stacks according to how well they satisfied the assignment. I tried not to let handwriting influence my judgments, because clear handwriting does not always indicate clear thinking, and vice versa. After obtaining four stacks, I read the papers a final time and rank ordered them. I now had tentative information to help me determine how well each student could meet certain outcomes with the one textbook. After forming my own opinion, I consulted the portfolios of students' work Yetta Maverick had sent up from last year. The portfolios contained representative samples of literacy products, and they certainly informed my understandings of individuals' proficiencies.

Based on my group reading inventory and my examination of the portfolios produced in fourth grade, I came up with a tentative list of students and their abilities to benefit from our classroom social studies text. I seem to have four students who cannot be expected to learn from the text. Daisy, Jeff, Mike, and Paul appear to need special lessons and materials if they are to benefit from reading in social studies. If I don't provide them special lessons and materials, then they are doomed to two situations: (1) frustration with an incomprehensible text, and (2) reliance on class lectures, presentations, videos, and other nonprint media in order to obtain information.

I seem to have 14 students who can be expected to learn from our text and increase their reading abilities while doing so, as long as they receive some direct guidance from me. I realize that learning from text is not an all-or-nothing affair and that students can acquire some knowledge, even from quite difficult materials. However, it seems these 14 children will learn the most information and best improve their reading abilities at the same time if I provide them clear guidance before and after they read the class social studies text.

The remaining eight students look as though they will be able to understand the text with ease. They still will require my help to lead them to even better understanding and insight into what they read. But from what I can tell, they should have little difficulty with my typical assignments based on the text.

I will observe my students' reading abilities throughout the year, but for the present I have a tentative idea of their relative levels. Sometime in October I will look at the permanent files of those students whom I am especially concerned about, and perhaps I will talk with some of their past teachers. I like to form my own opinions first, however, before I solicit other people's opinions about my students.

The morning after the parent meeting, most of the children had obviously heard from their parents about the new computers. "Where are they?" Mike wanted to know. "Still in the boxes," I replied, and received a chorus of groans in response. "You are not completely ready to use them yet, but I will help you finish getting ready over the next few weeks," I promised. Everyone wanted to know what they had to do to get ready. "Get better at typing on a keyboard," I answered. Almost everyone declared they were already really good at that!

TENTATIVE RANKING OF ABILITIES TO BENEFIT
FROM INSTRUCTION WITH
SOCIAL STUDIES TEXTBOOK

Relative Ability	Student
Independent level (little guidance)	Betty
	Danielle
	Hilda
	Larry
	Mandy
	Pat
	Rita
	Roberta
Instructional level (some guidance)	Alex
	Anthony
	Carl
	Chip
	Daphne
	Horace
	Joyce
	Manuel
	Mitch
	Steve
Instructional level (much guidance)	Alexander
	Butch
	Mort
	Tanana
Frustration level (needs accommodation)	Daisy
	Jeff
	Mike
	Paul

That afternoon, I took them as a class to the school's computer lab for the 45-minute period that Mr. Topps had reserved for me there every day this month. I subtracted 15 minutes each out of science, social studies, and opportunity hour to make time for it. It is only temporary, and I am sure the learning students gain will make it well worthwhile.

Even though the computers in the lab are rather different from the ones we will have in our classroom, the children can still learn to improve their keyboarding on them. The computer lab is networked, and there is an excellent keyboarding tutorial available on the network. All of my students this year had worked in the lab during past years, so they knew how to turn the computers on. I showed them how to download the tutorial from the network into their individual machines and walked around the lab as they did so. I explained to them how the introductory lesson would work and how they should proceed at their own pace. After Larry explained to me that he had already completed this tutorial at home and proved it by jumping to the last lesson and typing with impressive speed and accuracy through the first part of it, I had him help me move around among the other students to help them with the tutorial.

Every afternoon for the rest of September, Larry and I assisted the class as they moved through the keyboarding tutorial. We played down competition between students as much as possible and tried to emphasize the concept of "personal best." Of course, students still compared themselves with each other, but we were able to keep it to a minimum. When the amount of assistance being sought decreased markedly after the first week, Larry also spent most of his time at a computer with the tutorial, increasing his speed and accuracy even more.

While the students vary tremendously in their speed and accuracy of keyboarding, the only ones whose typing was still inadequate by the end of the month were Jeff and Paul. They have made some progress, however.

October

As I get to know my students better, I always am amazed at how different they are! Larry has an exceptionally quick mind, and his knowledge of the world is actually astounding. Occasionally I wonder if he couldn't teach the class. The students ask him for help almost as often and as willingly as they ask me. Mike either cannot or will not stay at any task or in any one place for more than a minute or two. He does not defy me, but he does require constant reminding. Betty, Tanana, Daphne, and Joyce are fast friends, which is not unusual of course, but individually they are such diverse people. Betty is a perfectionist who almost always succeeds. Tanana's interest in nature has dominated all her other interests. Daphne has a tremendous imagination, as does Joyce.

We got off to a good start this month working on different reading-writing activities in social studies, health, and science because of the care I took getting into them. I always am careful to keep my class together as a large group during the first few weeks of school. This allows the students to learn what my limits are in regard to acceptable behavior, and it allows the class routine to become established. After a time, I gradually begin allowing the students to control some of their own learning activities. This is a yearlong process, and some classes go further than others in their independent learning.

The way I opened up my science period by balancing whole class, small-group, and individual work is a good example of how I promote independence. We spent the first week exploring our class science textbook, noting its table of contents, skimming through the chapters, and becoming familiar with the special parts of the book such as its index, glossary, and footnoting system. I then began whole-class lessons on our first unit of study, which dealt with motion.

To kick off the unit, I posed an overall guiding question: "What would be needed to have a perpetual motion machine?" Questions such as this one provide students an overarching purpose for study, turning the facts and ideas they encounter into facts-in-action and ideas-in-action. Thinking is essential to reading and writing, and guiding questions elicit good higher-order thinking. After posing the guiding question, I presented the idea of perpetual motion, showed illustrations of previous attempts at rendering such a machine, and brainstormed possibilities. With this overall direction set for the unit, we began focusing on specific components related to motion such as acceleration, momentum, velocity, and friction.

When reading materials were used at first, I kept the class together, preparing them for each passage, setting specific purposes, and discussing the material afterward to make sure that the purposes had been met. I balanced lessons with purposes such as "Read to determine what new information this passage contains," and "Read to find out how friction affects motion" to move students forward in a clear common direction.

When assigning writing tasks, I made them one at a time and held everyone in the class responsible for each one. As expected, some students did better than others; differences are to be expected, although all are expected to succeed. Larry and Pat turned in papers that could have been displayed in a showcase, Alexander had some terrific insights, but they were not stated very clearly, and Tanana and Daisy appeared to jot down whatever came to their minds.

Later in the unit, we watched a video and worked through a CD-ROM on motion, and I read aloud a short article on "Moving Machines." Then I listed four reading-writing activities on the board:

1. Draw arrows around a diagram of an airplane wing to show the direction and relative amounts of force pushing on the wing.
2. List names of pictured machines.
3. Construct a "web" of the information that is contained in the article "Moving Machines." (See Mr. Dunn for a copy of the article and a taped version of it.)
4. Complete the experiment described on page 83 of our science textbook.

"But, Mr. Dunn, some of those activities have nothing to do with our textbook," Hilda patiently explained to me.

"That's right. They all are connected to our study of motion, but they include a variety of materials. Try it, you'll like it," I assured her. "But wait until you hear the real surprise."

I then told the class that each person was responsible for completing all four activities, but that they could choose the order in which to complete them. They would have the normal amount of science time each day to complete the tasks. Friday of that week was set as the final due date.

Most students handled this choice making quite well. (Again, they reflect their previous training!) The biggest exception was Mort, who told me that he chose not to do any of the assignments. However, I reminded him firmly that he could choose the order of doing them but not the actual doing of them. He got the message.

We culminated our study of motion with a unit test (a conventional, yet necessary, aspect of teaching, I think) as well as poster displays of perpetual motion machines that students produced either as a group or individually. The posters represented futuristic, science fiction devices—typically involving transportation—that the students drew and labeled. We put them up in our room, then circulated among them to admire what had been produced and to inquire about whatever came to mind. The posters stimulated positive feelings about what had been learned; several of the more artistic children seemed quite pleased that others recognized their talents and realized that luck had nothing to do with what they produced.

Now that the class was accustomed to choosing the order of reading-writing activities during science period, I extended this procedure to the other subject areas. I had different due dates for the various projects in the different areas so that I didn't get totally snowed evaluating papers that came in all at once. I will need to see about cutting down on the paper load, though. I am sure that planning creative lessons for which the students give each other feedback is time better spent than my evaluating uncreative lessons. Somehow I need to get the youngsters in on the act.

During read-aloud time this month, I finished *Year of the Panda* and began *The Haunted Igloo* by Bonnie Turner. The main character of Turner's novel is a 10-year-old Inuit boy named Jean Paul. I first checked with Tanana to see whether or not she would be comfortable with me reading a book to the entire class based on her culture, and she indicated that she was quite willing—and even curious about the book. As we went through *The Haunted Igloo*, Tanana became bolder about making comments and even disagreeing with the book at times. Other children began asking her questions about things in the story that they wanted to know more about. Sometimes she could answer the questions and sometimes she couldn't, but she seemed to enjoy being the center of attention, and she had a chance to celebrate her cultural heritage.

The real excitement this month was caused by the new computers. The first Monday morning of October, the students straggled into the room to find seven carts with computers on them against the back wall. Each computer was mysteriously hidden beneath an opaque dust cover. As soon as everyone had arrived, and the lunch count and roll were completed, I pulled one of the carts into the middle of the room and allowed the children to gather around me. I removed the dust cover and the room was filled with exclamations of "wow," "bad," "cool," and "awesome!"

Briefly, I first explained to them how our class computers are like those in the computer lab; they all have a hard drive and a floppy drive. I then showed them how our computers are different from the lab's by turning this one on and demonstrating. They soon saw that each of our new computers has a color monitor, a CD-ROM drive, and an upside-down mouse that is called a track ball. Each of our computers can have several windows open at the same time, and all major commands can be accessed by clicking on pull-down menus. I showed them that the cart has lockable wheels so that it can be moved easily but has the stability of a stationary table when we are working with the computer. By this time they were all pleading to take a turn.

Quickly, I announced the seven mixed groups of three or four students that I had previously selected and written on a piece of paper. One at a time, I had each group move a computer and enough chairs to a particular place in the room, lock the cart wheels, plug in the computer, and wait to begin. I explained that the members of each group would go in alphabetical order of last name. I then led them to turn on the computers and open the hypermedia tutorials that had come installed on the hard disks. One at a time, amid much kibitzing, they proceeded individually through the tutorial, learning how to open applications, maneuver the track ball, and pull down menus. After 35 or 40 minutes, everyone had had a turn. I then directed them to return the computers to their places against the back wall as they pleaded with me to let them continue to explore them.

Except for having to switch two children to improve the discipline of one of the groups, I kept the students in the same seven computer groups for the rest of the month. Every day, the groups worked cooperatively to learn how to use these more sophisticated computers. While the students have had some access to computers in their classrooms and in the lab since kindergarten, those computers were simpler and more basic than these are. Also, the students have generally had more supervision than they will have this year. I intended for them to learn to be more mature, sophisticated, and responsible with these new computers. There were several stages of this learning, each one with several phases. The first stage consisted of the following phases:

> Learning to set up the computers in working condition around the room and then return them to their permanent condition against the back wall
>
> Learning the basic operation of these more complicated computers (using the track ball, opening more than one application at a time, clicking on a pull-down menu, shutting down all applications, etc.)
>
> Learning to follow the checklist of rules for good computer care posted on the back wall

Each day at computer time, a different group member was responsible for doing each phase, and I observed them carefully. The groups were told that they would not be able to move to the next level of computer use until every member had mastered every phase of this level. I was thrilled at how helpful they were to each other. Having only seven computers has certainly fostered cooperation and teamwork among students. The three groups of three that had either Paul, Daisy, or Jeff as a member each allowed that student a larger proportion of time at the computer without me even hinting that it might be necessary! By the end of the first week, everyone had learned to operate the computers individually at a stage-one level.

The second stage of learning how to use the new computers consisted of these phases:

> Learning to open the word processor and begin a new document
> Learning to name and save the document you are working on in *your* folder on the hard disk
> Learning to back up the document you are working on before closing it by saving it to *your* floppy disk

Each of the seven computers was numbered on the side with an adhesive metallic numeral, so each group could work with the same computer every day. I placed a folder for each student in the group on the hard disk of that group's computer. The folder was labeled with the given name of the child (e.g., Mandy, Horace, Joyce). I also labeled a floppy disk with each student's name and gave it to him or her to keep in the student's cubby except when needed.

By the middle of the month, every student had written, saved, and backed up at least two documents, however short, that they had written during computer time. The difficulty for most students was in avoiding the impulse to save without making sure they were saving to their folder or their floppy, rather than to the top level of the hard disk. Again, the cooperation and support being given within the groups was the crucial factor in the success students were having.

At this point, I felt that it was time to begin integrating the computers into writing/language arts time. The students had apparently become as comfortable writing and sharing for me as they had last year for Ms. Maverick. There was no one who refused to write. Everyone had shared something they had written, at least in pairs. I announced to the class that it was time for each one to choose a piece of writing from their folders that they wanted to publish. They should share it with at least two other students and get suggestions for changes to their content (no comments on form were allowed during this initial sharing). When they were ready for my evaluation, they placed it in the box on my desk designated for that purpose. The next day, I met with each student for a few minutes and discussed what I would require before the paper could be published. First, we agreed on what the content must be, then on what form conventions I would require. After our discussion, I typed the requirements we agreed on in the form of a rubric and printed out a copy for the student.

From that time on, we would set up all seven computers in the morning and leave them set up all day. That way, when a student has individual time, he or she can go to a computer and work on the paper. We also usually connect each computer to one of the two printers, so students can print when they think they have a final draft to show me.

November

This class and I are moving steadily toward a balance among whole-class, small-group, and individual projects. About one-third of the time I want to be in front of the whole class presenting lessons, leading discussions, and providing directions or guidance. I like to spend another third of my time circulating about the class, dealing with individual problems and questions that occur as students work through their various assignments. Finally, I want to spend the other one-third of my time instructing students in small groups and individually.

My small-group and individual instruction calls for me to meet with selected students and have what I call instructional conversations. For instance, during self-selected reading time I follow a schedule for meeting with book-club group members. The students in each group receive my attention along with suggestions and general comments, and I gather good information about the groups' dynamics as well as individuals' reading strategies, interests, and attitudes. During mathematics, I sit with some students and help them compose word problems that fit the mathematical operation we are studying at that time. In social studies, I frequently review vocabulary with students, and I have done several small-group lessons on reading maps.

The keys to maintaining this balanced instruction are to present clear expectations, provide necessary instructional support, and ease the class into working responsibly on their own. In all six subject areas, my students are choosing the order in which to complete their assigned tasks. In fact, the children had been completing their activities in whichever order they chose and turning them in by the deadline quite well, so this month I began allowing the children to choose among the assignments.

It was Larry who pointed out to me that the time had come to begin allowing more decision making. "I would like to try this experiment on page 115 of our science text, Mr. Dunn," he said, "but you have us doing this other one. Would you mind if I did the one on my own?"

Did I ever love that question! The next day, I told the class that they could choose any three of the four activities listed on the board. They were to complete the activities in whatever order they liked. They could do all four if they wanted, but the assignment was to complete three. I purposely included activities that varied in difficulty. This way, students like Paul and Daisy could participate fully with the class on simpler tasks, and students like Larry and Hilda could be challenged by more difficult ones.

In social studies this month we studied the Middle Ages, and the class focused on the guiding question, "What might be a better name for the era commonly called the 'Middle' Ages?" Everything we learned could be applied to forming and justifying an answer to this question; it engaged students in high-level thinking. As usual, I offered choices in reading materials and tasks. The tasks were always related to the topic and guiding question we were pursuing, but they varied according to how difficult they were and the type of ability they required. I regularly offered choices of what to read in order to accommodate reading abilities, along with choices of how to respond in order to accommodate multiple intelligences. For one assignment, the class could choose to read one of three short stories that were about King Arthur and the Knights of the Round Table. The stories ranged in difficulty from about a third-grade level to seventh-grade level. After reading their story, each child could respond to it either by writing a summary or by describing how Camelot differed from our town. I made it very clear that this was one task for them, but that they could decide among the variety of task options. I should mention, too, that I had taught summarizing in our writing/language arts period along with the computer activities, so everybody knew what to do if they chose that activity. We culminated this unit with debates among panels of students about a better name for the Middle Ages.

Report cards for the first nine weeks went out the middle of this month. Mr. Topps has long contended that a teacher's grading system is one of his or her most important professional creations. My first couple of years here, I constantly complained to everyone about the difficulties of grading, about parents' attitudes toward the school, and about students' lack of motivation. Mr. Topps would usually ignore me, but sometimes he patiently explained that my main tool in overcoming these three universal problems of teaching was the system I chose to use in assigning grades to my students and their work. At first, I defended myself by arguing that I really didn't have much leeway in how I graded. After all, there were state laws and state board policies, district policies and guidelines, and even a few schoolwide policies and restrictions. Grades were objective indicators of student learning, and I just delivered the news to children and their parents, whether good or bad! Finally, as I became a better teacher with more experience, I began to see how certain grading practices seem related to either causing or solving problems in my classroom.

With the help of Mr. Topps and teachers like Mrs. Wise, I came to understand how a grading system can either complement or undermine a teacher's instructional program. For example, a friend teaches fifth grade in a school where she has to give students a number grade in every subject every nine weeks. School board policy in that district requires that a certain minimum number of grades be averaged each grading period for each subject. I don't see how I could teach if I were forced to grade my students that way. Certainly, Paul, Daisy, and Jeff would be assured of low grades regardless of their efforts, and Betty, Larry, and Roberta would be assured of high grades without really having to try.

When I first became disenchanted with the traditional grade-everything, average-the-grades, and let-the-chips-fall-where-they-may system, I tried to move to the other extreme. Through a long, laborious process, I developed a checklist of knowledge and strategies for every subject I teach, for each grading period. When Mr. Topps saw my checklists, his face betrayed both admiration and discouragement. "Ed," he said, "this is very thorough, but let me ask you a question. Why do we send report cards home to the parents of the children we teach?"

"Obviously, so they will know how well their children are doing in school," I replied.

"Yes, you're right. Do you think most parents will know how well their children are doing if you send them these checklists filled in?"

Part of me had the impulse to declare impatiently that they would know much more than they had in the past, but his serious expression caused me to reconsider.

After a pause, he continued. "Ed, the problem with checklists and any other indicator of what students actually know is that parents have to understand the curriculum in order to determine their child's progress. Even if they were to understand the curriculum, they don't know how well their child is doing compared with the other children in the class."

"I don't understand." There was frustration in my voice. "Don't you think I should try to improve my grading system?"

"Yes, I do. You have worked very hard, but I'm afraid that what you have produced is too different from what parents want, expect, and can understand. It creates new problems while it solves only a few of the old ones. Many changes in education are like this. We fail to recognize the strengths in what we are doing. Rather than try to keep the strengths while overcoming the weaknesses, we throw everything out and start again from scratch. That's one reason the educational pendulum continues to swing."

"What do you suggest?" I asked pointblank.

"See if you can figure out a way to modify your current grading system so that you continue to give students letter grades, but reward student effort more than you do now, and emphasize application of knowledge and strategies rather than minutiae."

The grading system that I have in place this year is not perfect, but it has developed over the years since that conversation with Mr. Topps to become quite workable. It is a system that I can manage with a reasonable commitment of time, parents seem to understand how well their children are doing, and I am able to motivate students across a broad range of initial achievement levels. The system is really quite simple. It consists of daily grades, tests, small-group projects, and individual performance assessments. Daily grades and small-group projects are where everyone who makes a reasonable effort does well. (I monitor the group projects especially carefully and have the students write brief reports characterizing their peers' input to make sure that everyone in the group is contributing.) Tests and individual performance assessment are also designed so that students who have paid attention and made an effort can obtain satisfactory grades. Every test and performance assessment, however, has an aspect that challenges the most capable, creative, and hardworking student in the class. I use the following chart to determine the letter grade a student receives in each subject. During a particular grading period in a particular subject, one of the columns may be missing (e.g., individual projects). If so, I just use the other columns to determine my grades.

Grade	Daily Grades	Group Projects	Tests	Individual Projects
A	S+	S+	A	A
B	S or S+	S or S+	A-B	A-B
C	S−, S, or S+	S−, S, or S+	A-F	A-F
D	S−	S−	D-F	D-F
F	S−	S−	F	F

Because tests are an important component of my grading system, I use test formation when I want to be absolutely sure that the children's products come only from each child. Tanana told me about test formation, saying that it was the way they took tests at her old school. I first tried it when I administered the group inventory in social studies last month, and I intend to use it more and more often. In test formation, the children spread throughout the room, and each child sits at an isolated position. I moved a few children at first just to make sure that they could not easily see another's paper. I explained to them that I occasionally needed an uncontaminated measure of their performance so that I would know exactly how they were doing. We discussed the differences between an inventory (when I want to find out what they know for the purpose of planning lessons) and a test (when I want to find out what they know for the purpose of assigning a grade). I then explained that I would not trust even my own mother in the seating arrangement we normally used because even she would not be able to resist sneaking a quick peek at another's paper. Thus, I said flatly, "When I need to take inventory or administer a test, the class needs to get into test formation." They seem to have accepted this procedure.

This month closed with a visit from Daphne's grandmother. Mrs. Fields was concerned that Daphne was developing some very bad habits. "Mr. Dunn, maybe you can help us decide what to do. This fall my husband and I have noticed that Daphne is hard to wake up in the morning. Every year before, she's always jumped right out of bed. The other night I went to her room after midnight and there she was under the cover with a flashlight reading a Baby Sitters Club book! I asked the public librarian, and she said that Daphne has checked out over nine of them in the past two months. We want her to read better books than that. What do you think we ought to do?"

I tried to reassure her. "Daphne has been reading Baby Sitters Club books in self-selected reading every day since school started. We've had some very productive conversations about her reading abilities and the sense she is making of what she reads. Frankly, I think you should encourage her to read even more."

Mrs. Fields frowned slightly. "You mean you allow them to read those series? Aren't all the books alike? What about their low level of content?"

"Series books have some positive attributes," I explained. "They interest many children in reading. Once the reading habit is formed, books of greater literary quality can be introduced. These books also provide lots of predictable story structures, which is the way many children practice the skills they have learned in reading instructional time at school. Don't worry, every good reader I've known read comic books and one or more juvenile series at Daphne's age. If these books didn't cause them to be good readers, they at least didn't prevent them from becoming good readers.

"I would suggest that you give Daphne time to read before she goes to bed so that she won't miss her sleep. I agree with you that she needs proper rest, but please don't be alarmed about these books." I haven't heard any more about it, but Daphne has continued to read about the Baby Sitters Club during self-selected reading.

Many of the other students have locked onto a favorite author or two and are reading them exclusively. Betty, Tanana, Daphne, and Joyce have discovered Beverly Cleary; Horace, Mitch, and Alex are going through Gary Paulsen's books; Mandy and Pat are trading stories by Richard Peck.

This month the students have continued to improve in their individual writing on the computers. To provide some variety and a sense of audience, we produced two class newsletters, published two weeks apart. Each of the students chose to write an editorial, a feature article about another student in the class, or a sports article. We had peer response groups on the first drafts, peer editing groups on the second drafts, and my response to the third drafts. The fourth drafts were all published in one or the other of the two newsletters. I used my desktop publishing program on my home computer to compile the newsletter, promising to get students involved with this later in the year. Every student was given a copy of each newsletter to take home. The excitement and sense of accomplishment was tremendous.

December

My attempts in the six subject areas to achieve a balance among whole-class, group, and individual instruction continued moving steadily this month. I still move gradually because I've seen some quite chaotic classes where the teacher one day simply opened everything up to learning centers or cooperative learning without preparing the class. If anything, I may move the class to independence too slowly.

I've been able to spend extra time emphasizing meaning vocabulary in the subject areas now that the class is working so smoothly. This month I used capsule vocabulary to develop understandings of geometry terms during math period. This practice capitalizes on language, which is the foundation of reading and writing. For the first part of the lesson, we sat as a group and discussed the topic of geometry. I had selected the following 10 words that the group needed to know:

point	plane
polygon	perpendicular
line segment	ray
angle	triangle
parallel	line

As we discussed geometry, I made a conscious effort to introduce the 10 terms in meaningful context, even though I had to occasionally force the conversation in order to allow the word to fit. "The wall in front of me can be considered a *plane*," I said at one point. "The wall behind me is a *parallel plane*, then, and the walls on either side are *perpendicular planes*." The students copied these words into their math notebooks, and we continued using them in discussion until everyone felt that they understood their meanings.

In the second part of the lesson, the students paired off for one-to-one talk sessions. The requirement was that each student use each one of the new words in a meaningful context at least once while talking to the other. For instance, I overheard this part of the conversation between Manuel and Steve:

Manuel: Yesterday, when we played softball during recess, the ball came off my bat at a funny *angle*. It didn't go *parallel* to the ground; it went straight up.

Steve: Yeah, it almost went *perpendicular* to the ground. As for me, I hit a ball that broke the *plane* between second base and third base. I actually got a hit into left field!

Manuel: Uh huh. Well, I played second base, and I was looking at the base paths. Did you realize that some form a *ray?* Well they do! The one going from second to first and the one going from second to third form *rays*. What do you think about that?

This activity seems to foster Manuel's vocabulary acquisition especially well. He is able to interact with the words and with his classmates in a semi-structured and meaningful format. He does rather well with the language differences he brings to class, so although capsule vocabulary helps him, it is not as crucial as it might be for other children acquiring English.

I always set a timer when we do one-to-one conversations; they tend to get a little loony if I allow them to just go on and on. When the children know that they have only a little time, they usually work in a much more concentrated manner. Indeed, Larry and Danielle really got going, and I'm sure that they used each term at least four times in entirely different contexts.

After applying the new terms in conversation, each student then wrote a short paper using all the new words in a meaningful context. Sometimes I collect the papers and check them for proper inclusion of the specific words, and sometimes I have the original pairs of students look over each other's papers for proper use of the words. With this lesson, I include reading, writing, speaking, and listening development along with the math content that I am responsible to teach.

In order to review the 10 geometry terms a few days after our capsule vocabulary lesson, I had the students web them. The students formed their pair groupings again and graphically organized the 10 words. This was meant to provide needed variety to the word learning task. Anthony and Steve, my whizzes in math and science who are so-so in the other areas, produced a very logical web. Both boys were able to explain why they grouped the words that way.

Good news! I think a breakthrough is being made with Mike! That boy certainly has his good and bad days, but lately his good days are beginning to outnumber his bad ones. Just last week he made it through an entire day without picking on Rita even once! I'm sure that there are a number of reasons for this change in his behavior, but I believe his tutoring the second-grader is part of it.

I had looked into his permanent file for some additional information and saw that he was not here at Merritt for third and fourth grade. As a result, we

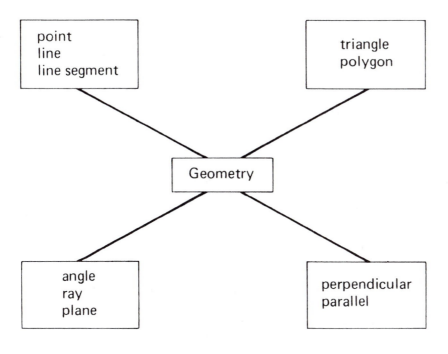

Geometry Web

don't know what type of instruction he was getting at his other school. The file confirmed that he could be a bit of a behavioral problem. With this information about Mike, I decided to see about having him tutor a younger child. I figured this way Mike could work with quite simple reading materials and still save face. I also thought that the responsibility of caring for a younger child might help him mature a bit. However, when I contacted Norma Flame about my proposal, she was dubious, to say the least.

"Ed," she exclaimed, "you don't realize the nights I spent in tears because of the mean things Mike did in my classroom!"

She eventually agreed that we could set up Mike with a second-grader who had some reading abilities but who could benefit from some extra individual attention with word identification. (I do believe that Norma has come a long way since her first year of teaching as Miss Nouveau!) We established a three-day-a-week schedule for Mike and Jimmy, the boy to be tutored. Norma provides lessons for the boys for two days; the third day is devoted to Mike reading books aloud that Jimmy wants to hear. All I can say is that feelings definitely energize literacy learning, and having special responsibility for another person and being able to work comfortably with easy materials without losing self-esteem seems to have given Mike a boost that he sorely needed. He seems to be realizing that he can take responsibility for and control his own actions—that he is not a helpless victim of external forces.

My other youngsters with major difficulties in reading are involved in their special programs during our 8:45 to 9:30 reading/literature period too, but changes with them are not so obvious as with Mike. Jeff is reading and comparing animals at present. Since his word identification is rather well developed, we decided that he would read about a certain topic and that we would get together once a week in order to compare the information he is learning. Miss Page, the librarian, was able to help Jeff find a good number of books and magazines about animals, since that was the topic he chose. He reads and we discuss animal books such as *What's the Difference? A Guide to Some Familiar Animal Look-Alikes*, *Hiding Out: Camouflage in the Wild*, *Wolves*, and *Arctic Summer* along with informative magazines like *Ranger Rick* and *National Geographic World* that contain features on animals.

Daisy and Paul were started in a rather structured program largely because they seem to need clear goals and tangible evidence of progress. Daisy, especially, won't budge unless she knows exactly what she is to do. She then will do the activity at a minimal level of acceptability. On the other hand, Paul is willing to extend himself, but he seems to get lost once he does so. He will read a passage all the way through, but then he has great difficulty manipulating the ideas in a thoughtful or creative way.

The program I've devised for them is based largely on materials from a commercial book series for reluctant readers and on collections of short stories and informational passages. The book series consists of hardcover books made up of about eight chapters each, with word identification and comprehension activities that correspond to each chapter. I have a chart for Daisy and Paul to keep in their personal folders. They fill in a section of the chart each time that they complete a chapter of the book and its corresponding activities. After finishing an entire book, they choose and complete at least one written composition and one artistic response. Although I worried that this program might seem rather mechanical and dry, these two students seem to benefit from it. Again, the structure is important, and there is enough variation to promote high levels of thinking.

In addition, Paul and Daisy regularly choose at least one short story or informational passage from a collection to read on their own and discuss with me. I meet with these two at least once a week for about 20 minutes in order to discuss what they have chosen and to provide specific word identification and comprehension instruction with those materials. The two typically take something away from our sessions to complete as follow-up and practice to my instruction.

Because it is December, the new book I chose for teacher read-aloud this month was *Latkes and Applesauce* by Fran Manushkin. The book centers around a Jewish family's difficulties celebrating Hanukkah because of a blizzard. It's a simple story, but it's one that fifth-graders enjoy while learning about a distinct culture.

In science we have been studying the solar system, and for this unit I presented a writing prompt to guide thinking rather than a question. I displayed the following prompt on poster board decorated with a space motif:

Pretend you are the captain of a space ship. Your ship has recently made a voyage through the solar system. Now that you are back on earth, an admiral has asked you to write a speech for cadets at the space academy. In your speech, explain to your audience of future space ship captains how to travel safely and quickly through the solar system.

After reading the prompt aloud, I explained to the students that, before beginning to write their speeches, they would have an opportunity to learn more about how to equip, supply, and pilot a space shuttle. The class again became quite engaged in the big idea generated by the prompt; they boldly ventured into the unknown.

After kicking off the unit with the prompt and a brief video of space travel, I began its components by reviewing the names of the planets and their distances from the sun. I also made sure the class understood the technical differences between planets, moons, asteroids, meteors, and comets. Finally, I talked through the various references available in the class—encyclopedias, brochures, newspaper clippings, the Internet—for students' use.

The way students acquired most information for this unit was through a computer simulation called There and Back. This program simulates travel throughout the solar system. The graphics are quite detailed and accurate in their representation of each of the planets, each of the moons, the asteroid belt, the sun, and several meteor showers and comets. The challenging aspect of the simulation is trying to explore as much of the solar system as possible within the shortest period of time. A number of decisions have to be made, and incorrect decisions can result in a very long voyage. Moreover, a number of dangers have to be anticipated or dealt with, and it is possible that the ship will be destroyed or marooned in space. Because the positions of the planets relative to each other are constantly changing, the simulation is somewhat different each time it is played.

Before long, students were in their computer groups completely engaged with the simulation. They were very excited about learning a new computer program, being quite sophisticated at working together, helping each other, and discovering the ins and outs of a new piece of software without needing to rely too much on the manual. This was a good way to balance my literacy and subject matter instruction while providing a variety of ways to learn. When I informed students that they needed to begin their shutting down routines, there were groans and pleadings from all over the room.

The next five days were devoted to the groups either conducting simulated voyages through the solar system or reading the available materials. We regularly held whole-class discussions about this unit at the end of the sessions, and these typically amounted to a sharing of tips and insights about There and Back. Mike was amazingly insightful and successful with this program. Before long, students were asking him specific questions, and he was giving specific answers. This discussion really seemed to help the groups that were unable to complete their voyage safely.

I began science class the seventh day of the unit by explaining that this was when they were to plan what they intended to say about traveling safely and quickly through the solar system. Tomorrow, during science, they were to write their speeches. As I walked around the room, I was asked a number of substantive questions about the solar system and about the nature of space travel. I was extremely pleased at the level of involvement with science concepts that the simulation program and the writing prompt together elicited from almost all the students.

The next day, everyone remained at their seats to write their speeches. Part of fading to independence is eventually requiring students to work alone on a project. They had been engaged in writing all fall, including producing two class newsletters, and they had several days of science instruction time to prepare for this particular individual effort. Now was the time to produce a composition of their own. Their diligence and concentration during the writing demonstrated that all the time and activity spent in preparing them to do it were well worth it.

The culmination of this unit consisted of students sharing their speeches by reading them aloud in small groups. I used a different arrangement of students so that the four students in each sharing group came from four different computer groups. I did not want the students evaluating how well a piece of writing conformed to the actual simulated voyage through the solar system. This sharing time naturally led into a whole-class discussion on the solar system and the possibility of one day being able to explore it with manned spacecraft. More than any of the other students, Hilda yearns to be an astronaut. She really enjoyed this five-day adventure. I expect to hear one day that she has fulfilled her dream.

January

January often seemed like September; at times after returning from the winter holiday, it felt as though we were starting anew. The first few days after the holidays were a bit hectic as we reestablished the routine that was so carefully nurtured the first four months of school. After a while, though, everyone got back into the swing of things.

This month I continued my quest for independence by emphasizing learning strategies. I reminded the class that thinking is the essence of reading and writing, and I told them we would focus on predicting what could be learned from a passage. My plan for doing this began in the second week of January. One day during reading/literature period, I kept the class together and showed them a picture of an aircraft carrier that I had cut out of a magazine. "If I had a book about aircraft carriers, what could I learn?" I asked.

Finally, Larry spoke up. "I think we could learn how something that big and heavy can float on top of the water."

Pat thought she would learn the name of the carrier and how many sailors it held.

Mitch was tentative, but he finally blurted out, "We could learn how the ship can get close enough to shore so the guns and airplanes can blow up a town!"

When the time was up for suggesting what we might learn about aircraft carriers, I explained how each student could become a better reader by following this same procedure with material that he or she was reading.

After putting the picture away, I presented a short, expository passage that was about the U.S. Navy's battleships. We surveyed the passage as we normally did before reading any informative materials, and then I asked the class, "What do you think you can learn from this passage?" I listed their responses on the chalkboard. Because this activity was so similar to what we had just done with the picture, the responses came much more easily.

"I think we can learn how many ships the navy has," ventured Alex.

Larry was sure that we would learn something about the U.S. Navy's submarines because he noted the picture of one along the side of one page and he saw the subheading titled "Submarine Warfare." When I probed for a specific aspect to learn, he decided that we probably could learn the advantages and disadvantages of submarines versus surface craft.

Roberta suggested that we could learn when women first were allowed to join the navy, even though she could not point out any evidence in the passage that indicated coverage of that topic.

After the children listed what they thought could be learned from the passage, I read it to them. This way, everybody was able to receive the information, and they finished receiving it at the identical time. We then followed up the list on the board by noting which items actually were covered in the passage.

The next few days during reading/literature period, I conducted this same activity using another passage with groups of randomly assigned students. They seemed to become rather good at determining what they thought they could learn from the passages.

As a follow-up, I had the class get into test formation, and I projected an overhead transparency that was made from a page in the social studies textbook. My question to the class was, "What do you think you can learn from this passage?" I collected the papers and took them home in order to see who needed further work with predicting meaning from a passage.

Although I've been emphasizing prediction throughout the subject areas, I continue to place a large emphasis upon meaning vocabulary. We perform capsule vocabulary lessons frequently, and I always have students identify unfamiliar words they encounter and attempt to determine their meaning by noting the information that is contained in the passage about those terms. We spend time relating past experiences and previously encountered concepts to the new concepts encountered in passages. Word origins are discussed (Betty informed us just recently that *boycott* comes from a British army officer, C. C. Boycott, who was the first victim of this tactic), and the special meanings of technical terms are pointed out. For example, while studying "Coal Mining and Steel Manufacturing" in social studies, we encountered that troublesome term *coke*. I brought in a piece of charcoal as a rough example of this substance. I explained that coke is distilled from coal and that it can produce the terrific heat necessary to separate iron ore from waste rock. After this rather thorough explanation and demonstration, Jeff volunteered the opinion that he would never drink another Coke now that he knew where it came from. I'm still not sure if he was kidding or not!

One vocabulary activity that we regularly pursue during subject-matter instruction is to note words that contain frequently occurring morphemes. Rather than use the terms *morpheme, prefix, root, suffix, contraction,* and *compound,* we use the phrase *meaningful word part*. Whenever subject-area vocabulary emerges for special attention, I make sure the class examines the meaningful parts. Sometimes I simply underline the meaningful parts if the words are written on the chalkboard, and sometimes I ask a group of students to identify the parts in words.

I always point out how the meaningful part contributes to the formation of the word. For example, one of the geometry terms that we studied last December contained a meaningful word part that occurred in other parts frequently enough to warrant attention, so I pointed it out to the class. I underlined the *tri* in *triangle* and explained how it contributed to the meaning of the word. Next, I listed *tricycle* and *triplane* underneath *triangle* in order to reinforce the way *tri* functioned. We constructed sentences with the words to keep this exercise meaningful. Then, as one of the choice activities for this unit, the students were to list at least five words that contained *tri* as a meaningful part and make up sentences that included their words.

Alexander and Steve got together and produced the following list:

"TRI" WORDS

trilogy	triplet
trio	triennial
triple	trilingual

Later I put these words on the board, and we noted how the pronunciation of the part could change drastically but that the meaning stayed the same. Hilda was quick to point out that the *tri* in *trilogy, triple,* and *triplet* was pronounced one way, that it was pronounced another way in *trio,* and still another way in *tricycle, triennial,* and *trilingual.*

Daisy got a little angry with me because she had recorded *trial, tribe,* and *trigger* among her *tri* words. When I explained to her that *tri* did not refer to "three" in those words, she became sullen. What a shame! I have shown this class that *father* is not made up of *fat* and *her* and that looking for meaningful word parts doesn't always work. I've tried to demonstrate how this word-analysis technique is useful when it is used while attending to the context of a passage. Looking for meaningful word parts doesn't always help students figure out words, but pronouncing words, recognizing them at sight, and attending to the way they are used in a passage don't always work in isolation either. However, word analysis techniques are worthwhile when readers learn to let them interact with each other. Besides, meaningful word parts frequently occur in technical, content-area vocabulary, and noting them helps students get a handle on the new terms.

I was totally surprised when Larry, Horace, and Danielle took *poly* from our geometry term *polygon* and created a list of *poly* words. They came up with *polygamy, polyester, polyglot,* and *polyhedron.* They were quite proud of themselves and assured me that they understood the meanings of all their terms. They also pointed out that the *poly* in *polygamy* was pronounced differently than in the others, even though it meant the same in all four. I was impressed! I had decided not to introduce *poly* to my fifth-graders because even though it occurs frequently as a meaningful part in many words, those words are rarely encountered by students in the fifth grade. If I were teaching ninth-grade math or science, then I probably would have presented it. At present, highlighting more common, meaningful parts such as *tri* allows students to attend to that particular element, and it helps children become accustomed to noting meaningful word parts. And students with advanced vocabularies certainly can explore words on their own.

Erik Haugaard has always been one of my favorite children's authors. Last summer, I read *The Boy and the Samurai* for the first time. What an exciting story! That is the book I began reading aloud the first day back after the holidays. It is a historical novel set in ancient Japan. Again, this was a culture few of my students knew anything about. Before long, however, they were really caught up in the story, and they became attuned to the similarities and differences among their cultures and the one described in the story.

Since our state's standards for education became effective January of this year, I consulted them especially carefully to determine expectations for writing. I concluded that I had better get moving on the six traits the state presented for considering children's writing. I had addressed the traits in one form or another during the past months, but now I decided to be a bit more systematic and explicit about them. The traits are:

Ideas and content
Organization
Word choice
Sentence fluency
Conventions
Voice

After school one day, I placed a chart above the chalkboard where every student in the room would be able to see it. I entitled the chart "Dimensions of Writing," thinking that my fifth-graders would grasp the term *dimension* better than *trait*. In math we learned that length, width, and height were some dimensions corresponding to geometric shapes, so I figured the class could apply the concept of dimensions to what corresponded to writing.

When the students came in the next morning, they immediately noticed the chart. During writing/language arts period I explained that I was very pleased with how well they were writing and liking to write, and that now it was time for them to concentrate on specific dimensions of their writing. I explained that the six dimensions listed on the chart provided a common vocabulary for talking about what they wrote. Attending to these dimensions would promote control over their writing. I explained that writers wrote well when they felt the need to convey thoughts—rather than demonstrate knowledge of dimensions—so we still would emphasize authentic communications. But now was the time for us to focus a bit more attention to some specific dimensions of what they produced.

Over the next few weeks, I spent a small amount of time each day presenting the dimensions. For instance, I explained that "organization" meant showcasing what was important; I showed how well-organized compositions led readers to the main points. Stories had clear beginnings, middles, and ends, and informational passages had clear main ideas.

Because our language arts textbook presented paragraphing rather well, I focused attention on it as an aspect of organization. I presented paragraphs as the building blocks of ideas, telling the class that if they have two things to say, say one thing first, then the other. When we were reading from the same book in a subject, I often pointed out the paragraphing used by the author, and we spent a few minutes discussing it. I showed them how a web they had used to plan a piece of writing could help them decide when to begin a new paragraph (i.e., they started a new paragraph when they began writing another part of the web). I also showed how a new paragraph begins each time the speaker in a written conversation changes.

Once the class seemed to have a good grasp of paragraphing as a concept, I began having them proofread their own papers or each other's for this aspect of organization. This self-evaluation of writing according to the dimension listed on the room chart seemed especially effective. The discussions students had about particular instances helped everyone understand paragraphing better and realize that it is not an exact science.

February

Paula Danziger has been discovered. After reading the first chapter of *Amber Brown Sees Red*, Pat, Rita, and Joyce came up and wanted to know if the author, Paula Danziger, had written any other books. When I told them that Danziger had been writing books since before they were born, they wanted to go immediately to the library and check out all her books. They eventually found some of Danziger's early work like *The Cat Ate My Gymsuit*, *There's a Bat in Bunk Five*, and *It's an Aardvark Eat Turtle World*, as well as some of her relatively newer ones such as *Earth to Matthew* and *Make Like a Tree and Leave*. So now there is a minor craze for Paula Danziger books.

I still am amazed at how people select one author and read everything that person has written. This seems true for series as well as nonseries books that are written by the same person. For example, during self-selected reading I've noticed that Daphne still is reading her *Baby Sitter Club* stories. Horace, Mitch, and Alex switched to the best selling *Animorphs* series. Mandy and Pat have discovered J.R.R. Tolkien. There clearly is more to developing readers than imparting skills; developing readers must have the desire to experience authors' worlds.

Another interesting point about these fifth-graders' feelings about reading is their fascination with informative books. Butch has been perusing books on Egypt, and he takes the time to really study some of the entries. Anthony has his own collection of science-oriented books at home that he brings in, and Paul has taken to the *Magic School Bus* series. Students at this age like to read to learn as well as to be entertained.

My plan for developing independent learners is continuing still. The guided reading and listening activities that I do with the whole class and with small groups is devoted more and more to helping them with the essential thinking strategy of determining what deserves attention. I want them to decide beforehand, and afterward, what they should attend to in a passage. The activities I conducted last month on predicting meaning with the U.S. Navy passages is one way to get children to do this.

I go through the same steps for each of my guided comprehension lessons. First, I present general background that is needed to understand what will be read. In this step, I teach the vocabulary students might need to make sense of the passage, or I tell them to discover the meaning of particular key words they will encounter. In the second step, I set a purpose for students' reading. I select my purpose to be congruent with the kind of reading they are doing. I wouldn't want them to read for sequence if there were little in the passage to be organized in that way. I frequently have students produce some kind of graphic organizer as a way to help them organize the information they are reading. I always follow up the set purpose to monitor their ability to meet the purpose. I plan reading-writing activities to extend comprehension and to help them become independent readers.

One form of guidance I provided involved turning a short story with lots of conversation into a readers' theater by actually doing it step-by-step with one of the first stories we read. We ended the month by producing another readers' theater version of one of the short stories in the book. The students did much better and enjoyed it much more the second time. They seemed to especially enjoy the variety involved in transforming passages into theatrical productions. I plan to do many more before the year ends.

One practice, The Mag Bag, that we performed during writing/language arts period got the class quite involved in independent learning. I brought in duplicate copies of popular magazines. The class divided themselves into groups based on interests such as sports, fashion, and the environment, and each group went through the magazines and found an article they thought interesting. After locating an appropriate article, they had three tasks. First, they created a poster to advertise the article. Headlines, blurbs, and pictures were included in the posters. (I brought in duplicate copies of the magazines partly because they had to be cut up to make these posters.) Second, the students prepared a six-by-eight-inch file card that contained complete bibliographic information about the article. I gave them a model of how to cite the articles. An identical number was written on the poster and on the card, so other students could match them later. Finally, on the back of the cards, each group wrote a question or two that would guide a person's reading of the article. For instance, Horace and Mitch worked together on an article about the human heart. They decided that the most important information in the article was about heart attack, so they asked two questions: "What are the most common causes of heart attacks?" and "What can people do to guard against heart attacks?"

After preparing the posters and file cards, these two items and complete, original issues of the magazines were placed in the classroom library area. The file cards were placed in a box by numbers. This way, just before self-selected reading, individuals not in book clubs could study the posters to locate an article that seemed interesting. Then they noted the number of the poster, got its corresponding file card, and used the bibliographic information on the card to locate the correct magazine. This was a good precursor to locating information in the library, and it got the class to independently figure what was important in the articles.

Another practice that addressed important information also used index cards. I guided the class through a science passage about invertebrates in the ocean, and the students then formed pairs. To begin this activity, each person wrote four questions that he or she thought dealt with the most important information in the passage. For instance, Joyce wrote the following questions:

1. What are sponges?
2. How do jellyfish get food?
3. How do sea anemones get food?
4. Why is a coral really an animal?

After writing the questions, the partners traded cards and attempted to answer each other's questions. Then, after writing down their answers, the partners decided which questions would be best for a whole-class quiz. They rank ordered their questions and turned them in to me. As promised, I gave a short quiz the next day using the class's own questions.

That day Tanana came up to me and complimented me for allowing them to write their own questions. I asked why she liked doing it, and her reply showed a lot of insight. "For the first time I felt like I was in charge of the book," she said. "I had to decide what we needed to know; I couldn't just wait for you to tell us what to study for."

I knew that I had the state-level standards and the district curriculum guide to help determine important content, and I knew I had my own opinions about what was important, but Tanana's mature comment helped remind me that children need to develop strategies for themselves for thinking about what they read.

As February ended, my students were becoming better at evaluating papers according to all six dimensions of writing. However, this clearly will be an ongoing process, carried into middle school and beyond, because the dimensions, or traits, are quite open ended and somewhat vague. These fifth-graders have a good grasp of the conventions such as capitalization, punctuation, spelling, and usage that they need; they're reasonably proficient identifying ideas and content, organization, and sentence fluency; but they still are unclear about voice and word choice. We refer to these dimensions when good examples emerge in class—some newspaper columnists are especially strong with voice and word choice—so they are slowly but surely catching on.

February was the month that the writing we have been doing in math really began bearing some fruit. I often stopped and had students record the difficulties they were having with particular aspects of math or write what they knew. Back in November, I started having students work in small groups to compose word problems that fit whatever mathematical operation we were studying at that time. I worked with different groups on different days to help them improve their problems. I presented writing lessons, modeling for the whole class how to compose a word problem before having them work together in their groups. Later, the groups would share one or two of their problems with the whole class. It was slow at first, but by December they were able to produce weekly word problem "tests" for each other over all the mathematics we had studied since the beginning of the year. After a while, I would vary whether they composed word problems in small groups, pairs, or individually. Once this process was operating well, it served three functions: (1) It reviewed mathematical computation from earlier this year and previous years; (2) It lowered the resistance to and fear of word problems on the part of almost all the students; (3) It helped students improve in solving word problems by understanding how a word problem is put together and how it can help or mislead the student. This month it became apparent to me that the class's attitude toward word problems and ability to solve them definitely improved compared with past years' classes. I credit our writing in mathematics with this improvement.

March

This was the month to emphasize locating information independently. We continued our study of the ocean during science period, and as a group we watched videos and laser disks, read passages from the text and from magazines I had saved, discussed our various experiences at the beach, and performed several activities such as webbing. In addition, I listed five activities for individual or small-group work and allowed the students to choose any three. The final thing they were to do was choose any animal that lived in the ocean, gather all the information they could about that animal, and report what they had learned. As usual, I stated an overarching guiding question—"What should be our national ocean animal?"—to help energize and direct their thinking.

To prepare the class for their individual reports, I listed categories of information about animals so that the class would know what to look for and so their reports would be well organized. The following list of categories was put on the board:

INFORMATION ABOUT OCEAN ANIMALS

Type of animal (fish, mammal, mollusk?)
Appearance (How big is it? What does it look like?)
Location (Where is it found? Describe its habitat.)
Eating habits (What does it eat? How does it eat?)
Relation to humans (How does it help or harm humans?)

After describing these categories of information, I passed out copies of an ocean animal report that was completed last year in my class. This provided a model for this year's class. Everyone seemed to be getting a fairly good idea of what to look for. Since we had worked on selecting important information in passages throughout the past few months, I figured most students would be able to identify what should be included in each category from what they were reading. I asked students to write on each of the five categories of information. Additionally, they were to produce a visual—of their choice—that portrayed what they had learned. I suggested visuals such as posters, collages, illustration, and murals, saying that individuals could produce one of these or something else of a visual nature. Balancing the visuals with the written work seemed like a good way to accommodate students' preferred modes of learning.

The component of this project that needed the most instruction was locating materials that contained appropriate information about particular animals. With this in mind, I told them all to remember which animal they had chosen to study, but that we had some preliminary things to learn. Then I turned to Miss Page, our librarian, for help.

Miss Page said we could have a 45-minute period each afternoon in the library for two weeks to work on our projects. But first, she said, she would show the class how to locate information. On our first day in the library, she taught the class for me and reviewed the concept of subject indexes. First, everyone was given a photocopy of the index of a book on animals. To see if everyone could use an index, she dictated 10 topics for each student to find. She gave topics such as "skeleton," "teeth," and "veins," and the students wrote down the page numbers where information on each topic could be found. Everyone then traded papers, and she read out the correct page numbers. No one missed any, of course, since this task required only the ability to locate a word and the ability to copy its corresponding page number.

Next, she showed them how to locate information on the library's computer. She projected a computer screen onto a movie screen, then took a topic suggested by a student and looked it up for them as they watched. First, she located books the library held, then she showed how to use a search engine for examining the Internet. She gave another list of topics, and the class spent the rest of the period at computer terminals writing down bibliographic information from the articles that were found under Miss Page's topics.

At the beginning of the next day in the library, Miss Page checked the students' references for the topics she had provided. Eventually, everyone had listed the correct materials that the library had listed under the topics. Then she showed how to obtain the various books from the library's collection.

Following this lesson, Miss Page and I figured that this group of students had the prerequisites for locating information in a library. They knew what subject indexes were and the principle on which they work. Moreover, they knew how to use the computers.

For the next few days, either Miss Page or I helped the students locate a book given as a source or refine their searches on the Internet. We were into our ocean animals research full blast now. Most of the students could already find books by the Dewey Decimal System, which reflected their experience with this and other libraries.

A problem did arise, however, with selecting topic words. Chip wanted to investigate conches because his grandfather had brought him a conch shell from the Indian Ocean. He had that shell on top of his dresser in his bedroom, so he knew that there was such a thing. However, he couldn't find *conch* listed anywhere.

"Now what am I supposed to do?" he moaned. "I'm stuck."

I helped Chip locate information about conches by going through the key words *shellfish* and *mollusk,* and then I raised Chip's predicament with Miss Page. She agreed that predicting key words to locate information was a problem and suggested that I prepare a lesson to develop that ability. I mentioned that I thought that she might have a "predicting key words" lesson handy, but she assured me in her good-natured way that she didn't.

"Mr. Dunn," she said, "I'd love to help you, but I'm afraid you'll have to do this one on your own. I am totally inundated trying to keep up with my cataloguing. But be a dear, and do let me know what you come up with. I'm sure it will be very useful to me in the future."

"Boy, is she smooth! I thought. "Not only do I need to come up with an entirely new lesson, but I need to share it with her. I guess flattery *will* get you everywhere."

Like many abilities that are part of reading to learn, the ability to predict key words for locating information is a complex one. The lesson I used to develop this ability had two parts. First, the class tried to think of all the possibilities for key words, given a particular topic. Then they tried to determine which of those possibilities would most likely yield the desired information.

The sample topic we chose was last month's holiday, Valentine's Day. Using a chalkboard, they brainstormed all the possible key words that, regardless of source used, might yield information about Valentine's Day. We listed the following possible key words:

Hearts	Cupid
St. Valentine	romance
Valentine's Day	February
Holidays	February 14
Love	red
Candy	saints
greeting cards	

After compiling the list, we considered each item as a possible key word for use in researching Valentine's Day. After the discussion, everyone wrote down three topic words to consult and handed in these choices. I sorted the ballots and placed votes by the items in our list as they had been chosen by the group.

Four possible key words received the most votes by far: *St. Valentine, Valentine's Day, holidays,* and *February 14.* As a group, we then discussed why these four might be better than the others.

The follow-up activity for this lesson was to go to the library with the key words the class had selected, and to use those key words to see if information could be found about that topic. Alexander, Manuel, and Carl were selected, and they reported the next day that there was a wealth of information about Valentine's Day under *Valentine's Day* and *holidays* on line and in the library. Thank goodness!

This month closed with the students' reports on ocean animals being completed. Within the limits I had set, they had selected their own topics, organized their search, located appropriate sources of information, gathered the important data, reported it in one paper which they had typed on the computer, and produced a visual. I used the six writing traits when evaluating the written reports. Of course, the finished products varied in quality quite a bit, but even my students with the least proficient reading and writing demonstrated some abilities to learn independently.

We closed with a stimulating discussion about a national ocean animal. The class produced good issues about selecting such a thing: Should it be something that we eat lots of (tuna, lobster)? Should it be something that is associated with the world more than just our country (whale)? Should it be something that is approachable (dolphin) or a predator (shark)? The general consensus finally centered on salmon as our national ocean animal. Most class members seemed especially well impressed with this fish's navigational abilities and its instinct to return home, but I did not declare salmon the choice. I keep units' guiding questions open all the time to stimulate thinking and show how individuals need to produce their own closure on some issues.

The book I have been reading to the students during most of this month has been *The Middle of Somewhere* by Sheila Gordon. Like the first book I read to the class back in September, it is a wonderful book set in South Africa under the system of apartheid. The main character is a nine-year-old African girl named Rebecca Gwala. The situation at the beginning of the novel is that the planning department of the White-only government has decided that a village for Black people is to be destroyed, the people transported to a new town, and a new town for White people built on the site of the village. Rebecca and her family live in the village. The new town to which the Gwalas and their neighbors will be transported is so far away that Rebecca's father will lose his job. This book has really raised my students' sensitivity to issues of fairness in government toward people of different races or nationalities.

April

What a great month! I just love April, with all of nature springing back to life! In class everything seems to start coming together during this month.

To add variety to my instruction on predicting key words to locate information, I brought in a collection of telephone directories. I listed the types of phone calls I wanted to make, and the class found the page numbers in the yellow pages where I should look. For instance, the class discovered that to locate a doctor, one looked under the key word *physician;* to locate a kitchen oven, one looked under *appliances;* and to locate a store that sold baseballs, one looked under *sporting goods.* I discovered that my "predicting key words" lesson actually was a good lesson on organizing information. It's amazing how so many language arts abilities are interrelated!

Independent inquiry projects were conducted in social studies this month according to the same general plan that we followed in science. I still was rather directive about the general topic and the report format, but there was enough room for individual decisions that allowed each final product to be unique. The general topic this time was the 50 United States—a common fifth-grade undertaking—and each student chose a different one to investigate. No one was allowed to choose our state.

Again, we set out a common outline so that everybody would work toward the same general goal, and I made this unit's central question somewhat personal by asking, "If your family had to move, would you recommend moving to this state?" I had the class decide what specific aspects of the topic deserved investigation this time. I knew they had examined our home state last year in Ms. Maverick's class, so I thought they would be in a good position to decide. Mort suggested researching amusement parks in the other states, and Daisy wanted to do restaurants.

"Very funny," I replied. "Let me give you a better perspective on why you are investigating your state. Let's say that your family is going to move out of our state, but they haven't decided where to go. They have asked you to help. Your mission, class, should you decide to accept it, is to convince your family either to move to or else avoid the state you have chosen."

Well, this livened things up a bit because this new perspective helped them focus their thinking. After all, "doing" a state is a rather global and abstract task; convincing your family of the relative desirability of moving somewhere is a much more compelling endeavor. Like all the guiding questions we had addressed this year, this one positioned students as problem solvers rather than fact getters.

"We need to find out about the weather," Tanana volunteered. "My family likes the cold."

"What about hunting and fishing?" asked Mitch. "My dad won't go anywhere unless he can get outdoors."

Larry suggested that we had better find out about job situations since that was important, and Jeff wanted us to be sure to figure out how far the state was from where we lived because he gets carsick. Mike, the old pro who actually had moved out of state, suggested that we find out about the various cities so we would know exactly where to move once we had gotten to the state.

We kept this up for five minutes, and then we organized the categories of information on the chalkboard. Again, these categories, allowed each student to pursue an individual topic within a set of common guidelines. Some teachers prefer having individuals establish their own parameters for their inquiries, but I like a bit more structure. We decided that the following areas deserved special attention:

> Location (How far away from our state is it? How long would it take to travel to by car? Where is it in relation to neighboring states?)
>
> Weather (What are the temperature ranges in various locations? Is it warmer or colder than where we are already?)
>
> Business (What are the main industries of the state? How easily could your father and/or mother find a job?)
>
> Major cities (Where are the major cities? Which city seems best for your family to be in or near?)
>
> Vacation spots (Where could you go within the state for a weekend visit?)

With these categories of information in mind, we descended upon Miss Page once again. This time the group had a much better notion of how to locate the information that would satisfy their inquiries.

Talk about activity. Addresses for state and city chambers of commerce were located, letters were drafted on computers, newspapers were consulted for weather reports, and a multitude of reference books and trade books were checked out for information about specific states. Students were even using our social studies textbook as a reference, which probably is its best use.

I met with Mike, Jeff, Paul, and Daisy at individual times in order to provide as much direction as possible. These four, and a few others in the class, easily get lost in such research projects. I made certain that they got off letters to their respective chambers of commerce and helped them locate understandable materials about their states. Luckily, there were such materials!

These state reports ended up being much more elaborate than the ocean animal projects. When the class worked on ocean animals, they were rather intent on completing in a straightforward fashion the outline that I had presented. But this time many students completed the outline through some rather creative means. Mandy and Pat teamed up and put together a travel brochure of their state that was patterned after the ones they received in the mail. Several students produced relief maps of their states, following the procedure they had learned in Ms. Maverick's class. Posters of vacation spots were in evidence everywhere. Many students downloaded some stunning graphics from their states' web sites.

Everyone turned in a typed report dealing with the areas of investigation, but the compositions were directed toward their parents or guardians rather than me. Most students wrote their reports as personal letters to their families, detailing the advantages and disadvantages of moving to their chosen state. I believe the class found this perspective more meaningful, and their writing was even better planned and more complete than usual.

With regard to the six writing traits, I had the class break into two-person teams and edit each others' papers for the traits still posted on the wall. Each editor was to begin with a word of praise for the writer relative to each trait; they were to find at least one good example of ideas and content, organization, and so on. Then they were to identify a few examples of these traits that might be improved and offer suggestions. Such peer revision still requires much good will and trust on the part of the individuals, and I was pleased that such positive feelings seemed to predominate during the revision events. I also was happy to note the control several students exhibited over their papers. They seemed to realize that they governed what was on the page, so they shaped it according to their preferences.

We held an open house for the children's families to come and celebrate the state reports that had been produced. The room was exceptionally colorful and vibrant with all the maps, posters, and brochures portraying the states, and the students' recommendations about moving made for lively and engaging reading. The parents were impressed with the products, and they seemed to appreciate the opportunity to meet and greet one another again.

May

When spring comes, the sap rises, and it has certainly risen in my students! Pat and Horace are obviously in love, and Rita is constantly following Larry around and writing him notes. Daisy seems to have her eye on Mitch, but he pays absolutely no attention to her.

We performed one final activity this month to continue developing independent learning strategies. I called it an "open-notes" quiz. We had practiced writing notes that corresponded to outlines of passages throughout the year, so the idea of note taking was familiar to the class. Indeed, the independent projects they had undertaken with ocean animals and states had called for note taking. This particular application activity began with my telling everyone that they would have a quiz on a section of the science textbook that dealt with the formation of mountains. They were to be able to compare the effects of volcanic action, folding, and faulting on mountain formations. However, they had time to take notes on the section of the text that dealt with mountain formations, and they could use those notes during the quiz. I met in a part of the room with whoever wanted to read the section orally and decide as a group what notes to make. Most of the class found this activity worthwhile, especially after they all did so well on the quiz.

In reading/literature period, we completed a unit on prejudice that went over well. I began this unit by reading *Roll of Thunder, Hear My Cry* by Mildred Taylor to the whole class. Afterward, I set out multiple copies of various short novels and short stories for the class. For instance, William Armstrong's novel *Sounder* was made available, and Shirley Jackson's classic short story "After You, My Dear Alphonse" was provided.

Having students read these stories while focusing on prejudice was the perfect follow-up to the two books on apartheid in South Africa that I had read to the class earlier, *Journey to Jo'burg* and *The Middle of Somewhere*. When the racism being practiced was occurring in another country and culture, students were roundly disgusted and angered by it. By reading the materials I provided this month, the students confronted the racism of our own country and culture.

They were to record in journals the instances of prejudice that the materials portrayed. This recording had been modeled beforehand with *Roll of Thunder, Hear My Cry* when I displayed a journal one of last year's students had maintained about the prejudice Cassie encountered in this story. By providing this model, everyone had an idea of what to do. The students knew what to read for and how to record what they read, and they were able to choose materials that were written at various levels of difficulty. On preset days, students who had selected particular materials gathered in what we called book clubs to talk about what they had read and what they had recorded. I showed them how to converse with each other about the materials, exploring ideas rather than debating conclusions. Some of the clubs progressed better than others, but all seemed to like the idea of talking about materials they had chosen.

THE MEETING AT THE MIDDLE SCHOOL

Ed Dunn sat quietly by Tip Topps as the middle-school language arts teachers filed into the small meeting room at their school. The expressions on their faces indicated that they were as excited about going on vacation as he was. They were smiling and kidding each other about what they would do with their upcoming vacation.

Mr. Topps had known since April that he would be the new principal at Upton Hill, and he was meeting with small groups of teachers at that school ever since. He thought the meetings would help make for a smoother transition, and so far everyone agreed. This meeting was with just language arts teachers.

When all the teachers were present, Mr. Topps introduced Mr. Dunn. "Ed has done an excellent job with his students this year, and I wanted him to share some of his ideas with you. He has emphasized some of the areas that concern many middle-school teachers of language arts. Understanding his efforts promotes consistent instruction across the grades."

Mr. Dunn stood to address these teachers. "When the students who will begin sixth grade this fall graduate from high school, it will be well into the twenty-first century. Whether they go on to four-year college, community college, vocational training, or a job requiring only a high-school education, the reading, writing, and thinking they must do to succeed will be quite sophisticated by the standards of just a few years ago.

"My goal with this year's fifth-graders has been to build on what the Merritt Elementary K–4 teachers accomplished and to move the children closer to having the reading, writing, and thinking proficiencies their futures require. This has meant that I had to move the students beyond both what they learned in fourth grade last year and what they would have learned in fifth grade just a few years ago. In meeting that goal, I emphasized several areas.

"First, I stressed the gaining of knowledge. Students in middle school and above will not be able to read, write, or think well without adequate knowledge of the world in which they live. What students know already is a powerful determinant of how much they can learn. You are all language arts teachers who teach literature. Think about how much most poets, playwrights, short story authors, and novelists assume their readers will know about geography, history, politics, and the particulars of food, clothes, transportation, abodes, furnishings, or romance. To increase this knowledge, I placed special priority on students engaging important ideas encountered in multiple resources during units of study. The student examined ideas in order to solve problems more than to store facts for a test.

"Knowing that wide reading is the principal means by which most people acquire general background knowledge and word meanings, I provided time and encouragement for self-selected reading every day. Because the K–4 teachers at my school had already been doing that, my students were accustomed to reading on their own or as members of a book club. My conversations with the children about their readings regularly enhanced their experiences and understandings of the world. In addition, because the knowledge students will need is of a shrinking globe with many cultures, I read aloud every day from a book set in another country. As the year progressed, students discussed and wrote about the books I was reading aloud. Together, effective content instruction, meaning vocabulary building, reading multicultural literature aloud, and wide book reading served to build knowledge of the world."

Mr. Dunn paused. He sensed that he had the attention of the teachers before him. "I also emphasized my students' abilities to learn independently. Fortunately, the K–4 teachers at Merritt had students on the road to independent learning in topics they already were interested in and knew about. I worked to move them into independent learning of new, more challenging topics. I gradually released control of the class, having individuals select the order of assignments to complete, which assignments to complete, and eventually what the form of the assignments should be. This was to promote individuals' sense of self-sufficiency. Additionally, I emphasized strategies for learning independently. Even when there is only one book to read—the textbook, for example—a student must be able to determine what the main points of a selection are and what is most important to remember for a class discussion or a test. When one is inquiring into a topic, the ability to read independently becomes absolutely necessary.

"Finally, computer technology accounted for a large part of the fifth-grade curriculum. At the beginning of the year, all the students in my class learned to keyboard at a proficient level. After that, students worked in small groups and individually to learn how to better use the computer as a tool for learning. They produced several reports, using technology to access and display information. I think you will find your new sixth-graders from Merritt Elementary better able to plan, draft, and revise their papers compared with sixth-graders in the past."

Mr. Dunn nodded at Mr. Topps to indicate that he had finished his prepared remarks. From his seat, Mr. Topps looked around at the middle-school teachers. "Any questions or comments for Mr. Dunn?"

After a few seconds, Buzz Riley responded, "I have."

Turning to face Mr. Dunn, he quipped, "Seems like you could have left us something to teach them!"

Mr. Dunn laughed along with the others. "I'm sure you'll have your hands full with this group. They seem to be off to a good start, but they still have a long way to go. Sometimes I think we forget how complicated and abstract middle- and high-school content is. This group will require good instruction when they encounter that content.

"The students we are sending you are going to need what you have to teach them just as much as before, but you may find that they are better able to learn it and perhaps will be able to go further than groups in the past. I look forward to hearing from you next year about this very interesting group you are inheriting from us."

As Ed and Tip walked out of the middle school into the parking lot, both were silent. Tip focused on his preparation for the challenge of a new school. Ed was thinking of ways he could improve his program for next year's fifth-graders and wondering who his new principal would be. "One thing is for sure," he thought, "No one will top Mr. Topps!"

CHILDREN'S BOOKS/MATERIALS CITED

"After You, My Dear Alphonse," by S. Jackson. In *The Lottery, or The Adventures of James Harris.* Farrar, Straus, & Co., 1949.

Amber Brown Sees Red, by P. Danziger, Putnam, 1997.

Animorphs series, by K. A. Applegate, Scholastic, various dates.

Arctic Summer, by D. Matthews, Simon and Schuster, 1993.

Baby Sitter Club series, by A. Martin, Scholastic, various dates.

The Boy and the Samurai, by E. Haugaard, Houghton Mifflin, 1991.

The Cat Ate My Gymsuit, by P. Danziger, Delacorte, 1974.

Earth to Matthew, by P. Danziger, Delacorte, 1991.

The Haunted Igloo, by B. Turner, Houghton Mifflin, 1991.

Hiding Out: Camouflage in the Wild, by J. Martin, Crown, 1993.

It's an Aardvark Eat Turtle World, by P. Danziger, Dell, 1985.

Journey to Jo'burg: A South African Story, by B. Naidoo, HarperCollins, 1988.

Latkes and Applesauce: A Hanukkah Story, by F. Manushkin, Scholastic, 1992.

The Magic School Bus series, by J. Cole, Scholastic, various dates.

Make Like a Tree and Leave, by P. Danziger, Delacorte, 1990.

The Middle of Somewhere: A Story of South Africa, by S. Gordon, Bantam, 1992.

National Geographic World magazine.

Ranger Rick magazine.

Roll of Thunder, Hear My Cry, by M. Taylor, Bantam, 1978.

Sounder, by W. H. Armstrong, HarperCollins, 1969.

There's a Bat in Bunk Five, by P. Danziger, Delacorte, 1980.

What's the Difference? A Guide to Some Familiar Animal Look-Alikes, by E. Lacey, Clarion, 1993.

Wolves, by S. Simon, HarperCollins, 1993.

Year of the Panda, by M. Schlein, HarperCollins, 1992.

INDEX

A

Alphabet Books II-25, II-65, II-98
Anecdotal records, II-73, II-96,
 II-155–156
Assessment
 anecdotal records, II- 73, II-96,
  II-155–156
 conferencing, II-174–175,
  II-177–178
 grades, II- 230–231
 expectations, II-55, II-107, II-170,
  II-242
 holistic evaluation, II-221–223
 informal reading inventory, II-140,
  II-221–223
 portfolios, II-80, II-142, II-161,
  II-208
 oral reading records, II- 140
 testing, II-226, II-232, II-245, II-252
Audiotapes, II-77–78
Author's chair, *See* Shared Writing,
 Writer's Workshop
Automaticity, *See* High Frequency
 Words, Word Wall

B

Background knowledge. *See* Back-
 ground building, Prior knowledge
Big Books, II-29–30, II-35, II-39, II-45,
 II-61, II-65, II-68, II-89
Book clubs, II-229, II-232
Book publishing. *See* Publishing,
 Alphabet Books
Brainstorming, *See* Writing

C

Centers, II-113–114, II-197, II-205
Chunking (words). *See* Making Words
Comprehension
 and emergent literacy, II-42–43,
  II-49
 Comprehension strategy lessons,
  II-61–62, II-68, II-72, II-125–127,
  II-183–185, II-243–244
Computers, II-222–224, II-225,
 II-226–228, II-237, II-247
Conferences, student-teacher, II-229
Content-area reading, II-155,
 II-247–248, II-249, II-250, II-251

Content-area subjects
    and comprehension, , II-125–127,
        II-183–185, II-243–244
    focused writing, II-155, II-247–248,
        II-249, II-250, II-251
Critical knowings, II-15

D

Daily planning, II-17–18, II-114–115,
    II-117–119, II-168, II-217–218
Decoding. *See also* Phonics
    analytical approaches, II-82–85,
        II-95, II-102, II-147–148,
        II-183–184, II-240–241
    multisyllabic words, II-102,
    prefixes, II-240–241
    and rhyming words, II-187–191
    sorting, II-147–148
    strategies, II-187–191, II-240–241
    unfamiliar words, II-183–184
Diagnosis. *See* Assessment
Dictionaries, using, II-247, II-249
Discipline, II-111, II-120
Discussion, II-220–221
    groups, II-20, II-193, II-206
Drama, II-116
    Editing. *See also* Revisions (writ-
        ing) II-81–82, II-86–88, II-89,
        II-93, II-101, II-202, II-121–122,
        II-142, II-143, II-178–180

E

Emergent literacy
    and comprehension, II- 42–43, II-49
    and phonemic awareness, II-29,
        II-31, II-32–33, II-34–35, II-37–38,
        II-40–41, II-47, II-48
    and reading to children, II-29–30,
        II-35, II-39, II-45, II-61, II-62,
        II-65, II-68, II-89
    and shared reading, II-21–22,
        II-29–30, II-35, II-39, II-45, II-61,
        II-65, II-68, II-89

and shared writing, II-22, II-25–26,
    II-45
and writing, II-22, II-25–26,
    II-26–28, II-32, II-35, II-39
Expectations, II-55, II-107, II-170,
    II-242

F

Five Steps, II-26–28, II-32, II-35, II-39
Focused writing, II-146, II-154
    content-area subjects, II-155,
        II-247–248, II-249, II-250, II-251
Four Blocks, II-54, II-98–103
    Function of reading and writing,
        understanding of. *See*
        Understandings about print,
        Critical knowings

G

Grading
    creative systems, II-230–231, II- 242
    portfolios, II-80, II-142, II-161,
        II-208
Graphic organizers, II-235,
Groups
    discussion groups, II-20, II-193,
        II-206
    reading groups, II-61–62,
        II-107–108, II-110
    research projects, II-246–248
Group tests, II-221–223
Guess the Covered Word, II-75
Guided reading, II-61–62, II-68, II-72,
    II-125–127, II-183–184, II-243–244

H

High-frequency words, II-73–74,
    II-93–94
Holistic scoring, II-221–223
Homophones. *See* Word Wall, High
    frequency words
Identifying- sorting-classifying
    games, II-44–45

Informal reading inventory,
   II-140–141, II-161–162, II-222
Informational books, II-243
Instructional level, reading, II-
   140–141, II-161–162, II-172–173,
   II-222–223
Interests, II-173–174

J
Job charts, II-24

K
Key boarding. *See* computers

L
Language experience activities (LEA),
   II-25–26, II-31–32, II-128
   See also Shared writing
Lap-style reading, II-29–30, II-35,
   II-39, II-45, II-61, II-65, II-68, II-89
Learning centers. *See* Centers
Letter formations, II- 47–48, II-48
Letter names, II-19, II-37
Letter-sound relationships, II-40–41,
   II-43, II-47, II-59–61, II-71
List, Group and Label, II-92–93
Listening comprehension lessons,
   II-42–43
Listening/reading transfer lessons,
   II-203
Literature. *See also* Literature
   response activities
   acquiring for classroom, II-136–137
   classroom use, II-29–30, II-35, II-39,
      II-45, II-61, II-65, II-68, II-89,
      II-112, II-115, II-123, II-125,
      II-127, II-129–130, II-137,
      II-145–146, II-149, II-160,II-177,
      II-199, II-201, II-204–205, II-219,
      II-226, II-243, II-249, II-252
   and comprehension, II-61–62,
      II-68, II-72, II-125–127,
      II-183–185, II-243–244

and content-subject areas, II-89,
   II-125, II-127, II-129, II-199,
   II-236, II-239, II-244–245
and knowledge development,
   II-244–245
Literature anthologies, II-199
   Literature-based teaching,
      II-29–30, II-35, II-39, II-45, II-61,
      II-65, II-68, II-89, II-112, II-115,
      II-123, II-125, II-127, II-129–130,
      II-137, II-145–146, II-149,
      II-160,II-177, II-199, II-201,
      II-204–205, II-219, II-226, II-243,
      II-249, II-252,
Literature discussion groups, II-229,
   II-232
   Literature response activities,
      II-20, II-144–145, *See also*
      Discussion groups, Book
      Clubs, Literature response
      journals
Literature response journals, II-20

M
Making Words, II-82–85, II-95,
   II-102
Mapping (stories), II-149–150,
   II-152–154
Minilessons, writing, II-85–88, II-93,
   II-123
Miscue analysis, *See* Informal
   Reading Inventories
Morphemes, II-102, II-240–241,
   II-187–191, II-240–241,
   II-183–184
Motivation, II-209–210
Multilevel activities. *See* Making
   Words, Writer's Workshop
Multisyllabic words. *See* Making
   Words, Decoding

N
Names, II-22–24

O

Observation (assessment). *See* Anecdotal Records
On-the-back activity, II-94
Oral reading,
running records, II-140
Organizing (information). *See* Writing, reports

P

Peer conferencing. *See* Editing, Writer's Workshop
Phonics. *See also* Decoding
analytical approaches, II-82–85, II-95, II-102, II-147–148, II-183–184, II-240–241
multisyllabic words, II-102,
prefixes, II-240–241
and rhyming words, II-187–191
sorting, II-147–148
strategies, II-187–191, II-240–241
unfamiliar words, II-183–184
Phonemic awareness, II-13–14, II-29, II-31, II-32–33, II-34–35, II-37–38, II-40–41, II-47, II-48
Planning
content-area subjects, II-214, II-217
daily, II-17–18, II-114–115, II-117–119, II-168, II-217–218
weekly, II-17–18, II-114–115, II-117–119, II-168–170
Poems, II-20–21, II-34, II-41, II-46, II-157–158
Portfolios, II-80, II-142, II-161, II-208
Prefixes, II-240–241
Pretend reading, II-65–67, II-77–78, II-95–96
Process writing. *See* Writer's Workshop
Publishing, II-85–88, II-124, II-129, II-156, II-175, II-251
Reader's Workshop, II-138, II-143–144, II-151–152, II-154, II-159, II-161, II-174, II-187, II-209–210

R

Reading, pretend. *See* Pretend reading
Reading aloud. *See* Oral reading, Reading to children
Reading groups, II-199–200, *See* also Groups
Reading instructional level, II-140–141, II-161–162, II-172–173
Reading partners, II-199
Reading to children,
classroom use of literature, II-65–67, II-199, II-219, II-236
and emergent literacy, II-29–30, II-35, II-39, II-45, II-61, II-62, II-65, II-68, II-89
Record keeping, II-73, *See* also Assessment, anecdotal records, Grading
Reluctant readers,II-236
Repeated reading, II-76
Research for writing, II-247–248, II-249
Research groups, II-247–249
Responses to literature. *See* Literature response activities
Revising (writing). *See also* Editing II-178–180, II-202
Rhyme,
and phonemic awareness, II-14, II-34–35
rhyming charts, II-75
and spelling patterns, II-183–184, II-187–191, II-240–241
Rules, writing. *See* Editing, Writer's Workshop, Writing rules
Running records. *See* Informal Reading Inventory

S

Scheduling, II-17–18, II-114–115, II-117–119, II-168–170, II-214, II-217–218

Self-confidence, II-215, II-209–210, II-235

Self-evaluation (writing), II-215, II-242–243

Self-selected reading, II-36–37, II-43, II-62, II-65–67, II-77–78, II-95–96, II-112, II-121, II-130, II-177, II-220

Shared writing. *See also* Language experience activities (LEA), II-25–26, II-128

Sight words, II-22, II-73–74, II-93–94

Singing, II-16–17

Sound-letter relationships. *See* Letter–sound relationships

Spelling
  analytical approaches, II-82–85, II-95, II-102, II-147–148, II-183–184, II-240–241
  endings of words, II-89–91
  multisyllabic words, II-102,
  prefixes, II-240–241
  and rhyming words, II-90–91, II-187–191
  sorting, II-147–148
  strategies, II-187–191, II-240–241
  unfamiliar words, II-183–184

Story maps, II-149–150, II-152–154

Story webs, II-149–150

Syllable awareness, II-14, II-33. *See also* Phonics, multisyllabic words

T

Teacher read-aloud. *See* Reading to children

Technology. *See* Computers

Think Links, II-42–43, II-49

Time allocations. *See* Scheduling, Planning

Time lines, II-195–196

U

Understandings about print, II-21–22, II-31

Uninterrupted Sustained Silent Reading (USSR),
  Unit teaching, II-175, II-181–183, II-198–199, II-204–205, II-221, II-224–225, II-226, II-229, II-237–238, II-246, II-252

V

Vocabulary,
  content-area subjects, II-181, II-203–204, II-233–234, II-240–241
  notebooks, II-24–25
  reviewing, II-229, II-234
  strategies, II-240–241

W

Webbing, II-149–150, II-200, II-205, II-234–235

Weekly planning, II-17–18, II-114–115, II-117–119, II-168–170

What looks right? II-187–191

Word awareness, II-13

Word Books. *See* Vocabulary, notebooks

Word identification
  analytical approaches, II-82–85, II-95, II-102, II-147–148, II-183–184, II-240–241
  endings of words, II-89–91
  multisyllabic words, II-102,
  prefixes, II-240–241
  and rhyming words, II-90–91, II-187–191
  sorting, II-147–148
  strategies, II-187–191, II-240–241
  unfamiliar words, II-183–184

Words. *See also* Vocabulary II-24–25
  high-frequency words, II-58–59, II-70, II-73–74, II-93–94, II-123
  Making Words, II-82–85, II-95, II-102
  multisyllabic, II-102, II-240–241
  sight words, II-58–59, II-70, II-73–74, II-93–94, II-123

analytical approaches, II-82–85,
  II-95, II-102, II-147–148,
  II-183–184, II-240–241
endings of words, II-89–91
prefixes, II-240–241
and rhyming words, II-90–91,
  II-187–191
sorting, II-58–59, II-70, II-73–74,
  II-93–94, II-123, II-147–148
strategies, II-187–191, II-240–241
Word Wall, II-58–59, II-70, II-73–74,
  II-93–94, II-123
Writers' Workshop, II-56–58, II-64,
  II-68–70, II-81–82, II-85–88,
  II-143, II-179–180
Writing. *See also* Focused writing,
  Process writing
computers, II-216
and emergent literacy, II-22,
  II-25–26, II-26–28, II-32, II-35,
  II-39

editing, II-81, II-82, II-86–88, II-93,
  II-101, II-121–122, II-142, II-143,
  II-178–180, II-202
Five Steps, II-26–28, II-32, II-35,
  II-39
guided writing, II-159–160
organizing, II-250
portfolios, II-142
reports, II-155, II-247–248, II-249,
  II-250, II-251
revisions, II-81, II-82, II-86–88,
  II-93, II-101, II-121–122, II-142,
  II-143, II-178–180, II-202
self-evaluation, II-242–243, II-245
shared writing, II-22, II-25–26,
  II-26–28, II-32, II-35, II-39, II-220
traits, II-242, II-245
Writing prompts, II-237
Writing rules, II-81, II-82, II-86–88,
  II-93, II-101, II-121–122, II-142,
  II-143, II-178–180, II-202